The Culture
of Sports in the
Harlem Renaissance

The Culture of Sports in the Harlem Renaissance

DANIEL ANDERSON

McFarland & Company, Inc., Publishers
Jefferson, North Carolina

LIBRARY OF CONGRESS CATALOGUING-IN-PUBLICATION DATA

Names: Anderson, Daniel, 1965–
Title: The culture of sports in the Harlem Renaissance / Daniel Anderson.
Description: Jefferson, North Carolina : McFarland & Company, Inc., Publishers, 2017. | Includes bibliographical references and index.
Identifiers: LCCN 2017005430 | ISBN 9781476665184 (softcover : acid free paper) ∞
Subjects: LCSH: Sports—Social aspects—New York (State)—New York—History—20th century. | Mass media and sports—New York (State)—New York—History—20th century. | African American sportswriters—History—20th century. | American literature—African American authors. | American literature—New York (State)—New York. | Harlem Renaissance. | Harlem (New York, N.Y.)—Intellectual life—20th century.
Classification: LCC GV584.5.N4 A46 2017 | DDC 306.4/83—dc23
LC record available at https://lccn.loc.gov/2017005430

BRITISH LIBRARY CATALOGUING DATA ARE AVAILABLE

ISBN (print) 978-1-4766-6518-4
ISBN (ebook) 978-1-4766-2898-1

© 2017 Daniel Roger Anderson. All rights reserved

No part of this book may be reproduced or transmitted in any form or by any means, electronic or mechanical, including photocopying or recording, or by any information storage and retrieval system, without permission in writing from the publisher.

Front cover: Team photograph of the New York Lincoln Giants, based in Harlem, taken in 1911 (National Baseball Hall of Fame, Cooperstown, New York)

Printed in the United States of America

McFarland & Company, Inc., Publishers
  Box 611, Jefferson, North Carolina 28640
  www.mcfarlandpub.com

To my parents
Roger and Diane Anderson

Acknowledgments

I am grateful to the University of Minnesota for two research grants, a Doctoral Dissertation Special Grant from the Graduate School and a Monk-Marston Travel Award from the Department of English. A Research and Creative Projects Assistance Grant from Dominican University enabled me to conduct the additional research necessary to complete this project.

Thanks to all the faculty members who shared their advice and expertise at the University of Minnesota, particularly Edward M. Griffin, John S. Wright, and the late Kent Bales. I appreciate all the support I have received from Dominican University, especially my colleagues in the English Department.

My deepest gratitude goes out to all my family and friends, especially my parents; my sister and her family; and Anne Marie, without whose love and support the finish line might never have been reached.

Table of Contents

Acknowledgments	vi
Preface	1
Introduction: Examining the Harlem Renaissance Through the Prism of Sports	3

Part I: Literature and the Renaissance Intelligentsia

1. The "Discipline of Work and Play": Athletics, Education and the Harlem Intelligentsia's Concept of Culture	21
2. "Minds of Fleetful Thoughts": Negro League Baseball, Intellectualism and the Black Bourgeoisie	41
3. Escaping the Iron Cage: Sports, Art and Performance in Harlem's "Black Bohemia"	57
4. The "Lost Arts": Baseball and Boxing in the Historiography of James Weldon Johnson	80

Part II: Sportswriting and the Harlem Press

5. "Jazz Journalism": Sportswriting and Popular Culture in the Black Press	101
6. "A Course in the Curriculum of the Institution": Sports and Politics in the Harlem Press	118
7. "Race First" in the Sports Section: Romeo Dougherty and Harlem's Caribbean Circle	140
8. The Dean's Demise: The Sudden Fall and Long Disappearance of Romeo Dougherty	164

Table of Contents

Epilogue: Arna Bontemps, Sterling Brown and the End of an Era — 179

Chapter Notes — 187

Bibliography — 191

Index — 201

The Baseball Park is soon to be
    A place where players, white and tan,
Shall demonstrate pure sportsmanship
    And man will love his fellow man.
—*Andy Razaf, "Hail to the Continental League"*

◆

"To understand black baseball might give us some sense of what a black historical consciousness is and what the development of a form of racial consciousness has meant to America at large."
—*Gerald Early, "Baseball and African American Life"*

◆

"Renaissance Men, indeed!"
—*Ralph Ellison,* Shadow and Act

Preface

American sports reached unforeseen levels of popularity and influence in the 1920s, not only in the mainstream media capital of New York City but also in the African American cultural renaissance associated with Harlem. The present work examines the absence of sports in most of the literature of the Harlem Renaissance and in critical studies that attempt to capture the popular culture of the era.

My research explores the relationships between communities of writers—intellectual and popular, African American and Caribbean—that conceived of a renaissance in Harlem with distinctly different cultural ideals. Looking specifically at prominent writers such as W.E.B. Du Bois, Claude McKay, and James Weldon Johnson, I show how each used sports in a distinctive way to communicate their vision of an ideal culture. I juxtapose these intellectuals with the writers in the Harlem press, who not only promoted sports and other popular art forms but also argued unrelentingly for their importance in the fight for equality. The disproportionate number of Caribbean migrants in Harlem added to the complexity of this dynamic. Caribbean-born writers largely embraced athletics, celebrating them as community institutions and using them to debate issues such as Garveyism.

This analysis takes a multidisciplinary approach, applying methods drawn from cultural studies, sociology, and historiography; however, its primary focus is literary. I combine close readings of major Harlem Renaissance writers with extensive archival research in the sportswriting of the African American press, arguing that the intelligentsia largely dismissed the growing importance of sports to the younger generation while the press used athletics as a means to participate in the debates of the day. Sports and sportswriting played significant roles in the culture of the Renaissance, helping to create a model for racial discourse that shaped intellectual, artistic, and social movements in the ensuing decades.

Introduction
Examining the Harlem Renaissance Through the Prism of Sports

In 1921, the sports page of the *New York News*, an African American weekly, ran a poem by a young songwriter. Andrea Razafkeriefo's untitled poem paid homage to the Continental League, a proposed enterprise that would have circumvented both Negro League baseball and the all-white major leagues by fielding integrated rosters. The poem's opening stanza read:

> Hail to the Continental League
> The Champions of a nobler plan,
> Whose motto is "Democracy"
> Whose aims are true American.[1]

Belying his poem's lofty dreams for the new league and the patriotic potential of baseball, Razafkeriefo had just given up on a career as a pitcher. Although his semi-professional team, the Naco Giants, won the Cleveland city championship the previous season, Razafkeriefo's personal experiment was not a success: Forced to take a job as a porter on top of his responsibilities as the league secretary, he had no time to write (Singer 61). Facing every athlete's ultimate opponent—he turned twenty-five years of age that winter—Razafkeriefo returned to Harlem and the musical theatre.

Razafkeriefo dedicated himself to songwriting in New York, becoming famous as Andy Razaf, the lyricist of several popular songs by Fats Waller, including "Ain't Misbehavin'," and "Honeysuckle Rose," in addition to the lyric that Ralph Ellison would use as a recurring motif in *Invisible Man*, "What Did I Do (To Be So Black and Blue)?" He never lost his passion for baseball, however. According Romeo Dougherty, the sports editor who printed his poem, Razaf had organized a semi-professional team, the New York Black Sox, upon his return. "'Razaf,'" Dougherty wrote in that spring of 1921, using his friend's shortened name in print for perhaps the first time, "claims he has the fastest bunch of youngsters in town, who are going to make the 'old timers' sit up and take notice. The team is fully uniformed and is being booked."[2] (By 1923, "Andrea Razaf" was appearing in Dougherty's pages in the *Amsterdam News*.) Indeed, Razaf continued to contribute verse to the sports pages edited by Dougherty in the Harlem newspapers throughout the Renaissance years. "Man of the Theatre at a Baseball Game," for example, describes an exhibition game between Babe Ruth's team of white major leaguers and the New York Cuban Stars of the Negro National League (Andy Razaf Papers).

The working relationship between Razaf and Dougherty, the songwriter and the sportswriter, might seem rather unusual today, but few of their readers would have considered it strange. Harlem's newspapers, like most of those in the African American press, combined entertainment and sports coverage in a single section; moreover, Dougherty had a reputation as the "dean" of the black sports-and-entertainment editors and was known as a mentor to athletes and entertainers on the rise. Dougherty and Razaf continued a sort of partnership throughout the 1920s, writing concurrently for Marcus Garvey's black nationalist newspaper, *Negro World*. Later, as Dougherty moved to Harlem's leading paper in the Renaissance, the *Amsterdam News*, Razaf frequently contributed observations, witticisms, and poetry to the sports and entertainment pages. Their association, however, involved more than sports and entertainment: The political radicalism of their journalistic enterprises testifies to the power sports inspired and wielded in the Harlem Renaissance—a potency ignored by the artists and intellectuals of the era and largely neglected by scholars in the decades since.

The absence of sports in most of the literature of the Renaissance and in the scholarship on the period represents more than a stark omission in attempts to document the popular culture of the era; this neglect also tells us much about the attitudes that the leading figures of the Renaissance held regarding that culture—and about their concept of "culture" itself. Initially, the artists and intellectuals interested in defining the renaissance of the "New Negro," such as Alain Locke and W.E.B. Du Bois, had little interest in the culture that was actually popular among the younger generation or the working people of Harlem. While most artists and intellectuals looked the other way, the African American newspapers of the era embraced sports and other popular forms of entertainment while asserting a role for the press in the movement's attempts to re-define a culture. Despite their absence in the documentary record of the era, however, Negro League baseball and other sports played a prominent role in the life of the Renaissance. That prominence extended beyond social practices, exemplified by the popularity of the biggest boxing matches and college football games, to realms that were laden with more cultural heft, such as education and the arts. Radical publications such as *The Crusader* led the way in this regard, driven in large part by Caribbean-born writers even more inclined than were their American-born counterparts to question cultural traditions.

From different, distant backgrounds, both Razaf and Dougherty found their way into the overlapping worlds of sports, popular entertainment, political activism, and professional writing in the Harlem Renaissance. Razaf was born and raised in Washington, D.C., although his grandmother had once been the queen of Madagascar. In all likelihood, he and Dougherty first met in the early 1910s, while Dougherty briefly worked for a newspaper in Washington. Although Razaf—and, to an extent, Dougherty as well—became better known in the world of entertainment, they shared a passion and an idealism when it came to sports. Dougherty, who was born in the Virgin Islands but grew up in New Jersey, maintained his own measure of fame in both worlds for a time: He became well known as both as a music promoter in Harlem and as the "Dean of Colored Sports Writers." After moving to New York from Washington in the late 1910s, Dougherty and Razaf became frequent contributors to *The Crusader*, a radical leftist periodical that supported socialist revolt and black separatism. *The Crusader*, like several other radical magazines in Harlem, first appeared in the years immediately following the Great Migration and the end of World War I, emerging largely out of the strife that rose in the wake of those two events. While the magazine dedicated itself to black liberation, its editors also found space to argue for the merits of an emerging community institution in Harlem: amateur athletics. Dougherty argued against professionalism in African American sports as the architect of the magazine's "Fight to Keep Sport Clean."

Razaf, meanwhile, had attracted the government's attention as a contributor of poems and short prose pieces. One of his poems, "Don't Tread on Me," was considered so provocative that it was mentioned, along with Claude McKay's "If We Must Die," by J. Edgar Hoover in a Justice Department report on the "seditious" writings in the radical black press. In the report, Hoover cited Razaf as Andrea Razafkeriefo, adding insultingly, "if that is a name" (Vincent, *Voices* 34). The department presented the report,

"Radicalism and Sedition Among the Negroes as Reflected in Their Publications," to Congress in 1919, after which *The Crusader* reprinted it under the headline, "We 'Rile' the Crackered Department of Justice" ("We Rile" 5).

The political radicalism of these journalistic associations is clearly expressed in the poem Razaf published on Dougherty's sporting page in the *New York News* in 1921. After the opening stanza hailed the Continental League and its organizers as "Champions of a nobler plan," with aims that were "true American," Razaf continued:

> For they would save the nation's game
>   And free it from a selfish few;
> Who have dishonored it for gain
>   And barred the men of darker hue
> The Baseball Park is soon to be
>   A place where players, white and tan,
> Shall demonstrate pure sportsmanship
>   And man will love his fellow man.
> Where grandstand, box and bleacher crowds
>   Will feel a new and greater thrill;
> When pale and dusky Ruths and Cobbs
>   Will match their fleetness, nerve and skill.
> Proclaim the news from coast to coast,
>   Let every true, red-blooded fan;
> Support the worthy enterprise
>   Of Andy Lawson and his clan!

Like much of the cultural mythology of baseball, Razaf's poem is unabashedly patriotic. In the aftermath of World War I, he appeals to readers' democratic principles, perhaps in response to implications of sedition the Justice Department had attached to his name two years earlier. In a more timely fashion, however, less than year after the banishment from the game of the eight Chicago White Sox players who had conspired to throw the World Series, Razaf credits the founders of the Continental League with saving the American game. In the second stanza, Razaf directs his ire not at the conspirators or the gamblers, but at the lords of white baseball. Just as the White Sox players blamed the team owner, Charles Comiskey, for forcing them to act in desperation, Razaf depicts the owners as an avaricious ruling class that the new league will overthrow.

The language of revolution then gives way to pure praise of integration, which Razaf imagines flourishing in the pastoral utopia of the ballfield. Razaf predicts no less than purity and love emanating from the new league.

He also promises a previously unknown, thrilling experience: the league will raise baseball to a new level as the African American counterparts to the white stars join the competition. Appropriately, the progressive power of a league "whose motto is 'Democracy'" will reach fans in every part of the park—in every social class—equally. The league's founder, the Boston promoter Andy Lawson, made headlines in the black press that spring by offering Jack Johnson an "umpireship"—news that the *Chicago Defender* reported in a banner headline across its front page.[3]

In the final stanza, Razaf shifts from the discourses of progressive politics and patriotic fandom to a Biblical call to action. While Razaf uses several modes of revolutionary language, he stops short of Marxist rhetoric. Indeed, both Razaf and Dougherty discontinued their association with *The Crusader* in the early 1920s as its editors moved the magazine's editorial position closer to communism and away from racial solidarity. The major-league owners might be a "selfish few" who have dishonored the sport "for gain," but the revolt Razaf and Dougherty had in mind would bring about democracy and equality, not collectivization.

This confluence of cultural forces—Negro League baseball and popular songwriting—commanded attention among the readers of the Harlem press but went unnoticed or ignored by the most established voices of the New Negro movement. The Renaissance elite dismissed sports, like jazz, as frivolous—or worse, as anti-intellectual. While the intelligentsia paid scornful attention to the Cotton Club and other venues because whites patronized them and gangsters often owned them, the most prominent writers of the movement generally overlooked Harlem residents' favorite hotspots, such as the Rockland Casino, where the Renaissance Five played basketball and Duke Ellington's band played "breakfast dances" after the Cotton Club closed at 4 a.m.

African American intellectuals weren't alone in ignoring sports in the early twentieth century. While some European and Anglo-American philosophers, such as Georg Simmel and John Dewey, had begun to show an interest in the abstract idea of *play*, most white intellectuals who deigned to analyze specific sports usually did so dismissively. H.L. Mencken disliked sports, as he did most of popular culture, and he especially despised baseball. Mencken's bitterness, in this case, might have come from personal experience: In 1899, his father and uncle had tried unsuccessfully to purchase the Baltimore Orioles and prevent their relocation to Brooklyn (Light 57). Baseball's popularity and patriotic aura may

Introduction

well have had something to do with Mencken's distaste for the game. While critiquing the popular press, he noted: "I know of no subject, save perhaps baseball, on which the average American newspaper discourses without unfailing sense and understanding" (as qtd. by Light 505).

Mencken's characteristic irony seems mild, however, compared to the bile that the social critic and theorist Thorstein Veblen had released in his own dismissal of sports. In his pioneering, expansive treatise *The Theory of the Leisure Class* (1899), Veblen branded all modern athletic pursuits "barbaric," asserting:

> A strong proclivity to adventuresome exploit and to the infliction of damage is especially pronounced in those employments which are in colloquial usage specifically called sportsmanship ... the temperament which inclines men to them is essentially a boyish temperament. The addiction to sports, therefore, in a peculiar degree marks an arrested development of the man's moral nature [Veblen 255–56].

Veblen's assessment of sports forms part of the foundation of his theory of conspicuous consumption and the general barbarity of the leisure class. In his introduction, Veblen categorized sports alongside other pursuits that had been transformed by capitalist society: "The man's occupation as it stands at the earlier barbarian stage is not the original out of which any appreciable portion of later industry has developed. In the later development it survives only in employments that are not classed as industrial,—war, politics, sports, learning, and the priestly office" (4–5). Similarly, much of the intellectual disdain for sports in the early twentieth century stems from a circumspect attitude towards capitalism and the increasing professionalism and profitability of athletics.

Most notably, Max Weber cited sports as an example of a formerly pleasurable pursuit that had become, under capitalism, an "iron cage" (Weber 181–82). Van Wyck Brooks reduced this notion, placing it in a specifically American framework and arguing that business had subsumed sports, as it had religion and the arts. In *America's Coming-of-Age* (1915), Brooks compared the American businessman to a top sportsman, one who stands in "the centre of the field" (Brooks 136–37). In America, he lamented, too much talent and energy had been funneled into business:

> Just those elements which in other countries produce art and literature, formulate the ideals and methods of philosophy and sociology, think and act for those disinterested ends which make up the meaning of life; just that free, disinterested, athletic sense of play which is precisely the same in dialectic, in art, in religion, in sociology, in sport—just these, relatively speaking, have in America been absorbed in trade [137].

Just when intellectuals such as Brooks began to take notice, then, American sports ceased to be properly "disinterested" and became a business. From this perspective, it follows logically that the sheer pragmatism of the Negro Leagues would have turned the Harlem intelligentsia away. Throughout the 1920s, for example, Du Bois edited *The Crisis*—the NAACP magazine that reached a circulation of nearly 100,000 and was especially well-read in middle-class homes where, in the words of David Levering Lewis, it "lay next to the Bible"—without ever running a story that mentioned the formation of the Negro Leagues.[4]

In recent decades, the scholarship concerning the Harlem Renaissance has similarly overlooked the popularity and influence of sports, even as scholars have shed new light on popular culture and other related topics. In the preface to the second edition of his authoritative study *When Harlem Was in Vogue* (1988), David Levering Lewis noted that the arts and letters of the New Negro movement had been "talked about endlessly" but challenged "the widespread belief that what is usually called the Harlem Renaissance has also been extensively written about by students of social movements" (Lewis, *When Harlem* xxvii). The editors of *Double-Take: A Revisionist Harlem Renaissance Anthology* (2001), concentrating on women writers and homoerotic themes that were prevalent in the era, pointed out that popular music and the visual arts have been "neglected genres" in previous anthologies (Patton and Honey xxv). Still, while the work of Lewis and others has addressed this lack of attention to popular culture, social movements, and community institutions, sports and sportswriting in the Renaissance remain largely unexamined. For example, Anna Pochmara pointedly discusses the issue of masculinity in Harlem Renaissance literature and culture in her superb, wide-ranging study *The Making of the New Negro: Black Authorship, Masculinity, and Sexuality in the Harlem Renaissance* (2011), but she does not consider sports specifically; reflecting the scholarly and artistic focus on sports and popular culture in subsequent decades, Pochmara notes the references to boxing and bullfighting—and Ernest Hemingway—in the correspondence of Ralph Ellison and Richard Wright (Pochmara 191). Similarly, Andrew Leiter's *In the Shadow of the Black Beast* (2010) is an excellent analysis of the influence of primitivism in depictions of black masculinity in both Harlem Renaissance literature and the works of Southern white writers. Leiter does not focus on sports specifically, although he does refer to the rumors that were rampant in the 1920s about Babe Ruth's racial heritage; Leiter points out that this speculation likely explains Jason Compson's disdain for Ruth in William Faulkner's *The Sound and the Fury* (Leiter 90).

Just as masculinity and sexuality have been the subjects of recent scholarship on the Harlem Renaissance, the social significance of the African American press and its sportswriters has been the focus of notable research projects. Chris Lamb's *Conspiracy of Silence: Sportswriters and the Long Campaign to Desegregate Baseball* (2012) and Brian Carroll's *When to Stop the Cheering? The Black Press, the Black Community, and the Integration of Professional Baseball* (2007) are focused more specifically on the activist journalism that gathered steam in the 1930s and '40s, and they add immeasurably to the understanding of the black press and its impact on American society at large. Even more notably, Carroll's *The Black Press and Black Baseball, 1915–1955: A Devil's Bargain* (2015), considers the history of sportswriting in the specific context of the Harlem Renaissance. Carroll devotes a chapter of his study to the use of poetry by African American sportswriters of the era, drawing connections not only to the cultural movements of the Jazz Age, but also to the subsequent rise of rap and hip hop. Comparing their lack of critical scrutiny to that of Langston Hughes in the mainstream culture in the years before Hughes's death, Carroll asserts: "Similarly, black press sportswriters and editors have not been given the scholarly attention they deserve as rhetors, writers, and social activists, men who, through the medium of the newspaper, applied their artistic talents to describe and comment on issues and events of cultural and social importance" (Carroll, *Black Press* 23).

The sports and sportswriting of the Harlem Renaissance era have been largely left out of the academic conversation even as popular interest in the history of Negro Leagues and other African American athletic subjects has burgeoned. A museum dedicated to their history was founded in 1990 in Kansas City, while replica jerseys and caps have become popular. This popularity owes much to the scholarship that has been produced since 1970, when Robert L. Peterson published a history of the leagues, *Only the Ball Was White*. Peterson's book relied heavily on interviews with former Negro Leaguers and spawned a plethora of oral histories of the era. More traditional historical studies appeared in the ensuing years, while a research group under the auspices of the Society for American Baseball Research (SABR) has aimed to compile a definitive statistical record of the era. In a more recent example, the Sunday Review section of *The New York Times* featured a front-page story on the Anderson Monarchs, a Little

Introduction

League team led by the teenaged sensation Mo'ne Davis, whose coach, Steve Bandura, requires his players to learn about the Negro Leagues and their importance in American history (Bruni 1, 3). In the spring of 2015, the team toured the South and visited sites from the Civil Rights movement—including Selma, Alabama, and Little Rock, Arkansas—while traveling in a vintage 1947 bus.

Paradoxically, this sustained surge in popular historical curiosity has come at a time when interest in major league baseball among African Americans is in decline. The cultural critic Gerald Early, acknowledging the game's decreasing black fan base, points out that from the 1920s through the 1940s—that is, between the formation of the Negro Leagues and their decline—baseball was "by far" the most popular sport among African Americans. "There is, in fact, no sport," Early asserts, "not even boxing … that is more deeply enmeshed in the mythology and 'memory' of African American culture than baseball" (Early 413).

In the late 1940s, that cultural pervasiveness extended from literature to arts such as painting, as Jacob Lawrence applied the techniques of Harlem Renaissance artists to baseball images in works such as "Strike" and "The Long Stretch" (Campbell 29–31). Even in the 1960s and '70s, when boxing provided a powerful metaphor for writers such as Ishmael Reed in the Black Arts movement, Negro League baseball continued to occupy a prominent place in African American literature. The poet Samuel Allen, who was a student of James Weldon Johnson at Fisk and later a contemporary of Richard Wright in Paris, paid homage to Satchel Paige in "To Satch," which was widely anthologized in the 1960s; Allen's "View from the Corner"—not about boxing but street fighting—later appeared in *Black Poetry* (Broadside Press, 1969), edited by Gwendolyn Brooks.[5] A generation later, August Wilson's *Fences* (1986) depicted a former Negro League player coming to terms with integration and the opportunities available to his son, a highly recruited high school athlete. Although Wilson's play takes place in 1957, it comes as no surprise to his contemporary audience when the protagonist's son—significantly, a football player—swings awkwardly when he picks up his father's bat (Wilson 59). Despite its rich history and resonance in the play, baseball has been overlooked, even discarded, by the younger generation.

Early suggests a resolution to this paradox by reading the history of Negro League baseball as a process of "negotiating contradictions" (Early 414). In an essay that appeared in the companion piece to Ken Burns's documentary on baseball, Early argues that this process can be a key to understanding not only African American history but also American history in general:

> The current interest in Negro baseball is as much a reflection of a larger interest in black history as a critical revision of standard white history. Perhaps one way to try to locate the meaning of this interest, this fascination, for both blacks and whites is by positing the notion that we need to see Negro baseball as a partial exploration of the significance of the use and abuse of Negro history for black people and for black American life. ... Put another way, to understand black baseball might give us some sense of what a black historical consciousness is and what the development of a form of racial consciousness has meant to America at large [414].

Early uses Negro League baseball to explain this "historical consciousness" by aligning it, chronologically and structurally, with the Harlem Renaissance. Not only did both get their start around the same time (Rube Foster organized the first Negro League in 1920), but the same spirit of politically motivated organization also took hold then in the growing African American communities in the urban centers of the North, giving birth to each movement. Early connects the formation of the Negro Leagues to the rise of the "New Negro": Just as "intellectuals, writers, and journalists" were redefining themselves for the modern era, black baseball was reorganizing itself in a more modern fashion (414). The fact that professional sports were "enjoying an unprecedented popularity in the dominant culture," Early observes, "is a remarkable conjunction of racially self-conscious impulses with the creation of a mass-market consumer culture" (414–15).

Not all critics have found these impulses so remarkable or so self-conscious. The most controversial critic of sports as an aspect of African American culture in recent decades has probably been John Hoberman, who argues in *Darwin's Athletes: How Sport Has Damaged Black America and Preserved the Myth of Race* (1997) that the prominence of sports in African American life has served mainly to propagate the idea that the race has certain essential talents and limitations. Even more dourly, he contends that the achievements of black athletes have resulted in a general disdain for education and intellectual pursuits among African Americans. *Darwin's Athletes* sparked a range of responses, many charging him with a misappraisal of African American culture or downright condescension. Hoberman examines African American writing about sport in only one chapter of his book and never delves so deeply into the past as to reach the Harlem Renaissance; he does, however, specifically criticize Black Arts

Movement writers Ishmael Reed, Eldridge Cleaver, and Imamu Amiri Baraka for emphasizing a hypermasculine, embattled "boxing" ethos in their work. In his chapter, which he titles "Writin' Is Fightin'"—Reed's own phrase—Hoberman broadly attacks the "black male intelligentsia that has denounced almost every other form of cultural entrapment [but] has never mounted a campaign against the sports fixation" (Hoberman 76). He does, however, praise one of his primary critics—Gerald Early—as "the best" analyst among the members of this group.

Early, by contrast, gives a more nuanced reading to Baraka, who wrote nostalgically and nationalistically about Negro League baseball in his autobiography. Citing his comparison of the Negro Leagues' "aura" with African American speech and music, Early further suggests that Baraka "expresses perhaps better than he realizes the complex relationship between blacks and popular culture" (413–415). Early considers both the New Negro movement and the Negro Leagues examples of "the complex relationship between blacks and American popular culture, which reached its first culmination during the Renaissance" (415). This culmination came about, in his view, because of the transformation (or modernization) of folk-art forms such as "speech, music, and athletics." The resulting historical consciousness gave rise to the concurrent struggles that Early identifies in the era: one in the culture at large, between blacks and whites, over social, political, and cultural issues; and the other within the African American community, over the interpretation of the past and its use in dealing with the present. "Black baseball," Early contends, "has become a metaphor for both struggles" (415).

James Weldon Johnson, whose preface to *The Book of American Negro Poetry* (1922) called on African American poets to transform the popular idioms of vernacular poetry into high art, also figures prominently in Early's essay, as he must in any study of Renaissance sports. Early cites Johnson's *Black Manhattan*, a historical study in which baseball in the era before the organization of the Negro Leagues receives serious treatment, as "one of the black expressive cultural idioms that was to bring into being a new 'Black Community'" (415). Johnson helped establish the importance of popular art forms in the culture of the Renaissance, and he also stands as the only major figure of the movement to write extensively about baseball. In both *Black Manhattan* and his autobiography, *Along This Way*, Johnson wrote nostalgically about African American baseball in the era before the formation of the Negro Leagues, describing the game as part of the same

Introduction

Bohemian culture that gave rise to ragtime around the turn of the century as well as the popular musical theatre of the 1920s. A generation earlier, Johnson had sketched a portrait of New York's "Black Bohemia" populated by artists and athletes, in his novel *The Autobiography of an Ex-Colored Man*. After publishing his novel anonymously in 1912, Johnson labored virtually alone among the "old crowd" of Renaissance intellectuals as a promoter of sports and popular music as forms of folk art. Among the so-called "New Negro" generation, interest in folk art and Bohemian culture was more prevalent, although few writers and intellectuals demonstrated any interest in sports.

While the Renaissance elite kept its distance from the worlds of popular culture and sports, the African American press immersed itself in both. Combining sports and entertainment coverage, the Harlem sportswriters were Renaissance men of a kind, writing news and features, gossip columns and serious editorials. The sections produced by Dougherty in the *Amsterdam News*, for instance, included game stories and theatre reviews, analyses of the social influence of popular musicals and calls for integration in sports, investigations of the projectionists' strike at the Lafayette Theatre and firsthand accounts of the formation of baseball's Eastern Colored League. A Dougherty section might include a guest editor, such as Razaf. The section also featured news of events—sporting, theatrical, and social—from the historically black colleges of the South. These catholic tastes were driven by a conviction that everyone involved was part of the Renaissance going on around them.

While Harlem became the "mecca" of the movement, college campuses, even in the South, changed perceptibly in the era, as African American students enrolled in record numbers. In 1925, the special issue of the special edition of the *Survey Graphic* examining "Harlem: Mecca of the New Negro" included, on its back cover, a Winold Reiss illustration titled "A College Lad" (the cover featured tenor Roland Hayes, a Fisk University graduate). The subject of the portrait was Harold Jackman, but a more prototypical embodiment might have been Paul Robeson, the All-American football player and a Phi Beta Kappa graduate from Rutgers. By the end of the decade, Robeson had played three seasons of professional football, earned a law degree from Columbia, starred in several plays by Eugene O'Neill as well as three major productions of *Othello*, and sung on classical stages in both the United States and Europe (Stewart 4).

Although sports first made Robeson famous, he only occasionally referred to them in his writings and speeches. After he stopped playing professional football, his primary foray into professional sports came in 1943, when he joined a delegation of African American journalists and publishers in meeting with major-league baseball commissioner Kenesaw Mountain Landis to urge baseball to integrate. In his brief (128-page) autobiography, *Here I Stand*, published in 1958, Robeson mentions playing a sport only once, briefly recalling his brother teaching him to play football (Robeson 13). In the "Author's Foreword," however, he describes moving back to Harlem and remembering the Renaissance, giving sports equal status with music and his entrance into drama:

> Every street and landmark around here is rich with memories of the good times and dreams of young manhood.... Harlem after the first world war. Here I met and married Essie; here lifelong friendships began; here I started my career as an artist. Just a few blocks away, at the YWCA, I first walked on the stage in a play; and here I sang, for fun, in the clubs and cabarets; here were the thrills of the big basketball games, the dances, the social life... [Robeson 2; ellipses in original].

While his accomplishments in the high arts and his leftist politics endeared him to the intellectual elite, Robeson's broad-based popularity grew largely because of his celebrity as an athlete. His personal life, for example, was the "subject of perennial fascination for Harlemites" (Lewis, *When Harlem* 264). Robeson was the sort of Renaissance man that the image of the New Negro conjured up for many ordinary folks in Harlem, as well as for their spokesmen in the press.

This ideal shares much with the one described by Ralph Ellison in his autobiographical introduction to *Shadow and Act* (1964), in which he describes his own conception of a "Renaissance man." Ellison, who played football in high school, moved to Harlem in 1936, interested in painting and photography after having studied music at Tuskegee. Describing his youth in Oklahoma in the 1920s, Ellison applies the term "Renaissance man" to himself and to his boyhood friends, whose imaginations expanded with "voracious reading" and a "vicarious identification" with the possibilities of adventure (Ellison xiv–xv). Ellison explains:

> We were seeking examples, patterns to live by, out of a freedom which for all its being ignored by the sociologists and subtle thinkers was implicit in the Negro situation. ... Gamblers and scholars, jazz musicians and scientists, Negro cowboys and soldiers from the Spanish-American and First World Wars, movie stars and stunt men, figures from the Italian Renaissance and literature, both classical and popular, were combined with the special virtues of some local bootlegger, the eloquence of some Negro preacher, the strength and grace of some local athlete, the

ruthlessness of some businessman-physician, the elegance in dress and manners of some headwaiter or hotel doorman [xv–xvi].

Ellison admits he self-consciously created these archetypes, explaining further that "*culturally* play is a preparation" for the performance that life as an African American artist would entail (emphasis in original). That "performance"—not a word he uses pejoratively—was driven by a "sense of obligation" and an awareness of style, in this case "Negro American style."

This awareness of "style" connects the artist and the group, in Ellison's view. He describes it as a microcosm of popular culture. "And we recognized and were proud of our group's own style wherever we discerned it," Ellison elaborates, "...in jazzmen and prize fighters, ballplayers and tap dancers; in gesture, inflection, intonation, timbre and phrasing. Indeed, in all those nuances of expression and attitude which reveal a culture" (xvii). The ostensible improbability of those on the margins of society achieving such cultural status serves to underscore the importance of Ellison's point. Comparing the "incongruity" of African American cultural achievements to those of white Southerners, he suggests an even deeper resonance in such organic American products as baseball and jazz:

> Surely our fantasies have caused less damage to the nation's sense of reality, if for no other reason than that ours were expressive of a more democratic ideal. Remember, too, as William Faulkner made us so vividly aware, that the slaves often took the essence of the aristocratic ideal (as they took Christianity) with far more seriousness than their masters, and that we, thanks to the tight telescoping of American history, were but two generations from that previous condition. Renaissance Men, indeed! [xvii–xviii]

While the intellectuals of the Renaissance failed to recognize the value in these cultural "nuances," most of Ellison's contemporaries in the 1930s and 1940s did not. The integrated Federal Writers Project, for which Ellison and Brown worked as part of the New Deal, employed several Harlem sportswriters in producing its social and cultural history of African Americans in New York; meanwhile, the Chicago chapter included Nelson Algren, Arna Bontemps, Jack Conroy, and James T. Farrell, all of whom showed an interest in sports and games.

Increasingly, as the Depression gave rise to proletarian interests, writers and other intellectuals recognized the social significance of sports. Dr. Edwin B. Henderson, a Harvard graduate and the head of physical training for high schools in Washington, D.C., published a book-length study of the subject, *The Negro in Sports*, in 1939. *The Crisis*, under the leadership of Roy Wilkins, covered sports more extensively and joined the sportswriters of the African American press in calling for the integration of baseball. The communist *Daily Worker*, which published articles by Richard Wright on Joe Louis and Satchel Paige, also joined the call for integration in baseball, taking partial credit when the Brooklyn Dodgers finally signed Jackie Robinson to a professional contract in 1946. The interracial membership of such organizations gave rise to the idea that the agitation of the Depression era, along with a common interest in sports, had briefly aligned the white and black working classes.

In the bleak light of the Depression, sports and other pursuits with popular appeal seemed to hold more political promise than ever before. That promise—that sports could compel powerful white interests to integrate and recognize unheralded performers—had lived throughout the Renaissance as a shadowy possibility, especially in the ballparks of the Negro Leagues. On those playing fields, symbolic as they were of institutional segregation, the chance that talent would win out over racism remained a vivid goal for ballplayers and fans alike. Even more vividly, that victory was the explicit goal of the sportswriters of the Renaissance, who not only considered it their purpose as sportswriters to debate such issues, but also saw their talent as undeniably worthy of attention. And why not? As writers in Harlem, they were imbued with the spirit of the Renaissance.

PART I
Literature and the Renaissance Intelligentsia

1. "The Discipline of Work and Play"
Athletics, Education and the Harlem Intelligentsia's Concept of Culture

Despite the burgeoning popularity of sports in the American culture of the 1920s, and in the African American community in particular, the intellectuals of the Harlem Renaissance generally ignored the exploits and influence of the era's black athletes. Amid their own calls for inclusion in American cultural life, the Renaissance intellectuals drew their own, often elitist, lines when confronted with increasingly influential elements of popular culture, from sports to jazz. If the intelligentsia had no interest in sports, however, ordinary folks certainly did. In the course of the decade, professional basketball shared bills with jazz bands in Harlem's dance halls, while football games between southern black colleges filled stadiums in northern cities. In 1923, when more than 400,000 fans paid to see the games played by the clubs in Rube Foster's Negro National League, the Eastern Colored League was organized to include New York City's two independent baseball teams. By the end of the decade, despite the onset of the Depression, Negro League teams were renting Yankee Stadium and other big-league ballparks for doubleheaders and all-star games. Only a generation later, however, after the triumphs of Jesse Owens, Joe Louis, and Jackie Robinson, did the African American intellectuals who came of age during the Renaissance turn their attention to the influence of sports in society.

During the New Negro movement that spawned the Renaissance, intellectuals took interest in sports only occasionally. Even sociologists such as W.E.B. Du Bois, the movement's elder statesman, rarely mentioned sports as anything more than a metaphor to be used in communicating to those beyond their social circle. Still, even in these brief mentions and glancing asides, one can extrapolate an attitude and an occasional analysis of the role sports played in the era. Beneath the debate over education between Du Bois and Booker T. Washington, for example, lay an additional disagreement over the value of recreation in an idealized culture. Increasingly, as athletics became widely ensconced in higher education and professional black sports were organized in the form of Negro League baseball, additional voices joined the fray, arguing not only that sports carried social significance but also that they could coexist with traditional cultural ideals. But these voices—especially in professional sports and the African American press—are rarely included in the body of literature that has come to represent the Renaissance.

Du Bois, as usual, represents both an example and an exception. His personal interest in sports seems to have been scant; in his vast body of work, one finds only a few references to collegiate or professional athletics. Although he promoted the benefits of exercise and recreation, his personal interest in them was apparently limited to walking. Filling out a questionnaire in 1938, he listed walking as his favorite outdoor sport; as his favorite indoor sport, he entered "reading" (*Correspondence* II 168). In a late essay looking at race relations in America between 1917 and 1947, however, he noted the importance of "some letting down" of the color bars in baseball and track and field and conceded sports "must loom large because of public liking for such recreation" ("Race Relations" 75). Although such references to sports are rare in Du Bois's work—in nearly a quarter-century as the editor of *The Crisis* (1910–1933), he published few articles on sports and none devoted to the organization of the Negro Leagues—these brief forays demonstrate his recognition of the social significance of athletics. While most intellectuals of the Renaissance era paid no attention to sports whatsoever, and the supremely practical Washington saw them as needless diversions from work and other forms of self-control, Du Bois acknowledged the popularity and potential of sports in African American culture. The trials of Jack Johnson and the triumphs of Jesse Owens in the 1936 Olympics were two subjects Du Bois used as springboards to comment on sport and its role in his concept of culture, while his long-running debate with Washington became another. In his analyses of higher education, beginning with an early essay that criticized the absence of recreation in Washington's vocational program and culminating with Du Bois's participation in a student rebellion at Fisk University at the height of the Renaissance, he gradually granted sports cultural status. Ultimately, Du Bois argued that sports could be not only productive play, serving as a necessary complement to cultural work, but also a field of achievement in their own right. Their value might be more symbolic than tangible, but their influence with the younger generation of the Renaissance convinced Du Bois they might play a role in social change, especially as he shifted political course in the 1920s and 1930s.

Du Bois and the Cultural Role of Sports

Du Bois's critique of the Jack Johnson controversy, which appeared in *The Crisis* in 1914, was trenchant but relatively brief, consisting of five short paragraphs. It also came rather belatedly: Johnson had won the heavyweight title in 1908; defeated the "great white hope," James J. Jeffries, in 1910; and fled the country in 1912 after being charged with violating the Mann Act for crossing state lines with his white girlfriend. In his editorial, Du Bois seemed less interested in boxing than in greater issues, whether directly related (racism) or not (war). After comparing the violence of the sport to that of football and boat racing (thereby demonstrating his distance from the tastes of the general public), Du Bois called boxing "a highly civilized pastime as compared with the international game of war which produces so many 'heroes' and national monuments" ("The Prize Fighter" 181). Writing as war was gathering in Europe, Du Bois noted ironically that the "brutality" of boxing had suddenly caused even liberal-minded newspapers to "roll their eyes in shivery horror" as they gave front-page coverage to Johnson's victory over Frank Moran in Paris. Du Bois kept his cultural gaze fixed on Europe in pointing out the absurdity of the sudden outrage over the "ancient sport," which was "mentioned in Homer's Iliad and Virgil's Aeneid and was a recognized branch of the celebrated Olympic games" (181).

For Du Bois, this connection between boxing and the achievements of western civilization became even more ironic as he shifted to his primary theme in the editorial, the persistence of racism in America. The driving force behind the furor, he pointed out, was not worry for the brutality of boxing but rather racism and the American obsession with Johnson's "unforgivable blackness." Du Bois contrasted the hatred shown by white America with what he cast as Johnson's own moral character, to which "some pretend to object." He pointed out that Johnson had not even knocked out Moran (though he fails to mention that the referee stopped the fight after twenty rounds), in fact "did not even try," and fought with "the utmost fairness and good nature." Meanwhile, Du Bois blithely dismissed the legal charges against Johnson as merely focused on his "marital troubles," which, he claimed, rarely affected the careers of celebrated white figures, be they "prize fighters or ball players or even statesmen." Du Bois intensified his sarcasm to end the editorial: "Wherefore we conclude that at present prize fighting is very, very immoral, and that we must rely on football and war for pastime until Mr. Johnson retires or permits himself to be 'knocked out'" (181).

Beneath Du Bois's sarcastic critique is an implied appeal to liberal ideals. Among supposedly cultured people, he suggested, racism is an absurdity that deserves as much mockery as rational analysis. In an even more sarcastic editorial in 1923, Du Bois took offense at the lack of outrage over Jack Dempsey's one-sided maulings ("This Law-Abiding Land" 151–152). Du Bois's anger at the failings of American culture could be expressed rationally or sardonically, but in either case, its intensity indicates his faith in the progress of an enlightened, educated society. According to Arnold Rampersad, Du Bois's middle age—roughly the first three decades of the 20th century—was marked by his "love of liberal idealism" (*Art* 182). Rampersad identifies a "triangulation among socialism, black nationalism, and liberal idealism" in Du Bois's work at the time, but he sees his liberalism as "drawing on" the other two strains and "becoming probably more influential than either" (182). In the Johnson case, Du Bois found the failings of American liberalism particularly outrageous, because they exposed the hypocrisy of the arguments against boxing. The racial persecution of Johnson lay hidden, even in the liberal press, beneath the supposedly principled outrage over boxing's brutality.

Like many critics of African American culture, Du Bois considered boxing a uniquely significant sport in racial terms. Even as late as 1945, in his plan for the *Encyclopedia of the Negro*, Du Bois's preparatory volume included only three entries dealing directly with sports, aside from a generic "Sports and Athletics" summary, but all three had to do with boxing: one devoted to the sport itself, and one each profiling Jack Johnson and Joe Louis. Even prominent subjects such as Negro League baseball (then enjoying a resurgence in popularity and influence that preceded Jackie Robinson's signing to a professional contract with the Dodgers the next season) and the 1936 Olympic victories of Jesse Owens were left out.[1] Still, Du Bois's responses to the Berlin Olympiad represent his shifting views on culture and the growing role sports had to play in it—particularly for African Americans. Although Du Bois's liberalism might have been dominant in the 1910s and '20s, by the time of the Berlin Olympics, his interest in economic factors had strengthened the strains of socialism and black nationalism in his writing. In the 1930s, Du Bois redefined his idealism as "liberal pragmatism" to emphasize these factors, though he argued for "a compromise short of a doctrine of revolution" (Rampersad, *Art* 220).

In two columns devoted to the Olympics, Du Bois elaborated upon the significance of sports in this pragmatic worldview. As it happened, Du Bois spent most of 1936 in Germany, posting weekly dispatches in the *Pittsburgh Courier*. However, in what David Levering Lewis has called "a costly decision for sports historians and biographers," Du Bois left Berlin for Paris just before the Olympics began on August 1; he then traveled to Bavaria and Austria, returning to Berlin only after the games had ended (Lewis, *Fight* 403). In his column of September 19, Du Bois began by observing, as if he had never left, "Berlin is settling down to normalcy after the Olympian Games" (*Newspaper Columns* 114). As he had done in his analysis of Jack Johnson, Du Bois showed more interest in the personal character of Jesse Owens and his teammates than in their athletic achievements. In this case, of course, the athletes were to be praised as "gentlemen" rather than defended in relative terms. In fact, Du Bois asserted, they "typified a new conception of the American Negro for Europe, and also a new idea of race relations in the United States" (114). The reference to character, however, raised another issue for Du Bois: "the whole question of amateur sport." How, Du Bois wondered, could the figure of the gentleman athlete be reconciled with the tenets of socialism?

Embarking on a brief history lesson, Du Bois summarized the development of sport in western culture, beginning with the leisure pursuits of the English gentry and concluding with the introduction of physical education, amid the rise of democracy and the middle class, in the 19th century. Du Bois located the modern rift between amateur and professional in higher education, specifically his own:

> The spread of sport in colleges arose from a mingling of the two ideas: the idea of Sport as a gentleman's diversion, and the idea of Sport as the development of health among the young. Thus in my day at Harvard one could easily see the two ideas in curious contrast: to get on the Harvard crew was then, and still is, an almost purely social function, for which no "mucker" need apply. This largely explains Harvard's defeats in rowing [*Newspaper Columns* 115].

Du Bois discerned the same "curious contrast" in the results of the Berlin Olympics. The Americans had taken the democratic approach, while the English continued to play the gentleman's game. The result was a lesson in pragmatism: "This explains why England, the land of Sport, cuts so poor a figure in the Olympics—she is picking her competing entrants from too small a class. On the contrary, the United States were compelled to pick even Negroes if they wanted to win" (115).

In this victory of pragmatism, however, Du Bois foresaw a pitfall—one that would resonate in future decades. The Olympic ideal of amateurism obtained only for those with the wealth and leisure to pursue it. At first casting this notion in classical terms ("To be an amateur, a man must not receive pay for his work"), Du Bois quickly returned to his pragmatic position. "Regardless of class or color," he pointed out, "the competing athlete must and does receive pay" (115). The likely result in America of a pursuit of achievement in sports, Du Bois argued, would not be the emergence of a new class of gentleman athletes but rather dishonesty. The stakes, as later Olympians and other amateur athletes have shown, would be particularly high for African Americans. Pragmatically, and perhaps presciently, Du Bois concluded: "It is to the clear interest of Negro athletes to help abolish the distinction between Professional and Amateur in athletic competition" (115).

Du Bois's second column on the 1936 Olympics ran in the *Courier* five weeks later. As if aware that he had conspicuously ignored the details of the most celebrated Olympiad in memory, Du Bois dealt with the events and the athletes more specifically this time, though with irony. The fact that the American team was integrated was remarkable enough to Europeans, he observed: "The man in the street has assumed that the chief industry of black men in America is being lynched" (*Newspaper Columns* 127). As a result, the African American athletes were featured and photographed by French and German newspapers—presumably, Du Bois's sources of information as he traveled during the Games—even before their victories on the track and the field. "That would be astonishing enough; but these black athletes are extraordinary performers," Du Bois continued (127). He then acknowledged the triumphs of the American team, as well as Owens's popularity in Germany. "He is without a doubt the most popular single athlete in the Olympic Games of 1936," Du Bois wrote of Owens (127).

Writing so soon after the conclusion of the games, Du Bois declined

1. The "Discipline of Work and Play"

to speculate on the lasting impression that Owens and his teammates would leave. He felt certain, however, it was "wide and deep" (127). The main point of his column, in fact, was the growing significance of sport, "which Europe is discovering and spelling with a large 'S'" (127). The confluence of the athletes' successes and the increasingly visible stage of sport had undeniable importance; the only question was whether other stages would follow. Looking ahead, Du Bois offered a suggestion steeped in cultural achievement: "All this is going to be big with promise for the future, but it must be followed by other things. We must be represented, not only in sports, but in science, in literature, and in art" (127). Although Lewis suggests that "perhaps a tinge of Du Boisian intellectual elitism was to be detected in his insistence" (*Fight* 403), the deference Du Bois shows to sports in his column remains significant. Victories in the high jump and the 100 meters certainly could not compare to accomplishments in the arts, but they could help clear a path that had been blocked.

Strangely, Du Bois neglected in either column to mention Hitler's refusal to follow tradition and greet Owens or his medal-winning African American teammates (Lewis, *Fight* 402–403). Lewis, who finds Du Bois's columns "decidedly more dutiful than interested," speculates: "A possible inference is that Du Bois regarded the games as a Nazi variation of the bread-and-circus diversions favored by dictatorships since ancient days" (403). Lewis also notes with irony that Du Bois spent the week after the conclusion of the Games in Bayreuth, where "for five nights uninterrupted he bathed himself in Wagner" (404). Although he conceded that he was no expert on opera, Du Bois devoted two columns in October to Wagner's *Lohengrin*, which he had also praised in *The Souls of Black Folk* (Lewis, *Fight* 649). Du Bois acknowledged the possibility that his readers might wonder what relevance Wagner had to them. However, as Lewis observes, "His answer—that Wagner's life exemplified the triumph of genius over adversity—may not have satisfied every reader, especially any who may have known of the Nazis' affinity for the composer and his music" (649).

Du Bois's attempt to bring Wagner to the masses helps explain his interest in examining the impact of the Berlin Olympics, even if he had little interest in the games. As Cornel West points out, although Du Bois turned to Marxism late in hopes of finding the key to equality, his deepest and most abiding faith lay always in the "inherently humanizing" effects of highbrow culture (West, "Black Strivings" 95–96). West specifically cites Du Bois's notion that "the educated elite can more easily transcend their individual and class interests and more readily act on behalf of the common good than the educated masses" (95). Certainly, Du Bois's effusive praise of Wagner—not to mention his decision to leave Berlin just as the Olympics were getting under way—attests to his cultural elitism. But Du Bois's concession to sports, in hopes that they might pave the way to greater cultural achievements, demonstrates his awareness that the Talented Tenth could include more than an educated elite.

Athletics, Education and the Du Bois–Washington Debate

Although Du Bois had little interest in sports as a spectator, he did support physical education as part of the liberal arts curriculum. As an undergraduate at Fisk University, he was among the students whose request for a gymnasium led to one being built in 1888, the year of his graduation (Richardson 155). Du Bois recalled in a letter to the editor of the *Fisk News* in 1940 that he had helped raise $700 to go towards the new gymnasium. That, he said, was his "only connection with athletics at Fisk" (*Correspondence* II 231–232). In 1948, Charles S. Johnson, the university president, converted the gym into the Carl Van Vechten Gallery; Georgia O'Keeffe had given Fisk part of a collection left by her husband, Alfred Stieglitz, and oversaw the conversion of the building (Powell 21).

In 1897, in a paper delivered at Hampton Institute and published in Hampton's magazine, *The Southern Workman*, Du Bois considered the role of athletics in education more specifically. In "The Problem of Amusement," Du Bois called for an equal emphasis on work and play in education, contending that the one enhances the other. "Boys and girls should be encouraged if not compelled," he wrote, "to run, jump, walk, row, swim, throw and vault" ("Problem" 235). Such a balance, he argued, is not only healthful but also cultural: "Where the balance between the two is best maintained, we have the best civilization, the best culture" (230–231).

Du Bois's work through the late 1890s had been primarily devoted to empirical and statistical analysis, but his argument in "The Problem of Amusement" represents a movement toward more subjective cultural studies. In the essay, Du Bois contended that the primacy of religion in African American life had created an ironic situation in which the church was the main source of recreational opportunities, even as it condemned most forms of amusement (234). Using billiards as an example, Du Bois noted that "taken in itself, a more innocent, interesting, and gentlemanly game of skill could scarcely be thought of," but because of the game's common connections to gambling and drinking, it was condemned by most ministers (231). It was thus left to the "social reformer" to rectify the paradox. "Is there any valid reason why the Y.M.C.A. at Norfolk should not have a billiard table among its amusements?" Du Bois asked. "In other words, is it wise policy to surrender a charming amusement wholly to the devil and then call it devilish?" (231–232).

Absolving the church of overreaching in its "untenable position," Du Bois turned his attention to educators, who he said had a special responsibility in teaching students the value of recreation. Addressing his comments directly to institutions, such as Hampton and Tuskegee, that had what he considered a single-minded focus on industrial education, Du Bois argued: "[A]thletic sports must in the future play a larger part in the normal and mission schools of the South" (236). Sports, Du Bois posited, provide more than simple exercise: they are also a means of channeling the need for amusement into productive, even intelligent, activity. "We must rapidly come to the place," he continued, "where the man all brain and no muscle is looked upon as almost as big a fool as the man all muscle and no brain" (236).

Despite this contention, Du Bois did not mention athletics, either as a part of student life or as a possible career for college graduates, in a related study, *The College-Bred Negro American* (1910). The monograph, edited by Du Bois and Augustus Granville Dill, his colleague at Atlanta University, was one of a series of studies that resulted from the annual conferences for the Study of Negro Problems, held at Atlanta between 1898 and 1914. *The College-Bred Negro American* was one such cyclical work, building on a briefer study, "The College-Bred Negro," of 1900 (Lewis, *W.E.B. Du Bois* I, 217–24). Although the idea for the conferences was not Du Bois's—Hampton Institute had already carried out a similar series of studies—he assumed control in its first year and laid out an ambitious plan, shifting the focus of the series to more urban problems. Du Bois had envisioned the project to span a century of decade-long cycles, with topics re-examined every ten years. The 1906 conference was devoted to "The Health and Physique of the Negro-American," featuring a presentation by Franz Boas on the cultural origins of racism, but otherwise its emphasis on physical characteristics such as brain size and the like "now seem mementos of largely discredited intellectual approaches" (Rampersad, "Art and Imagination," 55). Du Bois recognized the shortcomings of some of these studies but, given the difficulty of raising funds for such projects, "nevertheless felt that some information was better than none" (Green and Driver 15).

While he had not yet publicly broken ranks with Washington, Du Bois used the conclusion of "The Problem of Amusement" to hint at the split that was soon to come. The absence of play, he told his Hampton audience, was a particular failing of the Hampton-Tuskegee approach to education that Washington had developed:

> Instead of warning young people against an excess of pleasure, let us rather inspire them to unselfish work, and show them that amusement and recreation are the legitimate and necessary accompaniments of work, and that we get the maximum of enjoyment from them when they strengthen and inspire us for renewed effort in a great cause; and above all, let us teach them that there can be no greater cause than the development of Negro character to its highest and holiest possibilities [237].

Du Bois conflates recreation and amusement with "unselfish work," a connection that may seem incongruous at first blush, though no more so than his later insistence that "all art is propaganda" ("Criteria" 1000). Just as that pronouncement was spurred by his opposition to the "decadence" of the Harlem Renaissance, which he foresaw resulting from Alain Locke's apolitical fealty to beauty, the yoking together of contradictory drives in the service of a single ideal was characteristic of Du Bois's thinking. In *Darkwater*, for example, he described a chapter of his life as the "Discipline of Work and Play" (14).

That chapter of Du Bois's life stretched from 1897 to 1910, his years at Atlanta University, when his "real life work" began: "They were years of great spiritual upturning, of the making and unmaking of ideals, of hard work and hard play" (*Darkwater* 20). Ceasing to be a "cold and scientific investigator," Du Bois described himself perceiving and understanding life in its full breadth for the first time. "I saw life through all its paradox and contradiction of streaming eyes and mad merriment," he wrote (21). It was in this period, according to Rampersad, that Du Bois embraced more subjective approaches and wrote in a variety of genres as he overcame "an obsessive avoidance of the subjective and the racial" (Rampersad, "Afterword" 302). Rampersad sees Du Bois's willingness to work subjectively across genres as significant in the later movement towards interdisciplinarity in the academy and, particularly, in the development of American Studies (303). Rampersad continues:

> Above all, I would argue, race is the factor that made—and still makes—the complications that demand interdisciplinariness and multidisciplinariness as a necessary scholarly response. In grappling with race, with its overt but also covert power to complicate, subvert, and compromise virtually every important aspect of American life, Du Bois almost instinctively resorted to the unstable but highly creative patterns of investigation and adaptations of investigations that characterized his career as an intellectual and scholar [303–304].

Du Bois seems to have located this newfound subjectivity in "paradox and contradiction," particularly the complementary nature of work and play.

Du Bois's embrace of such complexities led him to oppose the leadership of Washington, which he found single-minded, especially regarding education. As Du Bois explained, "contrary to my dream of racial solidarity and notwithstanding my deep desire to serve and follow and think, rather than to lead and inspire and decide, I found myself suddenly the leader of a great wing of people fighting against another and greater wing" (*Darkwater* 22). Indeed, Du Bois's specific defense of play in "The Problem of Amusement," though stemming from a cultural tracing of the influence of religion, was ultimately directed at the vocational program of Washington. The program, as developed at Hampton and perfected at Tuskegee, was well-known for the rigidity of its daily schedule. As Washington explained in *Up from Slavery* (1900), this regimen was designed to keep students in line: "I have often been asked how we keep so large a body of people together, and at the same time keep them out of mischief. There are two answers: that the men and women who come to us for an education are in earnest; and that everybody is kept busy" (190). The tightly structured schedule that Washington then laid out, so detailed that it includes "five minutes with the daily news" at 8:55 a.m., included no time for exercise or recreation. By comparison, Benjamin Franklin's *Autobiography*, an obvious model for Washington's in many regards, also included no physical exercise or recreation in its "Scheme of Employment for the Twenty-four Hours of a natural Day"; Franklin did, however, include "Musick, or Diversion, or Conversation" among his suppertime evening business (Franklin 94). The Daily Order of Exercises at Hampton during Washington's time as a student there had been only slightly more forgiving: At 8:30 a.m., roll call included exercises; between 10:20 and 10:40, students enjoyed a recess (Harlan 62–63).

Washington's divergence from Du Bois, who valued both exercise and amusement, should come as no surprise in light of the general dismissal of games and play in *Up from Slavery*. "I am often asked how," Washington wrote, "in the midst of so much work, a large part of which is before the public, I can find time for any rest or recreation, and what kind of recreation or sports I am fond of. This is a rather difficult question to answer" (164). Indeed, the question went largely unanswered, as Washington explained that a love for work itself, and the ability to control it so that it never takes over one's life, led to "a freshness of body and a vigour of mind," as well as "a kind of strength that is most valuable." The only forms of physical recreation to which Washington assigned any value were gardening and caring for animals, both close to farm work and thus patently useful in the Tuskegee mindset. Games, beyond an occasional game of marbles with his children, were useless. "I have never seen a game of football," he asserted (166).

This emphasis on work and utility was elemental to the Tuskegee approach to education, which Houston A. Baker, Jr., sees as an attempt to control and purify the body. In Baker's view, this preoccupation with bodily control stems not only from Washington's depiction of racial uplift—that of rising up from the degradation of slavery and poverty by stressing cleanliness at each step—but also from the moral rectitude of the white missionary tradition of many Southern schools, which Baker brandishes "the containment of the beast" (Baker 46–50, 54–58). These attitudes had been ingrained in Washington as a student at Hampton: "The phrase 'containment of the beast' springs directly from the missionary imperatives of Hampton Institute, where General [Samuel] Armstrong designed a monstrously strenuous daily schedule for his black charges so that they would have no leftover vigor for nocturnal impropriety, sexual or otherwise" (Baker 57). This strictness did not extend to the faculty, of course: Armstrong would oversee sports and games played by the institute's white women teachers that sometimes grew so raucous as to disturb students who were in study hall (Baker 49–50, Harlan 69). Baker calls this "framed play," a departure from the model Armstrong presented to his students during working hours. Baker derives his concept of "framed play" from social psychologists Gregory Bateson and Erving Goffman (Baker 35). From Bateson, he draws the idea of play as "nonserious activity modeled on its serious complement," while Goffman provides his notion of frames as "spaces where cultural ideals are performed by human beings in commerce"

1. The "Discipline of Work and Play"

(35–36). Baker cites Victor Turner's notion of the "liminal" or middle stage in rituals as an example of framed cultural play (36).

Washington strove to emulate the model at all times, eliminating not only recreational play but also the "frame" that defines the fashioned self and delineates kinds of cultural "play" (Baker 35–36). According to Baker, "Washington never moved to a position where he could relax the boundaries of his self-created, performed identity as the 'son' of Armstrong. He had always to pay scrupulous attention to the line, the rim of the frame, allowing him minimal breathing room both for himself, and for 'the race'" (59). Indeed, the denial of games and recreation in *Up from Slavery*, along with the one-track daily regimen, are testaments to Washington's attempt to outdo the example of his mentor rather than to imitate it (Baker 59).

This use of "play" is slippery, of course. Baker's analysis of Washington shares much with Johan Huizinga's depiction of culture as something that is "played from the very beginning" (Huizinga 46). Specifically, it is a mimetic form of play, a display that takes on qualities of ritual in that aspects of the rite persist even after the performance ends (Huizinga 13–14). But Baker's critique goes much further, as he labels Washington's desire to control the body a "zealous aestheticization of slavery as 'modernity'" (Baker 60). Thus Baker comes closer to Huizinga's complaint that "civilization to-day is no longer played," as non-play and "false play" have spawned cultish movements such as Nazism (Huizinga 204–206). Like Huizinga, both Washington and Du Bois conceive of play dialectically. However, rather than opposing play to reality, as Huizinga does, their disagreement over "amusement" centered on its relationship to work: For Du Bois, it was complementary, for Washington, a distraction. As Jacques Ehrmann points out, this insistence on a dialectic between play and "seriousness" indicates the extreme rationalism of Huizinga's position (Ehrmann 34). Du Bois follows Huizinga's notion that play has a civilizing effect on culture, a notion that Ehrmann finds contradictory: Play civilizes, and yet our culture is constantly devoid of it (Ehrmann 51). In Ehrmann's view, to define play is to define culture: "In other words, the distinguishing characteristic of reality is that it is played. Play, reality, culture are synonymous and interchangeable. Nature does not exist prior to culture" (Ehrmann 56). Thus, while Washington placed little or no value in play, his inclination to see it in opposition to work reveals the rationalist viewpoint that he and Du Bois shared. For both men, the foundation of culture was work.

Cornel West points out a "procapitalist assumption circumscribing the Du Bois–Washington debate" (West, "Race and Modernity" 66). Within this assumption lay the overarching question of how best to instill a work ethic into the ensuing generation; more specifically, others asked whether organized play—intercollegiate athletics—should be a part of an educational institution. In time, as athletics became a central part of higher education, the debate continued through the Renaissance years. Du Bois, having outlived Washington, took part in this argument, further extending his concept of "the discipline of work and play." As protests erupted on the campuses of black colleges throughout the South, emboldened by the New Negro movement to challenge old notions of discipline, Du Bois turned to sports as a means of communicating with the younger generation. Consequently, at the height of the Renaissance, he began to widen his concept of culture, transcribing the growing importance of athletic achievements by African Americans into his ideal: a culture advanced by discipline, work, and productive play.

Athletics and Protest in Higher Education

The bold spirit of the Renaissance harbored little patience for the older generation's ideas of tradition and discipline. Enrollment at the historically black colleges exploded in the years immediately after World War I, growing from 2,641 in 1916 to 13,197 in 1927 (Holmes 160, 191). This emboldening gave rise to protests against antiquated codes of discipline at several southern schools in the mid-1920s. The most celebrated rebellion took place at Du Bois's alma mater, Fisk University, and it saw Du Bois revisit the issue of athletics and their role in higher education.

Discipline and regimentation had long been tenets of the South's segregated colleges, most of which were founded by white New Englanders in a wave of missionary zeal during the Reconstruction years. Even institutions that had evolved into independent, secular schools continued to be run by white administrators into the twentieth century. By that time, most white colleges, even in the South, had lifted or eased their own Victorian codes of discipline; as Raymond Wolters points out, the fact that the African American schools still retained such codes made their racialized underpinnings clear (13). Many faculty members at these schools, imbued with bourgeois ideals of scientific progress, believed students "could not learn unless they broke away from the black folk culture and assimilated the values of the white middle class" (Wolters 12).

According to Charles S. Johnson, "the missionary era had reached its apex by 1900" (286). However, strict codes of discipline—prohibiting, for instance, not just smoking and swearing but also the wearing of unapproved hats—remained in place into the 1920s, even at the more secular schools. The dress code at Fisk, as detailed in the 1920 catalog, required women to wear white uniforms in the summer and blue in winter; at other schools, even undergarments had to be approved. At almost all segregated schools in the South, leaving campus without permission was also prohibited—a rule that was widely supported by students' parents (Richardson 86-88). With support from both sides of the establishment's divide, the disciplinary codes generally persisted. The reasons ran deeper than residual religious tradition: Northern philanthropists, the primary sources of funding for the non-religious private colleges, agreed that strict codes of discipline were necessary; pragmatically, they feared an easing of the codes would have an inadvertent effect, causing state governments to tighten controls—and reduce funding—at state-supported black schools.

In the early twentieth century, this flow of money began to ebb: Philanthropists, presumably in an attempt to attack racism through "enlightenment," gave more money to private white institutions in the South. Predictably, this reduced the funds going to black schools, especially those that diverted from proscribed modes of operation (Wolters 14). Such ironies were not new, however: African Americans had long been excluded from the system of public schools in the South. As Negro Leaguer Dave Malarcher, a college graduate, recalled:

> You see, right after the Civil War, many white people from up in New England, Christian people, went South and founded schools. They founded my school, New Orleans University—Straight University, Talladega, Fisk—all those schools were founded by them. And then, of course, a few colored people that lived down in the cities where those schools were founded early learned to read and write and got a small amount of education, and they went out in the country and established 'pay schools.' A nickel a week, you know? ... This was a very common thing throughout the country down there in Louisiana. The whites had public schools, you know [Peterson, *Only* 6-7].

At the time of Washington's death in 1915, even Du Bois concurred with some of these convictions, for reasons that were as much moral as pedagogical (Wolters 13). But Du Bois's support for the southern schools and their disciplinary codes began to wane in the 1920s. While liberal arts institutions such as Fisk were beholden to an alliance of white supporters in the North and South for their survival, Hampton and Tuskegee had cultivated extensive support for their program among white philanthropists in the north. The Slater Fund, for example, which gave nearly two million dollars to forty-eight historically black colleges and universities between 1882 and 1932, awarded roughly two-thirds of that total to Tuskegee and Hampton (Holmes 170). By 1924, Hampton's endowment was larger than that of the University of Virginia (Lewis, *W.E.B. Du Bois* II, 133). As Du Bois saw it, a "new alliance of Northern Philanthropy and Southern white domination was in control" ("Fisk," 251–52). But there was also another, more publicized reminder of the widening gap between the two educational philosophies: In their 1924 football game, Tuskegee defeated Fisk by the score of 67–0—"the galling symbolism of which," according to David Levering Lewis, Du Bois could not bear (*W.E.B. Du Bois* II, 139).

The resounding defeat was no aberration. In spite of Washington's opposition to games, baseball and football had been introduced at Tuskegee in the 1890s, and the teams gradually became more organized and competitive after the players petitioned in 1897 to get more practice time (Harlan 282). The petition, which was signed by "several hundred" students, read in part: "We cannot finish a game of ball between the hours of three and four. We therefore petition that we be given Saturday afternoons, say from three o'clock till tea for base ball and other games" (as qtd. by Harlan 282–283). According to Louis Harlan, such grievances were usually filed when Washington was away from campus. By the 1920s, Tuskegee fielded dominant teams in almost every sport.

Meanwhile, the Fisk administration, looking for ways to save money, had eliminated intercollegiate baseball and track and slashed the budget for football (Wolters 45; Lewis, *W.E.B. Du Bois*, II, 139). The situation was a far cry from Fisk's glory days, not long after Du Bois's graduation, when the Bulldogs were part of college football's rise to national prominence. In 1899, the school named Yale graduate Warren G. Waterman its first coach (previously, the players had managed themselves), and the team lost only one game over the next six seasons. Fisk's preeminence was such that Walter Camp, the longtime Yale coach and the "Father of American Football," arbitrated a disputed outcome with Meharry in 1903 (Richardson 157). In 1907, John W. Work, a professor of Latin and history and the leader of the school's famed Jubilee Singers, took over as the head football coach; the singers and the team sometimes toured together (Richardson 157). By

1. The "Discipline of Work and Play"

1915, Fisk boasted of a broad-based, successful athletic program, winning the first baseball championship of the Southern Intercollegiate Athletic Conference.

Increasingly, however, the Fisk administration soured on sports. University President Fayette McKenzie, whose devotion to Fisk's code of discipline won him friends and funding from the white establishment in Tennessee, disdained the professionalism and gambling that had become prevalent at white colleges (Richardson 89, 157–58). The adherence to amateurism did not extend to the Jubilee Singers, however: In 1916, Work organized the Jubilee Quartet, designed to travel less expensively—and thus more profitably—than the entire company of singers. The Quartet sang at the White House that year (Richardson 80–81). Meanwhile, intercollegiate competition, which had been suspended during World War I, was reinstated in 1919, but the McKenzie administration remained "committed to a policy of no training table, no professional players, no players of wavering scholarship, and no athletic coach" (Richardson 89). In 1925, when Fisk students went on strike, resulting in the resignation of McKenzie and the emendation of the school's code of discipline, the reorganization of the athletic department was one of their central demands.

Du Bois was accused of fomenting the unrest by printing and defending the students' complaints in the pages of *The Crisis*. The issue of April 1925 included pictures of six student leaders, four of whom had been suspended, labeled "The Martyrs at Fisk." Although Du Bois's own complaint with McKenzie had originally been rooted in the president's accommodation of white philanthropic concerns, which Du Bois denounced unexpectedly in a speech to other alumni when he attended his daughter's graduation in the spring of 1924, by the time of the student strike he had expanded his critique to include McKenzie's approach to discipline. Acknowledging his own well-known support for a disciplinary component in education, Du Bois cited the president's opposition to competitive sports as one example that the code at Fisk had gone too far. "Discipline," Du Bois wrote, "does not demand the suppression of the student periodical, of the student athletic association and of practically every other student activity" ("Fisk" 247).

Du Bois's provocative argument—Raymond Wolters describes the *Crisis* editorial as "a masterpiece of polemical literature"—elevated the sports element of the debate beyond the level of simple self-determination (Wolters 59). The students had had that already, in coaching themselves;

indeed, they were to surrender it in their pursuit of intercollegiate athletic excellence. Rather, Du Bois suggested that athletics, like the campus newspaper and the student government (outlets of free speech and assembly), constituted a place of expression where individual freedom took precedence over authoritarian discipline. The playing field, unlike the classroom, became for Du Bois a place where Fisk students could express themselves freely.

Du Bois's defense of the students' demand for a formal athletic department assigns great social value to organized sports, countering McKenzie's support for intramural sports and an emphasis on exercise rather than on intercollegiate competition. Considering Du Bois's position on recreation in "The Problem of Amusement" and elsewhere in his voluminous body of work, this is one position on which he and McKenzie would seem to have agreed. Instead, Du Bois argued that sports are a means of self-determination, a status he neglected to elaborate upon in the "Fisk" editorial or anywhere else. In this singular editorial, he granted an importance to sport not as a complement to work but as an activity with its own cultural value. In connecting the athletic association with the student government and the campus newspaper, Du Bois not only argued for the social significance of sport, but he also acknowledged, uncharacteristically, its jazz-like qualities of freedom and self-expression.

Conversely, Du Bois generally dismissed the connection between social significance and popular entertainment when analyzing entertainment, especially jazz. Like many intellectuals of the era, he disdained jazz as lowbrow entertainment, popular with white audiences primarily because of its primitivistic displays of spontaneous physicality. According to Nathan Huggins, most Renaissance intellectuals "were so fixed on a vision of *high* culture that they did not look very hard or well at jazz" (Huggins 10; emphasis in original). As late as 1940, for example, Du Bois wrote of jazz and other "popular" art forms:

> Most whites want Negroes to amuse them; they demand caricature; they demand jazz; and torn between these allegiances: between the extraordinary reward for entertainers of the white world, and meager encouragement to honest self-expression, the artistic movement among American Negroes has accomplished something, but it has never flourished and never will until it is deliberately planned [*Dusk* 202–203].

Here Du Bois argued for a propagandistic approach to art, even as he bemoaned the lack of encouragement that African American artists receive when they aim for "honest self-expression." As in "Criteria for Negro Art," which was written soon after the Fisk rebellion, Du Bois consistently called for art that takes an explicit political position; the self-determination of the students in demanding an athletic department apparently qualified. By contrast, "self-expression" as defined by the musician, if not to say the athlete, rarely met with his approval.

The Fisk rebellion was one of those rare occasions. Its aftermath, however, was not pretty. The board of trustees eventually granted the reorganized athletic association, and football, in particular, revived after McKenzie's resignation (Richardson 95). Henderson A. "Tubby" Johnson, the school's dean of men, was named head coach and athletic director, and led the Bulldogs to conference championships in 1928 and 1929. However, these championships came not in the Southern Intercollegiate Athletic Conference, of which Fisk had been a charter member, but in the ad hoc Collegiate Athletic Conference (Hawkins 3). Along with four other schools, Fisk had left the conference in a dispute over the rules regarding transfer students. Much as McKenzie had feared, schools were luring star players from their rivals with scholarships and other perks; Fisk fired an assistant coach after he was accused of promising prospective players help with tuition and expenses (Richardson 158). Although Fisk returned to the SIAC after the conference adopted residency rules to prevent players from transferring indiscriminately, the football program never recovered. After several attempts to continue competing at a high level, the school eventually dropped out of the SIAC and continued as a lower-division program, without athletic scholarships (Hawkins 2–4; Richardson 159).

Du Bois's reaction to these controversies was vague and detached. An editorial complaining that other schools besides Fisk were violating transfer rules appeared in his "Postscript" column in *The Crisis* of June 1930. The entire editorial appeared in quotations, however, without attribution. At the end, Du Bois appended a disclaimer, acknowledging that he had not verified the charges in the piece and had no idea whether they were true. Judging by the style and content of the editorial, the author was probably George Streator, who wrote similar, bylined articles on college football for *The Crisis* in 1931 and 1932. Streator, who had been one of the suspended Fisk students lauded in the magazine as a martyr, accused Fisk of using professional players in the 1930 season (Richardson 158). After the Fisk rebellion, he became Du Bois's personal assistant and then the business editor and managing editor of *The Crisis*. He resigned with

Du Bois in 1934. Streator later became the first African American reporter on *The New York Times*.

By then, however, Du Bois seems to have considered it strictly a sports story, one that he felt content letting those who were interested in such things debate. Du Bois's reservations about athletics and athletes probably deepened in 1931 when his daughter, Yolande, married Arnette Franklin Williams. According to David Levering Lewis, Williams was "a football player who could take or leave poetry, was a bit of a rogue and the antithesis of Countee Cullen" (to whom Yolande had briefly been married in 1928). The Du Bois–Williams marriage ended in 1936 amid charges of alcoholism and abuse (Lewis, *W.E.B. Du Bois*, II, 281, 381). Still, despite his longstanding adherence to traditional discipline in education and his suspicions of exploitation in popular entertainment, Du Bois had supported sports as a central student concern in the Fisk rebellion. Perhaps he had merely stooped to assist the rebels in their fight; in the ensuing years, however, he turned to sports again when athletes commanded the social stage. Whenever discipline and a clearly complementary combination of work and play created the ideal cultural concoction, Du Bois recognized and seized upon sports as means of expression, advancement, and—at their best—education.

2. "Minds of Fleetful Thoughts"
Negro League Baseball, Intellectualism and the Black Bourgeoisie

The absence of sports in the documentary record of the Harlem Renaissance is particularly striking in light of the emphasis that many African American intellectuals placed on the normality of Harlem residents' lives. From the novels of Jessie Fauset and Walter White to the "Colored World Within" chapter of W.E.B. Du Bois's *Dusk of Dawn*, the movement's most established and influential writers endeavored to chronicle the existence of the African American middle class without mentioning the prevalence of sports among the popular entertainments enjoyed by its members. Only in the pages of the press, in fact, does one find reference to such events as the college football games that were so popular among the growing African American middle class—a sector of society that was sending its youth to college in ever-growing numbers.

The specific lack of intellectual interest in Negro League baseball as a sociological or economic phenomenon seems especially incongruous to the multidisciplinary reader of today. The Negro National League, organized in 1920 under the aegis of the enterprising and ambitious Rube Foster, achieved sufficient popularity to compel the formation in 1923 of a rival circuit, the Eastern Colored League, which included New York City's two independent teams. Still, the quintessential representation of the era, Locke's anthology *The New Negro* (1925), made no mention of the Negro Leagues—or of sports in general. Although this might seem unsurprising in light of Locke's highbrow aesthetics, his collection hardly looked down on the middle class or "bourgeois" culture: The final third of *The New Negro* consisted of essays devoted to African American history and an examination of contemporary black life; among the essays in this section was E. Franklin Frazier's profile of "Durham: Capital of the Black Middle Class." In this context, the absence of interest in Negro League baseball, even as

Part I: Literature and the Renaissance Intelligentsia

an economic factor in the era, stands out. Frazier's essay, for example, concentrated heavily on the North Carolina Mutual Life Insurance Company, the most successful African American business of the day. After insurance companies, however, the Negro League baseball clubs collectively composed the second-largest black business interest in the country in the 1920s (*Negro Leagues* 18). Considering its wide coverage in the press, Negro League baseball (taken as a single entity) was arguably the nation's most visible African American industry.

Meanwhile, the African American intelligentsia aimed to hold younger "New Negroes" to a higher standard. In *The Crisis* of March 1928, Du Bois ran Allison Davis's poem "The Second Generation," which sarcastically critiqued collegiate athletes, among others, for their lack of contributions to racial advancement. The poem comprises several sardonic tirades, but Davis reserved his ultimate ire for sportsmen. "College Athlete" concludes the sequence:

> You spend your winters
> Juggling basket-balls
> And women.
> You won't work,
> You won't study,
> You won't marry;
> But you have your four "letters,"
> And a fraternity pin.
>
> College education
> Of a hundred like you every year
> Will bring the race along rapidly [Davis 87].

The generation to whom Davis addressed his critique was his own. Moreover, Davis was addressing his fellow student-athletes: He had played tennis at Williams, with the poet Sterling Brown as his doubles partner (Brown, "A Son's Return" 10).[1] Having taken a master's degree in comparative literature from Harvard after being the valedictorian at Williams in 1924, Davis went on to become one of the leading sociologists of the "Second Generation." He earned his doctorate from the University of Chicago in the heyday of Robert Park and the Chicago School of Sociology and stayed on to teach there for more than forty years, becoming the first African American to receive tenure at a northern university. However, according to his son Gordon, Davis's original aspirations were literary (Oleck 38–41).

Davis embodied the "Talented Tenth" that Du Bois envisioned leading the way to racial pride and intellectual achievement. At a party in Chicago in 1940, Du Bois met Davis along with Arna Bontemps, Langston Hughes, and Richard Wright, and wrote of the experience: "One feels a certain sense of relief and confidence in meeting such sturdy pillars of the day to come" (as qtd. in Lewis, *W.E.B. Du Bois*, II, 471–72). In his poem, Davis attacks the stereotypical athlete for not achieving the balance between work and play that Du Bois had prescribed in "The Problem of Amusement."

Cornel West points out that Du Bois's position on racial advancement was always rooted in upward mobility. He sees the debate between Du Bois and Washington, for example, as one over relatively small turf, fought by "the two major spokesmen of the Afro-American petit bourgeoisie" (West 66). Similarly, Davis's complaint, that the athlete lacks purpose, is rooted in traditional, bourgeois concerns. The athlete in his poem has no interest in employment, education, or marriage—three building blocks of upward mobility. However, his first accusation, "You won't work," is more vague than the other two and less directly connected to a specific social convention (sequentially, one would expect "work" to come after school and before marriage). The idea that an athlete with "four letters" lacks a work ethic is patently ridiculous to anyone familiar with competitive sports, as Davis was. The issue in Davis's poem, then, is not really the athlete's willingness to work, but rather the connection of his work to the traditions and ideals of bourgeois culture. While Davis's contention seems at first to hearken back to Washington's dismissal of sports and games, his anger is more finely focused than that. The complaint registered by Davis, a disciple of Du Bois and his theories of culture, has more to do with the athlete's apparent rationale for working so hard at play: unless play can be clearly connected to a higher purpose—namely, the advancement of the race—it deserves only sarcastic applause.

Davis's sarcasm notwithstanding, the gap between student and athlete was generally ignored by African American intellectuals, rather than being a widespread source of concern. In a survey published in 1938 by Charles S. Johnson, another prominent sociologist of the "second generation," interest in athletics ranked only twentieth on a list of reasons for attending college cited by African American graduates. Johnson's rationale for this low ranking was succinct: "It is the experience of the colleges that most of those who come primarily for athletics drop out before they finish" (Johnson 217). Johnson's summary of recommendations included the suggestion that "less stress should be placed on athletics," but this was listed as one of fifty-eight recommendations and given no additional elaboration (364). However, Johnson also noted that half—two out of four—of those graduates who cited a love of athletics as a reason for attending college had gone on to become coaches; another was still in the educational system as a teacher (217).

In fact, most of the African American college athletes of the Renaissance era were drawn to higher education for the same reason that attracted their classmates: the chance to earn a better living. Even the rebellious students at Fisk and elsewhere, according to Raymond Wolters, wanted to "join the mainstream" (Wolters 341). Athletes in particular, especially Negro Leaguers, tended to have bourgeois aspirations that were rooted in a respect for education, which served as a means of social advancement even for those players who did not attend college. A disproportionate number of them, for example, married schoolteachers (Rogosin 91). The establishment of the organized leagues, bringing ballplayers respectability rather than notoriety, might have been responsible for this trend; a generation earlier, according to historian Steven A. Riess, the black middle class had generally considered ballplayers "unrespectable and irresponsible, and they were barred from better black homes" (260–261). Homestead Grays catcher Josh Johnson, who went on to earn a master's degree from Penn State, exemplified the status a college education carried in the Negro Leagues. In an interview with Brent Kelley, Johnson recalled the support he received from other ballplayers:

> We had an all-star team in New York—barnstorming—and at the end of that season the guys passed the hat among themselves. They did it while I was in the shower. When I came out, they had about $190 in a hat and the manager and the owner kicked in some money. They gave it to me to help me back in school. That's what they thought about education [Kelley 41].

Many Negro League players were uncomfortable with the social prestige their visibility and relatively high salaries gave them in the 1920s. In 1929, the *Amsterdam News* reported that the Lincoln Giants manager, John Henry Lloyd (previously a star shortstop and later elected to the Baseball Hall of Fame), noted that in the off-season he "spurns the limelight," preferring to work in a New Jersey post office ("'Pop'" 12). Lloyd's rejection of the celebrity life was not unusual, but neither was the newspaper's interest in his whereabouts during the winter. Still, the leagues' stalwarts became what Rogosin, in his book *Invisible Men*, calls "part of that 'missing' coterie of professionals, the invisible men of American history" (68). Within the

2. "Minds of Fleetful Thoughts"

community, however, they were anything but invisible. Foster and his successors, ever conscious of the bigger picture, taught their players that they were always representing the race. To this end, the ball clubs enforced strict dress codes, traveled conspicuously in Pullman cars whenever possible, and, in the case of the Kansas City Monarchs, trained their players in proper hotel etiquette (Rogosin 69).

During and after the Great Depression, the popularity of sports with the masses finally demanded the attention of intellectuals. Frazier, one sociologist of the Second Generation who considered athletics a subject worthy of at least passing interest, contended that Negro League baseball played a role in the migration of millions of African Americans from the rural south to the urban north. In "Recreation and Amusement among American Negroes," a research memorandum Frazier prepared for the Carnegie project that resulted in Gunnar Myrdal's *An American Dilemma*, he asserted that the development of the Negro Leagues was "one phase" of the Great Migration. "In every city," he added, "one may see groups about a radio listening daily to baseball" ("Recreation" 57). The study is arranged geographically, but Frazier's main interest was in social class, particularly as it affected the availability of recreational opportunities.[2] This interest is an offshoot of Frazier's extended analyses of the recreational habits of the middle class in particular, beginning in the 1920s and culminating with a book-length study, *Black Bourgeoisie*, in 1955.

In *Black Bourgeoisie*, Frazier traced the evolution of recreation in African American culture, concluding that "play" enjoys more prominence there than it does in American culture at large. Frazier argued that in antebellum America, the fact that black servants and slaves were often involved in social activities while being allowed little contact with the "serious" side of white culture led to an inordinately high level of emphasis on recreational activities and social life. As a result, Frazier contended, playing became "the one activity which the Negro may take seriously" (*Black Bourgeoisie* 170). To make his point especially fine, Frazier shifted from this generalized notion of play to sports more specifically: "Once the writer heard a Negro doctor who was prominent 'socially' say that he would rather lose a patient than have his favorite baseball team lose a game" (171–172).

Frazier's unflattering portrayal of the sports fan—in contrast to Davis's critique of the athlete—is representative of *Black Bourgeoisie*, which provoked controversy with its publication in 1955. Dismissed by many critics as more polemical and impressionistic than analytical, the study is a broad-based attack on the African American middle class, which Frazier believed had abandoned its own cultural heritage in its pursuit of assimilation and upward mobility (Edwards xviii). Whereas Frazier's essay in *The New Negro* anthology a generation earlier ("Durham: Capital of the Black Middle Class") had praised the traditions and manners of the middle class, in *Black Bourgeoisie* he criticized the same group categorically, relying to a large extent on personal observations and anecdotal evidence. Frazier specifically attacked educators and college professors—his peers—in claiming that African American professionals of the era had an excessive interest in "society" activities such as playing poker and policy numbers (174–175). Despite their "lowbrow" recreational pursuits, Frazier charged, the new professional class had distanced themselves from lower-class African Americans: "They were critical of what they called 'common Negroes' in literature and, on the whole, the black bourgeoisie either ignored the Negro renaissance or, when they exhibited any interest in it, they revealed their ambivalence towards the Negro masses" (107). Meanwhile, Frazier also criticized the "old upper class in the Negro community" for creating an "impenetrable barrier" between itself and the "'sporting' and criminal world." (109)

Frazier's critique of the middle class and its recreational habits, though somewhat convoluted in *Black Bourgeoisie*, is rooted in a theory of culture that owes much to that of Du Bois. As Jonathan Scott Holloway points out, Frazier, like most African American sociologists of his generation, had "little patience for Du Bois's bourgeois elitism" (204). Like Du Bois, however, Frazier maintained a stolid faith in education and western civilization. In 1961, the year before his death, Frazier named Du Bois among his personal heroes; the youngest member of his pantheon was Paul Robeson, the former athlete and lifelong activist (Platt 214). Although the lack of explicit references to sports in this context leaves Frazier's concept of their place in culture open to conjecture, his criticisms of recreation and play suggest that he, like Du Bois, assigned sports a certain value when—and only when—they were played with a higher purpose in mind.

The "Symbiosis" of Negro League Baseball and Higher Education

In the 1920s, baseball became a legitimate career option for African American college athletes who hoped to play sports professionally. Under the leadership of their founder, Foster, the Negro Leagues adapted the hierarchical structure of the historically black colleges and created a culture of intellectualism that exceeded that of their original model, the white major leagues. This culture, however, aimed at something more than careerism: the leagues' administrators, many of them college-educated, aimed to demonstrate the intelligence of the entire enterprise. The result was an attitude that adhered closely to Du Bois's classicist concept of culture.

Professional black baseball began to establish itself in the late nineteenth century, when independent teams formed in response to the drawing of the color line in the white major leagues. According to oral historian Donn Rogosin, the black professional baseball clubs, which frequently barnstormed through the South to play college teams, grew to have a "symbiotic relationship" with the historically black schools (47–48). This relationship grew even stronger after 1920, when Foster organized the first Negro League, which he envisioned as a self-supporting source of jobs in the community. Although this attempt was in some minds a failure—after expanding to add an eastern counterpart to the initial midwestern league, the organization collapsed amid infighting among the club owners, and Foster suffered a nervous breakdown from which he would never recover—the pipeline between the sport and the colleges remained strong. Even in 1930, after the onset of the Depression had disintegrated the leagues' original structure, a team such as the independent Harlem Black Sox was composed primarily of "Florida boys who have made good in college and semi-pro baseball" ("Black Sox" 17). The Black Sox folded before the summer was out, though notably, the team's manager was Nat Trammell, a former coach at Bethune-Cookman and Clark University. Trammell later edited a magazine, the *Colored Baseball and Sports Monthly*, which published two issues in 1934.

There were strong incentives for college athletes to pursue careers in professional baseball. For one thing, they were relatively well paid. Journeymen ballplayers in the Negro Leagues earned $250 a month in the late 1920s, while some stars made $400 monthly (Lanctot 162). The highest paid Negro Leaguer was undoubtedly Satchel Paige, whose top salary for a full season has been estimated as somewhere between $22,000 and $40,000 (Peterson 140). By comparison, the average salary earned by African American schoolteachers in the South in 1929 was $524 a year (*Negro Year Book* 203); the average annual salary for white teachers in the South during the same period was $1,020.[3]

While the existence of the leagues from year to year was precarious, this remuneration enabled Foster to groom an elite "managerial class" of coaches and administrators. In a column printed in the *Chicago Defender* in 1921, Foster described their off-the-field abilities: "They had the advantage of college education—all were graduates. They managed and handled the destiny of players of that day and had the future of the players of today in their hands" (Lester 133).[4] Rogosin refers to that group as the "Talented Tenth" of the Negro Leagues, further underscoring the leagues' connection to higher education:

> It was almost as if the traditional Southern black commitment to education, epitomized by the creation of the Negro colleges and the missionary role of education in the black community, had spilled over into baseball, an arena where such aims could prosper and pay dividends.... Teaching ability and a fierce commitment to spreading baseball information were the qualities which bound the talented tenth of Negro baseball together [83–84].

As for the players, the Negro Leagues attracted a familiar mix of athletes from across the social spectrum. According to Bill James, "Apart from skin color and the fact that there were even more southerners, the sociological mix of the Negro Leagues was probably not very different from that of the major leagues in the same era. There were some college men in the mix, some tough guys, some rubes and some slickers" (173). Still, the life of the Negro League ballplayer in the early Renaissance days—based in the largest northern cities, seeing your name in the newspaper alongside those of popular entertainers, spending most nights on the road in a Pullman car—perhaps appealed more to Du Bois's classically educated Talented Tenth, or even a Bohemian-minded roustabout, than to Washington's vocationally trained acolyte. To paraphrase the Wizard of Tuskegee, the Negro Leaguer did not have time to cast his bucket down for long.

Although most players in the Renaissance era, having been born before the Great Migration north, were southerners, relatively few of those who had played as collegians came out of Hampton or Tuskegee. Frank "Doc" Sykes, for example, was graduated from Howard with a degree in dentistry; George Sweatt, who was nicknamed "The Teacher," trained at Pittsburg Normal College and taught at Coffeyville Junior College in Kansas; and Andrew "Pat" Patterson took his degree at Wiley College and eventually became the superintendent of schools in Houston (Riley, *passim*). Patterson passed on offers to play football and basketball at New York University in order to play "serious baseball" at Wiley, indicating, in

Rogosin's words, "baseball's general preeminence at the time" (48). Dave Malarcher, a New Orleans University graduate, played for Foster and succeeded him as the manager of the American Giants. For his part, Malarcher recalled Foster as the greatest of all "teachers" in the game. When asked by another player where he learned "inside" baseball, he replied, "I went to Rube Foster's School" (Holway 40).

Foster attended the lab school at Tillotson, a historically black college in Austin, Texas; he was in the sixth grade when he was eighteen years old and began playing for the college baseball team (Lester 161). Despite his exposure to higher education and the collegiate background of many of his acolytes, he viewed the growing number of educated players in the Negro Leagues circumspectly. "They have proven to be the greatest whisky drinkers," he wrote in the *Defender*. "The greatest professional falsifiers, the biggest contract jumpers with whom I have come in contract [sic] are numbered among the boys that hailed from our colleges" (Lester 134). Ironically, the hierarchical structure of the league he formed and his emphasis on discipline as a team manager are reminiscent of the codes of conduct that were enforced at the segregated southern schools. Foster's code of discipline might seem related to Washington's Tuskegee approach in its strictness, but in fact it is more closely connected to Du Bois's ideal of a culture built on the complementary "discipline of work and play" (Du Bois, *Darkwater* 14, 20). The Negro Leagues, as Foster designed them, aimed to fill an important cultural role as a self-sufficient community institution. As a result, what Rogosin calls a "cult of professionalism" developed, sparked in part by a desire to emulate the white major leagues that caused the Negro League players to treat their work with the utmost seriousness. As Rogosin explains, "This circumstance focused their attention on baseball to a remarkable degree and resulted in one of the profound ironies of baseball history: Negro league baseball was a more thoughtful game than was white baseball (79)."

Foster considered himself a teacher who wanted his players to understand the principles that informed his decisions. In another *Defender* column, Foster explained his rigorous pre-season training regimen: "All of the men go over every detail, discuss it from every imaginable angle. We sometimes spend two weeks discussing plays without reaching a decision" (Lester 132). Under Foster's tutelage, one biographer notes, "black ballplayers had become careful students of the game" (Cottrell 51). Foster aimed to create players who were thoughtful but not single-minded. Similarly, his own approach to teaching was marked not only by discipline and a desire to make his theories transparent, but also by an attempt to understand his players psychologically. One of Foster's pitchers, Arthur Hardy, a college graduate who went on to earn a master's degree from Ohio State, considered Foster "a natural psychologist." In an interview with Robert Peterson, Hardy explained: "Now, he didn't know what psychology was and he probably couldn't spell it, but he realized that he couldn't fraternize and still maintain discipline. Rube was a strict disciplinarian. He wasn't harsh, but he was strict" (Peterson, *Only* 109–110).

Foster often accompanied his players out on the town to make sure they were spending their time in respectable places and also school them in the methods of moderation. His goals, however, were not restricted to a particular player's welfare. "I further inform them," he wrote, "that but few men can drink and think accurately, that I hope they won't let it interfere with my work" (Lester 133). Although Foster instilled in his players a sense of unselfishness, he left no doubt who had constructed the master plan. Foster's "work" was the larger project to which all of his players and partners in the Negro Leagues were contributing.

Foster's vision of the Negro Leagues went beyond staging games and making money, though those goals were never far from sight. His essays and correspondence reveal an emphasis on intelligence that extended beyond the game. As he was planning the expansion of the league in 1922, Foster explained to a prospective owner: "The time is ripe for such a venture and we need men who not only understand baseball but have the necessary intelligence to meet the public demands" (Foster correspondence). This "necessary intelligence" was not merely a reference to business acumen; Foster was also referring to the growth and appeal of the enterprise. According to one of his former players, *Indianapolis Freeman* sportswriter Dave Wyatt, the more organized African American baseball became, the more it appealed to "persons in all walks of life, who appreciate intelligence" (qtd. in Cottrell 57).

The Negro Leagues and Literary Tradition

One of the leagues' more celebrated intellects belonged to Foster's protégé and successor as manager of the American Giants, "Gentleman Dave" Malarcher. In 1970, he was interviewed by John Holway, who described

2. "Minds of Fleetful Thoughts"

Malarcher in his study, "surrounded by books ranging from Emerson and Shakespeare to Zen Buddhism" (Holway 40). In Holway's characterization, Malarcher was Foster's "scholarly" successor, who "went on to write a record as manager that rivaled if not surpassed that of his illustrious mentor" (39).

Malarcher, whose parents had been slaves, said he went to college because his mother, who had learned to read and write at an early age, "loved education" (Peterson 6). His own love for language and learning led him to literature after his retirement from baseball. Malarcher was a member of one of the literary clubs that Richard Wright had popularized on the South Side of Chicago, although Malarcher said of his fellow poets, "They used to come into the meetings and they would have those two-line two-verse poems, and I would come in with ten, twenty and thirty verses—long ones. Well, if you don't know much, you can't write much" (Holway 57). Malarcher's longest poem, sixteen years in the making, was titled "The Epic of the Second World Conflict: Man, War and the Gods," which he subtitled: "Poetic thesis on war and violent revolutions" (Holway 57).

Despite his predilection for lengthy treatises, Malarcher's most successful poem consists of just three stanzas. Malarcher wrote "Sunset Before Dawn," an ode to African American ballplayers who were born too early to play in the major leagues, after attending a game in 1948 that featured several former Negro Leaguers. "It was written in a melancholy moment," he later recalled, "when I thought of the host of Negro players now deceased—the great ones whom the great majority of America's fans did not see" (Holway 57). Malarcher's poetics were decidedly traditional, and, in the words of one critic, "histrionic" (Mote 265). However, Malarcher's eulogy for the largely unseen athletes who dreamt of escaping their fate hardly seems overblown. While most literature and oral history devoted to the Negro Leagues, like much baseball writing in general, celebrates physical achievement or devolves into tall tales about folkloric characters, Malarcher's poem articulates players' cognizance of their battles with fate, age, and mortality.

Much as James Weldon Johnson, in "O Black and Unknown Bards," eulogized the generations of slaves who had forged an American art form—the Negro spiritual—out of their suffering, Malarcher aimed to honor those who played in the earliest segregated leagues. As Sondra Kathryn Wilson says of the heroic subjects in Johnson's poem, "These creators didn't record

Part I: Literature and the Renaissance Intelligentsia

their creations themselves, but Johnson became the instrument for reproducing the black racial spirit in literary art form" (Wilson xxi).

Johnson's poem begins:

> O black and unknown bards of long ago,
> How came your lips to touch the sacred fire?
> How, in your darkness, did you come to know
> The power and beauty of the minstrels' lyre?

Similarly, Malarcher's poem records the artistry of men who labored in obscurity. In the first stanza of "Sunset Before Dawn," Malarcher addresses the players of the past and asserts that their achievements have been worthy:

> Thou wert among the best
> Who wrought upon this earth,
> O dead! Thine *endless* rest
> Is merit of thy worth ... [Holway 353].

Malarcher's description of the dead as those "who wrought" conflates work with play, elevating the ballplayer's effort to that of an artisan. The word further conjures images of Keats's Grecian Urn and its "Fair attitude! with brede/Of marble men and maidens overwrought." Although Malarcher's language itself might be considered overwrought, he effectively evokes the tone of a Keatsian ode; with its brief stanzas of trimeter, however, Malarcher's elegy probably owes more in influence to the impassioned lyrics of William Blake. (In terms of allusion, the closest antecedent for Malarcher's poem is probably an eighteenth-century work with Romantic harbingers, Thomas Gray's "Elegy Written in a Country Churchyard": "Full many a flower is born to blush unseen,/And waste its sweetness on the desert air.") In both diction and structure, Malarcher's evocation aims for the neo–Romantic effects mastered in the Harlem Renaissance by Countee Cullen. While Cullen's command of form made him one of the movement's most celebrated poets, it also tempered critics' enthusiasm for his work in later years. As early as 1931, James Weldon Johnson noted that although Cullen "has no desire or intention of being a Negro poet ... the best of his poetry is motivated by race" (Johnson, *Book* 220). More critically, Henry Louis Gates, Jr., in defining his theory of literary "signification," claimed that for Cullen, "form was a container into which he could pour a precious and black content" (Gates 50–52).

Gates cites Cullen as a cautionary example in his explanation of Signifyin(g), his rhetorical strategy for understanding texts and demonstrating

2. "Minds of Fleetful Thoughts"

intertextuality. As Gates explains it, Signifyin(g), or critical signification, is

> a uniquely black rhetorical concept, entirely textual or linguistic, by which a second statement or figure repeats, or tropes, or reverses the first. Its use as a figure for intertextuality allows us to understand literary revision without resource to thematic, biographical, or Oedipal slayings at the crossroads; rather, critical signification is tropic and rhetorical. Indeed, the very concept of Signifyin(g) can exist only in the realm of intertextual relation [*Figures* 49].

Gates mentions Cullen in explaining that Signifyin(g) is more than simply borrowing. Instead, the mediation between different discourses is at issue, as in the interplay and overlap among slave narratives, Confederate romances, and the fiction of the American Romantics (*Figures* 50–51). Similarly, the literature of the New Negro Renaissance "repeats and reverses the racist suppositions of turn-of-the-century American pseudo-science and social Darwinism" (*Figures* 53). As Houston Baker points out, this "rhetorical masking" shares much with his theory of "frames" and Booker T. Washington's performativity as well as with the "doubling, reflexive dynamics" of Paul Laurence Dunbar's poem "We Wear the Mask" (Baker 36). The intertextuality of the signifying figure encompasses two voices, as with "an archetype and a stereotype," in a dialectical relationship (*Figures* 52).

Although Gates dismisses Cullen as a mere imitator, he cites Phillis Wheatley, whose poetics have sometimes been criticized in similar terms, as a stronger example of his theory. As Gates explains: "The relation of Phillis Wheatley's poetry to that of Milton and Pope, and to the aesthetic theories of Kant and Hume, is a Signifyin(g) relation" (53). The importance of signification, Gates contends, is in the "plurality of readings" that are opened up by reading these writers in context of one another, readings that are "as various" as are the texts in the African American literary tradition, and "as black" (55). In this context, Malarcher's poem strives for the achievement of Wheatley's work, not only in its traditional approach to form, but also in its attempt to represent the intellect of its unheralded subjects.

Specifically, Malarcher's second stanza elucidates his main theme, the unrealized dreams of those who played in the segregated leagues:

> O, minds of fleetful thoughts!
> O dead who lived too soon!
> What pity thou wert brought
> To twilight ere the noon!

Malarcher affirms the artistry and intelligence of his subjects, recalling their "minds" and "thoughts." These thoughts are dream-like, or "fleeting," filled with ideas that will never come to fruition. However, Malarcher alters the word to describe them in athletic terms, as "fleetful." The unusual adjective recalls its common usage in sports parlance ("fleet of foot") and perhaps alludes to Moses Fleetwood Walker, the first African American to play in a major league, with Toledo in 1884. (Cap Anson's refusal to play on the same field as Walker in 1887 is usually considered the beginning of the apartheid that took hold in baseball until 1947; the story is largely symbolic, since Walker was not scheduled to catch the game, and any objection by Anson would more likely have been to pitcher George Stovey's presence in the line-up.)

The strange reversal in line 8 of Malarcher's poem, in which twilight precedes noon, not only underscores the lack of logic in segregation—exposing it as unnatural—but also gives the title of the poem a different aura. Whereas the image of the title, "Sunset Before Dawn," might initially seem to be a simple, pastoral image of evening bleeding into night, the more specific depiction of twilight coming before noon instead gives it the unsettled sense of time turned upside-down—or collapsed. The grounding of the image in nature is broadly Romantic, the declaration of its strangeness specifically Blakean. Indeed, the hysteria transmitted by the successive exclamations recalls the "Tyger! Tyger! burning bright," and Malarcher's poem does, in fact, conclude in Blake's "forests of the night."

Primarily, however, Malarcher's third stanza restores calm:

> But sleep thou on in peace,
>   As orchids which did bloom,
> Like pure unspotted fleece
>   Within the forest's gloom.

Here the pastoral aspect of the poem takes over. But despite its peaceful, funereal imagery, this is not the "cold pastoral" of Keats: this forest is laden with orchids, a tropical flower. According to Malarcher, "I compared them to the beautiful jungle orchids that bloom and die without ever being seen" (Holway 57). Again, the reference to nature is highly conventional, as the simile doubles up on itself, comparing the orchids to the purity of fleece. While this final image is stereotypically white, however, in the "gloom" of the forest its whiteness is irrelevant. Its "pure, unspotted" status is redeemed from the trope of color.

While Malarcher's poem certainly fails to approach the achievements of Wheatley and Cullen, it demonstrates the intellectual project and the cultural consciousness of the Negro Leagues. As Gates argues, "It is through such formal textual relations that we begin to understand the arbitrariness of both the signifier and the signified, the latter of which divides reality arbitrarily, culture by culture, language by language, discourse by discourse" (53). The double consciousness of Malarcher's poem, as in Foster's pedagogical approach to baseball, reveals their attempts to create a role for athletes, not only in mainstream American culture but also in the world of the African American educated elite.

Despite the self-conscious cultural appeals of administrators such as Foster and Malarcher, the organization of the Negro Leagues failed to move intellectuals such as Du Bois. *The Crisis*, under his leadership, was published monthly during the 1920s and failed to mention the Negro Leagues at all. Only in October of 1934, following Du Bois's resignation, did *The Crisis* take up the cause of integration in baseball, with a feature by *Pittsburgh Courier* sportswriter W. Rollo Wilson, "They Could Make the Big Leagues," and an accompanying editorial by Du Bois's successor, Roy Wilkins. Although many American radicals, black and white, began to embrace sports in the Depression years as a popular social force, the arguments put forth in *The Crisis* under Wilkins were more directly designed to appeal to the middle class. The bourgeoisie's affinity for sports was another in factor in maintaining the gulf between athletes and intellectuals; meanwhile, rifts in the community, such as the debate between Du Bois and Washington over education, resurfaced and widened in old arenas, such as sports.

Wilkins, whose second story in *The Crisis* had been a preview of the 1932 Olympics, held few reservations about the social significance of sports. By contrast, he approached sports with the uncritical enthusiasm of a fan. In his autobiography, he recalls attending a minor league baseball game in Kansas City and being shocked at the segregated seating in the ballpark; his initial interest was in seeing the visiting team from his hometown of St. Paul, where—he recalls somewhat nostalgically—the ballpark was free from such discrimination (Wilkins, *Standing* 60). In another anecdote that indicates the significance that he attached to baseball and the fight for integration, Wilkins recounts his mindset as he lay on a hospital bed in 1946, awaiting an operation to remove a malignant tumor. The morning of the operation, he called Walter White and left a message arguing that the Dodgers should make Roy Campanella, rather than Jackie

Robinson, the man to break baseball's color line. Wilkins added: "I suppose it's only human for people to prepare to meet their maker on such days. I would like history to record that what I thought about was the Brooklyn Dodgers" (191).

After taking over the editorship of *The Crisis*, Wilkins significantly increased the sports coverage in the magazine (Wilkins, *Standing* 118). In April 1938, he placed the Pittsburgh Crawfords' star catcher, Josh Gibson, on the cover. The issue also featured a brief history of the leagues, a preview of the upcoming season, and a strategy for forcing the integration of the major leagues. Reflecting the economic sobriety of the decade, *The Crisis* reminded its readers that only strong support for the Negro League clubs would get the attention of the white major leagues and force them to integrate. The authors advised: "On this topic, let the enthusiastic and over zealous colored fan remember that baseball is a big business, void of any sentimentality. The hope of Negro ball players getting into the major leagues does not rest in the development of the individual player, but in the development of our Negro leagues to the point where they will compete with the major leagues for their patrons" (Webber and Brown 137).

Although this pragmatism was in line with the economic self-help strategies Du Bois had begun promoting at the time, it stopped short of his ultimate emphasis on cultural achievements. Indeed, Du Bois considered the team of Wilkins and Walter White, who took the reins of the NAACP after Du Bois's departure in 1934, as "flawed in intellect and character" (Lewis, *W.E.B. Du Bois* II, 303). While Du Bois had helped established a role for athletics in education, he still seemed unconvinced of the larger significance of sports. His successors in the Talented Tenth of the Renaissance, however, had little doubt that "play" could be serious cultural work.

3. Escaping the Iron Cage
Sports, Art and Performance in Harlem's "Black Bohemia"

For most of the leaders of the Harlem Renaissance, the baseball diamonds of Negro League baseball and the basketball courts of Harlem, like the saloons and nightclubs of New York, suggested an unseemly netherworld that was best left unexplored. For other intellectuals of the era, especially those who reveled in the idea of Harlem as the capital of black counter-culturalism—the flourishing "Black Bohemia," as James Weldon Johnson labeled it—was something to celebrate, but only in the decidedly bourgeois African American press did organized athletics and popular culture co-exist on the printed page.

In the "Black Bohemia" described by Johnson, sports and the arts stood side by side, if only at the bar. Former boxers such as George Dixon, Joe Walcott, and Joe Gans owned saloons in the "black Tenderloin" west of Midtown that predated the migration uptown to Harlem; jockeys and other well-known athletes frequented the clubs (Anderson 15). To writers such as Johnson, these clubs were nerve centers, places where the spirit of the Renaissance took form. Not everyone agreed. In 1902, Paul Laurence Dunbar described one such nightclub as "a social cesspool, generating a poisonous miasma and reeking with the stench of decayed and rotten moralities" (as qtd. by Anderson 17). By the time of the Renaissance, however, amid the fervor of Modernism and the emergence of the New Negro, that "stench" had become widespread among the Bohemian aesthetes, and whether the saloons were cesspools or nerve centers became an issue of literary and intellectual debate (Anderson 17). In any case, the presence and popularity of the athletes remained largely unexplored.

Most of the artists and intellectuals of the Renaissance ignored the prominence of sports in Harlemites' lives. Writers such as Langston Hughes and, especially, Wallace Thurman were unflinching and non-judgmental in describing both the New Negro aesthetic and other aspects of Black Bohemia, but they rarely mentioned sports, even when they turned their gaze to Harlem's nightlife and numbers games. Indeed, many of the younger artists of the Renaissance aimed for social realism in their work, but the broad popularity of sports—and especially the professionalism of Negro League baseball—may simply have seemed more middlebrow and authoritarian than they could bear. As a result, the presence of sports in the everyday life of the Renaissance remains largely unexamined and creatively untouched in the literature of the period, even in those depictions of Harlem in which writers aimed for social realism and class consciousness.

Some self-proclaimed Bohemians, most notably Claude McKay, recognized the popularity and the importance of sports. They intertwined their desires to write about Harlem honestly and realistically, however, with their unabashed promotion of internationalism and opposition to American capitalism. For McKay in particular, sports seemed cages of capitalism, imprisoning the African American athlete. In two separate, book-length works of non-fiction—the Marxist treatise *The Negroes in America* and his autobiography, *A Long Way from Home*—he faced a conundrum, finding opportunities in sports for art and freedom, only to accept Max Weber's controlling metaphor for sports in the capitalistic industrial machine: the "iron cage."

Sports and the Bourgeoisie in Black Bohemia

The prototypical first-hand account of Bohemian Harlem appears in Langston Hughes's autobiographical *The Big Sea* (1940). Hughes departs frequently from the catalogues of partygoers and the literary anecdotes that characterize his portrait, emphasizing instead the unassuming everyday lives of most Harlem residents. Amid these snapshots of ordinary life, however, Hughes never mentions the sports that Harlemites watched and played. It would be a mistake to assume Hughes was a Bohemian aesthete who had no interest in athletics: He was a member of his high school relay team, which won the Cleveland city championship in both his junior and senior years, and he high-jumped five feet six inches, or "about two inches over his head" (Rampersad, *Life* 36).

Hughes pays special attention in *The Big Sea* to other "non-intellectual" elements that made up, one infers, the commonplace reactions to

Harlem's rent parties and theatrical offerings. "The ordinary Negroes hadn't heard of the Negro Renaissance," he points out. "And if they had, it hadn't raised their wages any" (Hughes 228). Hughes's delineation of ordinary and elite Harlemites is representative of the left-leaning politics he embraced in the 1930s, but he also sees a gap, even a tension, between "ordinary Negroes" and the Bohemian worlds of literature and entertainment. Although Hughes aims to align himself with the masses, the "nonintellectual, non-theatrical Harlem," he also castigates the African American press, widely seen as the oracle of the middle class, for not appreciating the efforts of artists. The tendency of the press to echo the old-guard intellectuals' disapproval of the era's Bohemianism was not so unusual: Tracy Mishkin, for example, notes that W.B. Yeats saw a similarity between the "sensitiveness" of the African American press and the negative reactions that some Irish Renaissance nationalists had to Abbey Theatre depictions of the Irish folk (Mishkin 21). Both the Harlem elite and the African American press come under fire in *The Big Sea* for their condemnation of the vulgarity they saw in novels such as Claude McKay's *Home to Harlem* as well as in Hughes's own work (266–68). Hughes specifically complains about what he calls "the strange inability on the part of many of the Negro critics to understand irony" (268).

Hughes, emerging from a decade of leftist activism, was criticized by some of his contemporaries for focusing inordinately on the cultural at the expense of the economic and the political. In particular, Ralph Ellison, then in his own period of Marxist idealism, objected to Hughes's lack of attention in *The Big Sea* to radical movements and "deeper meanings" (Rampersad, *Life* 389). Arnold Rampersad, who sees in Hughes's memoir not so much an inordinate emphasis on aesthetics as an explicit attempt to appeal to a mass audience, points out that the readers who were interested in the Renaissance in 1940 were relatively anti–Bohemian, if not necessarily "bourgeois" (Rampersad, "Introduction" xv–xvii). For example, Hughes sympathetically recounts a party at which several partygoers were astounded by their host's library of erotica, explaining that "Harlemites are not very familiar with erotic books" (250). He also describes with implied approval a staging of Eugene O'Neill's *The Emperor Jones* at the Lincoln Theatre on 135th Street, in which the audience "howled with laughter" (259). As for Harlemites' theatrical tastes, Hughes explains that they ranged from respected—but hardly highbrow—performers such as Ethel Waters, Jackie Mably, and Louis Armstrong to risqué vaudeville

Part I: Literature and the Renaissance Intelligentsia

shows. "But who wanted *The Emperor Jones* running through the jungles?" he asks. "Not Harlem!" (259). Even the extraordinary characteristics of Harlem's nightlife are explained by their mundane causes: Hughes notes that funerals in Harlem often took place as late as ten or eleven in the evening, "since Harlemites almost all work in the daytime" (274). For Hughes, whom Rampersad describes as "fastidious and yet bohemian, moral but determined never to judge his people," defending the popularity of sports was more difficult than expressing sympathy with the largely anti-Bohemian bourgeoisie—and thus better left undone.

One of Hughes's compatriots, Wallace Thurman, was similarly ambivalent about Bohemians, sports, and most matters. Hughes describes Thurman with a series of contradictions. Among them was the observation that Thurman "adored bohemianism, but thought it wrong to be a bohemian" (238). In *The Big Sea*, Thurman emerges as black Bohemia's most self-conscious, complex thinker, "capable of liking a book and then finding a million things wrong with it, too," while Hughes claims of himself, "I have no critical mind, so I usually either like a book or I don't" (234). Nonetheless, Thurman has been called "the focal point for black Bohemia in the late 1920s" (Walden 230). In 1928, Thurman published a Renaissance self-portrait of sorts, "Negro Life in New York's Harlem," a critique that explicitly dismisses both sports and the middle class. Subtitled "A Lively Picture of a Popular and Interesting Section," the essay is a precursor to Johnson's *Black Manhattan*, combining a history of African Americans in New York City and a sociological study of the contemporary scene in fourteen pages. In his summary of the movement of the African American community from Greenwich Village in the nineteenth century to Harlem in the twentieth, Thurman quotes extensively from Johnson's essay "Harlem: The Culture Capital," which had been published in 1925 as part of *The New Negro* (the essay subsequently became Chapter XIII of Johnson's *Black Manhattan*). Thurman includes sketches of upper- and lower-class life in Harlem and devotes separate sections of his essay to "social life," "night life," and "amusement life." However, even in his discussion of Harlem's amusements, Thurman refers to sports only in passing and strictly ironically. For example, he observes that playing the numbers "has become Harlem's favorite indoor sport" ("Negro Life" 141). Meanwhile, when discussing Harlem's nightlife, Thurman counters criticism of the seedier speakeasies in the area by ironically asserting that they are, at least, "good training grounds for prospective pugilists" (138).

3. Escaping the Iron Cage

Thurman's dismissive approach to sports as a cultural phenomenon, or even as a social curiosity, may be traced to their burgeoning professionalism at the time. For while the proliferation of professional sports in the Negro League era allowed some athletes access to the middle class, it also earned them the scorn of class-conscious critics such as Thurman. Thurman's description of Harlem's famous Strivers Row, the stretch of exclusive homes on 139th Street between Seventh and Eighth Avenues, mentions only one inhabitant: Harry Wills, a prominent boxer. "When one lives on 'strivers' row' one has supposedly arrived," Thurman observes. "Harry Wills lives there, as do a number of the leading Babbitts and professional folk of Harlem" (134). Indeed, Wills became a successful real estate investor after his retirement from the ring in 1932 (Roberts and Skutt 179).

Despite his pronounced attempt to critique all quarters, Thurman's point of view in the essay is decidedly anti-bourgeois. While mocking the pretensions of the "never-will-be-top-notch literary, artistic and intellectual strivers in Harlem" and complaining that "every other person one meets is writing a novel, a poem or a drama" (145), he aims his most biting and sustained attacks at the African American middle class, giving detailed and intense attention to the recreational habits of "dicty Negroes." Noting dryly, "these people have a social life of their own," he catalogues their dining habits and preferences in wedding arrangements (136). At this point, Thurman offers his only substantive reference to sports. Amid a comparison of Harlem's two primary dance halls, the Renaissance Casino and the Savoy Ballroom, he notes that the Renaissance "stages a basketball game every Sunday night that is one of the most popular amusements in Harlem" (138). These amusements featured the Renaissance Five, one of the prominent teams in early professional basketball. The Rens, as they were popularly called, staged regular games against such opponents as the all-white Boston Celtics and the Harlem Globetrotters, who were based in Chicago. (Their founder, Abe Saperstein, chose the name to indicate the team's racial make-up and attract African American audiences.) Thurman gives the Renaissance what seems to be due credit—he acknowledges its "exceptionally good orchestra"—but casts the backhanded compliment in lingo that hints at his own preference: "The Renaissance is, I believe, in good Harlemese, considered more 'dicty' than the Savoy" (138). John J. O'Brien, Jr., who played at the Renaissance Casino as a member of the white Brooklyn Visitations, later testified to the elite nature of the ballroom's basketball fans: "The fans were the wealthiest black people in

Harlem, dressed, believe it or not, in tuxedos. A good-looking crowd—handsome women, good-looking guys—and they loved the basketball game, but they loved to get the game over for dancing afterward" (Peterson, *Cages* 98). For Thurman, the quality of the entertainment at the Renaissance apparently could not mask the taint of its middle-class popularity, and that association seems to have obscured what scant interest Thurman might have had in casino's brand of late-night basketball—if not sports in general.

Similarly, the primary depiction of an athlete in Thurman's fiction is satirical and complex. The characterization appears in his novel *Infants of the Spring* (1932), in which Thurman satirizes the Bohemian art world and other aspects of Harlem in sharp and unapologetic detail. To many critics, the novel is a bitter obituary of a movement that helped bring about its own demise. Amritjit Singh, in his introduction to the 1992 edition of the novel, notes: "*Infants* has been read often as a satiric account of the Harlem Renaissance—as a measure of Thurman's final loss of faith in its possibilities and his despair at its failures" (Singh xiv). Langston Hughes compared the "bitterness and frustration of literary Harlem" represented in *Infants* to the similar depictions in Carl Van Vechten's *Nigger Heaven*; Hughes called Thurman's book "the only novel by a Negro about that fantastic period when Harlem was in vogue" (Hughes 227).

In *Infants*, Thurman lampoons the attitudes the aesthetes of the Renaissance held towards the middle class. A virile and pragmatic artist, nicknamed Bull, is particularly held up as the victim of such highbrow disdain. Lucille, one of the novel's more self-conscious characters and something of a social voyeur, compares her attraction to Bull to that of white women for boxer Jack Johnson: it is entirely physical and "primitivistic" (*Infants* 131). Later, at a party populated by caricatures of well-known Renaissance artists and voyeurs, a white woman is depicted "doing the Black Bottom with a famed Negro singer of spirituals" (178). The oblique reference, undoubtedly to Paul Robeson, conjures images of Robeson's physical stature and athletic exploits. The narrator clarifies the juxtaposition two paragraphs later: "She insinuated her scrawny white body close to that of her stalwart black partner and began performing the torrid abdominal movements of the 'mess-a-round'" (179). Bull's "primitive" nature is thus turned around, as it is the white woman who loses her reserve in his presence.

Such "primitivism" was a driving force behind white interest in the

Renaissance, partly as a result of the reductive voyeurism of the audiences who patronized segregated nightclubs in Harlem and made the controversial novels of Claude McKay and Carl Van Vechten best-sellers. The fad was an offshoot of the emphasis on African art that Howard University professor Alain Locke promoted as a basis for African American culture, as exemplified for the white audience by Winold Reiss's woodcut decorations in *The New Negro* anthology, edited by Locke in 1925. The critic Nathan Huggins, citing the Bavarian Reiss's influence on Aaron Douglas, the leading African American painter of the era, pointed out that "the Negro intellectual's fascination with primitivism was filled with ironies" (Huggins 187). In one such irony, Locke worked to advance African American culture along the European model by recruiting writers and artists for the wealthy patron and adherent of primitivism, Charlotte Osgood Mason, "dissembling masterfully and taking the cash" (Lewis, *When Harlem* 154). The reversal in Thurman's novel underscores the ironic prevalence of primitivism among those who considered themselves culturally elite and enlightened. Huggins argues that this irony prevailed across the color line in the 1920s: "Black Americans, like white Americans, dissatisfied with and unfulfilled by the selves that they had, sought escape in exotica" (189).

Although Thurman unquestionably took aim at the prominence of primitivism in the Renaissance, another implication of the party scene in *Infants* stands out: Artistic expression, the hallmark of Bohemian life, remains stereotypically opposed to physical prowess. For Thurman, the underpinnings of aestheticism and a devotion to high art as a way of life (the "scrawny" woman is the ex-wife of a playwright and a member of Manhattan's avant-garde) still seem to outweigh, if not mitigate, the excesses of primitivism. Unquestionably, Thurman offers variations on standard stereotypes. Bull, although rough-hewn and prone to violent outbursts, possesses intelligence; in fact, his interest in the profitable side of art comes off as practical and unpretentious. But in the end, he is dismissed as a passing fancy of Lucille's, as she ultimately chooses a relationship with the Thurman's less physical (even non-sexual) protagonist.

Such ironies and stereotypes flourished amid primitivism, a fad that also influenced many of the Renaissance writers' white counterparts. The poet Vachel Lindsay, sometimes credited with "discovering" Langston Hughes, was a "professional primitivist," while Sherwood Anderson attempted to get at "that primal something" in his novel *Dark Laughter*

(Lewis, *When Harlem* 99). While many "Negrotarians," as Zora Neale Hurston nicknamed them, were seriously interested in social equality and racial "uplift," some were more interested in the physical, "primal" urges that they believed had been drained out of a sterile white civilization. Anderson, for example, feared Jean Toomer would be "spoiled" by sophistication, success, and white influences (Lewis, *When Harlem* 59).

As David Levering Lewis points out, these desires were not held by white writers exclusively, but most Renaissance intellectuals recognized the superficiality of the attention white audiences were paying to primitivism (*When Harlem* 99, 92). Some, such as George Schuyler, cynically labeled the entire New Negro movement "hokum." Still, the celebration of folk art forms, as well as supposedly "natural" performing arts such as dance, flourished during the Renaissance era, even as the classically intellectual achievements of the race were emphasized. Hurston, defining the characteristics of African American dancing, aligned dance with speech and music as an idiomatic "suggestion." Significantly, she found it intrinsically different from the white form:

> The difference in the two arts is: the white dancer attempts to express fully; the Negro is restrained, but succeeds in gripping the beholders by forcing him to finish the action the performer suggests. Since no art can ever express all the variations conceivable, the Negro must be considered the greater artist, his dancing is realistic suggestion, and that is about all a great artist can do [Hurston 26–27].

While Hurston's theory seemed to some a paean to aficionados of primitivism, such as Mason (who was also Hurston's patron), its emphasis on self-consciousness demonstrates its strategies for liberation or, at the very least, survival. Susan Meisenhelder, citing Hurston's assertion that African American folklore is "not a thing of the past," argues that such "characteristics" were not naturally atavistic or primitively performed; rather, they were to be applied as "a self-conscious manipulation for rewards" (Meisenhelder 4). Meisenhelder reads Hurston's descriptions of the manipulation of one's audience as a "way of doing battle" for African Americans in a white-dominated culture and also for women when dealing with men (15). Similarly, Henry Louis Gates, citing Hurston's definition as an example of his own theory of signifying, asserts: "Zora Neale Hurston is the first author of the tradition to represent signifying itself as a vehicle of liberation for an oppressed woman" (Gates, *Figures* 241).

A generation earlier, in *The Autobiography of an Ex-Colored Man* (1912), James Weldon Johnson had praised the "natural" talents of popular musicians, admiringly contrasting their ignorance of musicology with his own knowledge. Describing a ragtime pianist, Johnson's narrator muses:

> I began to wonder what this man with such a lavish natural endowment would have done had he been trained. Perhaps he wouldn't have done anything at all; he might have become, at best, a mediocre imitator of the great masters in what they have already done to a finish, or one of the modern innovators who strive after originality by seeing how cleverly they can dodge about through the rules of harmony and at the same time avoid melody. It is certain that he would not have been so delightful as he was in ragtime [74].

While Johnson's praise for the musician's natural talent could be considered reductive, it remains nonetheless in the realm of the aesthetic: in the end, the ragtime musician is inarguably an artist. But Johnson was rare among the intellectuals of the era in striking this balance.

Claude McKay and the "Iron Cage" of Sports

It may be that for self-proclaimed Bohemians, the structure and rules of games equaled conformity rather than liberation. Max Weber famously described modern, capitalist society as an "iron cage" from which only art and other aesthetic pursuits offer actual release (Weber 181). For Weber, capitalism and sport both represented the tyranny of rationality and order in modernity: "In the field of its highest development, in the United States, the pursuit of wealth, stripped of its religious and ethical meaning, tends to become associated with purely mundane passions, which often actually give it the character of sport" (Weber 182). While noting an ironically Puritanical tone in his admonishments, critics have also pointed out the elitism in Weber's preference for music and art as opposed to elements of popular culture, such as sports (Jarvie and Maguire 50–62).

In a decade that gave rise to organized professionalism in African American baseball—and still saw basketball played within "cages" of rope or wire—the possibility of sports serving as a release, much less a means of liberation, was indeed becoming tenuous. However, for those in Harlem who were more practical than theoretical, Weber's metaphor of incarceration must have seemed ironic. Thurman, describing the prevalence of rent parties in Harlem, defended their social virtues as well as their financial practicality with a similar metaphor: "[T]hey also give lonesome Harlemites, caged in by intangible bars, some place to have their fun and forget problems of color, civilization, and economics" ("Negro Life" 141). Claude McKay, who helped usher in the Renaissance as one of the era's most committed Marxists and eulogized it in the 1930s by declaring himself doctrine-free (though a convert to Catholicism), found both freedom and frustration in sports—as he did in art. McKay's writing on sports, especially boxing, attempts to subvert the Weberian metaphor with Marxian analysis, stressing the freedom of performance and play while critiquing the modern emphases on professionalism and profit.

For McKay, political doctrine represented its own kind of cage. He imagined the theories of Marx himself as imprisoning, though more for the theorist than for the practitioner. In his autobiography *A Long Way from Home* (1937), McKay recalls first reading Marx:

> I saw a picture of the man, imprisoned by walls upon walls of books and passionately studying the history and philosophy and science of the world, so that he might outline a new social system for the world. I thought that Marx belonged even more to the institutions of learning than to the street corners from which I had so often heard his gospel preached [*Long* 69].

The passage demonstrates not only McKay's ambivalence about Marxism, but also his disillusionment with promises that had turned out to be false. McKay, especially in his non-fiction, used sports to demonstrate an opportunity tantalizingly open to African Americans but ultimately confining because of its susceptibility to exploitation.

In *A Long Way from Home*, McKay recalls meeting George Bernard Shaw, whose "athletic appearance" and "interest in boxing" had impressed him (Cooper, *Claude McKay* 127). Upon meeting Shaw in person, however, McKay was disappointed that Shaw's youthfulness was rather elfin and not so rugged. Shaw asked McKay why he had chosen to be a poet rather than a boxer (McKay, *A Long Way* 61). The query—a pragmatic rather than an insulting one, in McKay's depiction—reconstructs the social layers that constitute Bull's interaction with white aesthetes in Thurman's *Infants of the Spring*: The African American athlete and artist might find their way into well-heeled society, but both will be marginalized as naturally, physically talented. Like Thurman, McKay sees the superficiality of such social access (and financial success). Shaw, he concludes, "no doubt imagined that it would be easier for a black man to win success at boxing than at writing in a white world. But looking at life through an African telescope I could not see such a great difference in the choice" (71).

The title of this section of McKay's memoir, recounting his travels in

Great Britain in 1919 and 1920, is a sports metaphor: "An English Inning" (undoubtedly referring to cricket rather than baseball, especially considering McKay's Jamaican birth). Throughout the section, references to sports abound. Writing on race relations in England, for example, McKay recalls bringing his racial compatriots in London to the International Club. He offers the anecdote as evidence of the open-mindedness and communitarian flavor of the club and of internationalism, both of which the young Marxist McKay was then so enamored. However, the proletarian aspects of the club are strongly implied in the reactions of his friends: A sailor and a student, as well as some soldiers and boxers, return for additional visits, while a doctor and a minister do not (70). Similarly, McKay emphasizes the non-intellectual appeal of the club's "social diversions," namely dancing and exhibitions of boxing.

McKay's descriptions of the boxing matches reflect the fascination with physical performance and the "primitive," so common among Harlem's Bohemians:

> One was a coffee brown, the other bronze; both were strapping broad-chested fellows. Their bodies gleamed as if they were painted in oil. The darker one was a stout bamboo, smooth and hairless. They put on an entertaining act, showing marvelous foot and muscle work, dancing and feinting all over the stage [70].

The description recalls passages from McKay's novels *Home to Harlem* and *Banjo*, which established him as an "expert on primitivism" (Lewis, *When Harlem* 239). But while McKay considered such imagery a "source of cultural renewal for the African of the diaspora," he was also aware that its prevalence in the Renaissance had contradictory effects, both politically and aesthetically (Lewis, *When Harlem* 239). Looking back at those years in his autobiography, McKay qualifies his descriptions of such imagery with attention to the performers themselves and the high price they pay for their apparent success.

In one such description, of an "official" fight between black and white boxers, McKay emphasizes the violence of the match (in contrast to the more frivolously entertaining exhibitions). Still, he notices the performance rather than the result—"they fully satisfied the crowd with the brutal pleasure it craved"—and his account is more descriptive than narrative: he thinks, but cannot recall for sure, that his friend won (McKay, *A Long Way* 71). Ultimately, McKay expands his account of the bout into a narrative with deeper social significance. After the fight, a white observer congratulates the boxer in condescending terms ("Shake, Darkey, you did a clean job"), but when the boxer introduces his white wife to the man, the fan calls him a "damned nigger" and the boxer punches him in the mouth. The scene takes on an ironic tone as the victorious boxer concludes, "I guess they don't want no colored in this damned white man's country" and begins to sob "like a child." The incident stands as a metaphor for English racism, as McKay says of the black boxer: "I thought that that was *his* knockout" (71).

McKay extends this metaphor in other sporting terms, as intimated in the title of the section, adding: "No boxer can compete for a championship in the land of cricket" (71). In spite of the fact that an English marquis had defined the rules of boxing, McKay considers the sport international in character, with multicultural, working-class appeal. Conversely, cricket remains intrinsically British, colonialist, and white. Like most racial rules, this one is unwritten. McKay charges that the race-based regulations of the sport in England "have nothing to do with the science of boxing or the Negro's fitness to participate" (71). As such, they are especially confining, in much the same way that he envisioned Marx's books imprisoning him. McKay ends his "English Inning" by rejecting professional sports on internationalist, Bohemian grounds. Contradicting his earlier response to George Bernard Shaw, McKay asserts the artist's relative freedom from such restraints: Even the black poet, he declares, "has more potential scope than the pugilist" (72). McKay casts organizations and rules, like dogmatic thinking, as instruments of control.

McKay's art had not always been so free from dogma. His calls for racial solidarity led George Schuyler to brand him a "black fascist," after which McKay was forced to defend himself in print. In 1937, McKay responded in the *Amsterdam News*:

> My faith in the cause of social justice and a new social order broadly based on the dignity and democracy of labor had never wavered. But my intellect is not limited to the social interpretation of Marx and Lenin. It … finds its roots in the logic of the Greeks who actually used their brains to think, who approached social theories and problems with open minds; and from them extracted the genuine and rejected the spurious [as qtd. by Cooper, *Claude McKay* 337].

In the early years of the Renaissance, however, McKay was a committed Marxist and, in doctrinaire terms, he used sports as an example in a more explicit argument for internationalism and against the perils of bourgeois professionalism. In 1923, while visiting the Soviet Union to attend the Fourth Congress of the Third International, he wrote *The Negroes in America* (published only in Russian until 1979) after addressing the Comintern regarding the "Negro Question." The book exhibits a style that McKay eventually rejected. Wayne Cooper points out that in 1923, McKay was "trying to convince the Russian authorities that he was in fact a revolutionary" (*Claude McKay* 90). Recalling the experience a generation later, however, he wrote bitterly: "Russia has a great lesson to teach. And Negroes might learn from it just what they should not do. They can learn enough at least to save themselves from becoming the black butt of communism" (*Harlem: Negro Metropolis* 262). By the time he wrote *A Long Way from Home* in 1937—a time when many African American writers had turned to a more overtly political art—McKay was concerned to conclude the reminiscence of his "magic pilgrimage" to the U.S.S.R. by asserting his artistic independence. "I had no radical party affiliations," he wrote, "and there was no reason why I should consider myself under any special obligations to the Communists. I had not committed myself to anything. I had remained a free agent" (*A Long Way* 226).

Whether he was beholden to the State Publishing Department in Moscow or not, McKay's adherence to Marxism in the Renaissance years was well established in New York. He worked as an associate editor for Max Eastman's leftist magazine, *The Liberator*, between 1919 and 1922, when McKay's dedication to artistic independence provoked a falling-out. McKay's initial disagreement was with the magazine's chief editor, Mike Gold, who McKay thought was "sentimentally enthralled" with proletarian literature and "myopic" about racial issues; when McKay complained that the two could not work together, Eastman agreed but kept Gold on while McKay resigned (Cooper, *Claude McKay* 161). Gold was a former boxer and offered to settle his disagreement with McKay in the ring, an offer to which McKay initially agreed but soon found pointless (*Long* 141). Eastman and McKay, on the other hand, quickly reconciled and remained correspondents throughout their lives.

Despite his recurrent jousting with Marxism, McKay places his doctrinaire views on internationalism squarely at the heart of *The Negroes in America*. In a chapter titled "Negroes in Sports," he attributes nationalistic traits to sports and athletes. In one of the few critical analyses of *The Negroes in America*, William J. Maxwell calls "Negroes in Sports" one of the book's "cultural chapters." Maxwell notes in McKay's treatment of sports a "cultural conflict" between races and classes, and calls McKay a precursor to other Marxist critics who have analyzed sports, namely C.L.R.

James (Maxwell 86–87). Specifically, McKay uses the controversy surrounding a boxing match between Louis Phal "Battling" Siki and Georges Charpentier to compare the oppression of blacks in the United States, Europe, and colonial French Africa.

In 1922, Siki, a Senegalese light-heavyweight, had defeated the white Charpentier in Paris for the world championship. McKay begins by noting ironically that amid the protests that erupted afterward in both the United States and Europe, one of the French voices criticizing the racist reactions of whites had been Blaise Diagne, a conservative deputy from Senegal in the French parliament. Diagne summarized the controversy by commenting: "The white man refused to accept the idea that the black man can be equal to him physically or spiritually" (McKay, *Negroes* 49). McKay cites Diagne, who had been a critic of the Pan-African Congress organized by Du Bois in 1919, as an unwitting example of the potential of internationalism and the limitations of bourgeois values. Although Diagne had argued that Africans born in French colonies should consider themselves loyal to France above all else, his critique of the racist reaction to Siki's victory was for McKay evidence that France's ethos of equality was ultimately more potent than bourgeois conservatism or the evils of colonialism. Despite his conservative stance on the issue of colonialism, Diagne had been a strong critic of the lack of respect the French government had shown to its African soldiers after World War I; he was instrumental in arranging for monuments to be erected, first in French West Africa in 1919, and then in Reims in 1924 (Berliner 31–32). "For the Negro masses," McKay writes, "it is good that even black-skinned servants of the oppressors of these masses like Deputy Diagne, who is so proud of his French origin, be forced to recognize that Negroes have to carry on a difficult and unequal struggle for existence in the conditions of contemporary civilization" (52). Thus McKay sees the victory of Siki as a "slap" suffered by Diagne and bourgeois blacks everywhere (50).

McKay concedes, however, the uniqueness of Diagne's example. After observing that "American Negroes are beginning to believe that one imperialist exploiter can be better than another," McKay compares the conditions of blacks in different nations and colonies on both sides of the Atlantic (50). Although he accounts for similarities in the treatment of Siki in France to that of Jack Johnson in the United States, a significant difference remains: France, McKay argues, offers an equality among the races that does not exist in the United States, mitigating the colonialist crimes committed by the French in Africa. Some critics, however, argue otherwise. Brett Berliner, in a study of exoticism in France between the wars, points out that while France did not officially discriminate on the basis of race in the 1920s, the French "brutally subjugated their colonial populations, economically discriminated against blacks in the metropole, and commodified and denigrated blacks in the cultural arena" (Berliner 238). Berliner suggests that the "myth of a racially tolerant, indeed unprejudiced France" partly arose from the welcome given to African American artists, who were considered not only exceptional but also unthreatening; unlike French Africans, these artists were not arriving in France to compete for jobs (237). In Berliner's view, the arrival of highly visible African American artists, coupled with the publicity surrounding the contributions of the 200,000 French African soldiers in World War I, gave rise to a wave of exoticism, "both the affinity for and repulsion of the black other" in postwar France (235).

McKay's cultural analysis in "Negroes in Sports" extends further, however, bleeding into nationalistic essentialism. Because of their long history of "experience and contact with black-skinned peoples," he contends, Catholic and Latinate countries such as France are tolerant and friendly to people of color. As evidence, McKay—who would later convert to Catholicism—offers only the fact that "Jack Johnson was the subject of general interest in the Spanish capital" (50). By contrast, he argues, the Germanic countries have combined Protestantism with imperialism "in their justification of the enslavement of the black man." Thus McKay sets up his critique of capitalism in Weberian terms, concentrating on cultural rather than economic factors.

While McKay spends roughly two-thirds of "Negroes in Sports" discussing racial equality in—and the essential natures of—various countries, he does not use the controversy surrounding the Siki-Charpentier match as a mere starting point. The rationale for this lengthy set-up becomes clear when he shifts his focus to racism in American sports. Specifically, McKay argues that racism is encouraged and exploited by the business interests that control athletic contests, both professional and amateur, and that these interests have bourgeois roots. McKay's condemnation of those who run sports—he generically identifies them as "the bourgeoisie"—for their exploitation of athletes as commodities might seem prescient to the reader of today. For McKay, the exploitative nature of boxing in particular explains its status as the only professional sport in which African

Americans were then allowed to compete professionally with whites. Although he makes no reference to the professional Negro baseball leagues, McKay might have had their recent formation in mind as he contrasted the isolated, exploitative opportunities available in boxing to those in segregated sports. More often than not, he notes, the African American athlete is "locked in his own private sports world," adding sarcastically: "Only in the national American sport called lynching, is he assigned first place" (53). Whether athletes are locked out of professional competition or occasionally used for commercial purposes, the overriding concern for McKay is that the white bourgeoisie is in control and collecting the profits.

McKay briefly offers ironic examples from other sports. For example, even in the national game of baseball, blacks are barred; dark-skinned players of Native American and Caribbean origin are allowed to compete and are treated better than African Americans; and competition between teams from northern and southern colleges are often protested in the South (54). Similarly, James Weldon Johnson would write in his autobiography about baseball's ability to bring Southern fans of both races together (Johnson, *Along* 37). However, the situations Johnson would describe were all examples of segregated competition; mixed-race contests were rarely allowed, especially after the establishment of Jim Crow, and were considered by many to be dangerously inflammatory.[1]

At the end of "Negroes in Sports," McKay turns to boxing, the sport to which he would give the most attention in his autobiography. He does so—and here again he cites the example of Jack Johnson—to argue that the bourgeoisie uses sports to divide white and black workers who might otherwise unite. Here the Marxist argument of *The Negroes in America* takes prominence and supersedes McKay's discussion of racism, as Johnson is identified as a fighter not from segregated Texas or the deep South but rather the "milieu of the very poor proletariat" (54). Similarly, McKay contends that Johnson has been attacked not by a racist society or the white press, but by "influential bourgeois newspapers" (54). For McKay, pitched racial battles such as those between Johnson and Jess Willard—or between Willard's successor, Jack Dempsey, and the black challenger he forever avoided, Harry Wills—were more than exploitative entertainments staged for their sheer profitability. Such profits are assured by the racialized spectacle, but McKay sees interracial athletic competition more significantly as a sort of opiate offered to the masses:

The entrance fee will be high, the proceeds will be huge, both sides will place large bets, and at the same time that part of the black and white proletariat which has not been imbued with class consciousness will think that those radical differences which exist between them can be settled by fist fights arranged for a commercial purpose [55].

Though McKay's argument at first seems rooted in racism, it becomes clear by the end of the essay that he blames bourgeois capitalism for cynically keeping racism alive to profit from professional boxing. Initially, he promotes internationalism, as defined by the Third International, as the antidote. However, his attempts to expand his argument to include sports other than boxing—then, as now, a unique institution—become increasingly reliant on presuppositions. Ultimately, McKay's tendency to assign cultural characteristics to nations and peoples undermines his argument.

Sports, Literature and Class Consciousness

While McKay's discussion of sports and nationalities in *The Negroes in America* would seem to stem from his adherence to Marxist doctrine in the early 1920s, in fact this cultural essentialism persisted in McKay's writing, especially about sports, even after he broke from the Communist Party. In *A Long Way from Home*, he recalls a visit to Barcelona with a Senegalese boxer—it is unclear if it is Siki—during which he notices "the magnificent spectacle of the sporting spirit of the Spaniards" (*A Long Way* 295). McKay describes the response of Spanish crowds, concluding, "I had never been among any white people who gave such a splendid impression of sporting impartiality, and with such grand gestures" (296). Such purely subjective observations, representative of the "free agent" viewpoints McKay admitted and unapologetically held, drive his autobiography, just as they enliven his achievements in fiction and poetry. However, these characterizations also seep into his ostensibly objective analyses, whether economic or political, and their persistence mars the few discussions of sports that were offered up by Harlem's Bohemian radicals.

McKay's praise of the Spanish, including his claim that no matter the game, the interest of audience "lay in the technical excellences of the sport and the best opponent winning," echoes the "grace under pressure" ethos of Hemingway's encomium to bullfighting, *Death in the Afternoon* (1932). Indeed, elsewhere in his autobiography, McKay praises Hemingway at length, confessing to "a vast admiration" of him and praising the essentially American qualities he sees in Hemingway's style (*A Long Way* 250). McKay aligns himself with Hemingway as a social realist, though he bristles at the suggestion that he has imitated Hemingway and takes care to point out the differences between them. "I fail to find any relationship," he asserts, "between my loose manner and subjective feeling in writing and Hemingway's objective and carefully stylized form" (250). Hemingway's achievement, as McKay sees it, lay in his "artistic illumination" of "the hard-boiled contempt for and disgust with sissyness expressed among all classes of Americans" (252). This one unifying characteristic—masculinity, encoded as "roughness"—is described in athletic, proletarian, even Bohemian terms, as Hemingway has taken it "from the streets, the barrooms, the ringsides and lifted it into the realm of real literature" (252). More important, Hemingway accomplished this feat "with four-letter Anglo-Saxon words." For McKay, it is as if the English-speaking proletariat rose up in Hemingway—who rarely had a word to say about the working class, much less about racial reconciliation—to overthrow the exploitative bourgeoisie. Such, apparently, was the revolutionary power of his treatises on boxing and bullfighting.

For his part, Hemingway dismissed the relevance of cultural factors in determining a person's reaction to bullfighting. Early in *Death in the Afternoon*, he points out: "I will go into the way some of these people acted in detail later but let me say now that there was no difference, or line of difference, so that these people could be divided by any standard of civilization or experience into those that were affected and those that were not affected" (Hemingway 4–5). Hemingway also includes an appendix that lists, in the style of a demographic survey, the reaction of several different spectators to "the integral Spanish bullfight" (495–501).

The appeal of bullfighting to the Bohemians of the Renaissance seems to have been established even before Hemingway devoted a book to the subject. Langston Hughes recalled attending bullfights in Mexico in 1919, though his recollection is self-deprecating and devoid of the emphasis on masculinity exhibited by Hemingway and McKay. However, one could read Hughes's failure to describe bullfighting in detail as further evidence of his relative lack of interest in sports (or, perhaps, in the trappings of masculine culture). "I tried to write about a bullfight, but could never capture it on paper," Hughes recalled in *The Big Sea*. "Bullfights are very hard things to put down on paper—like trying to describe a ballet" (70). For

Hemingway, writing about bullfights was equally problematic, requiring great diligence and study, but his interest was spurred by violence rather than beauty: "The only place where you could see life and death, *i.e.*, violent death now that the wars were over, was in the bull ring and I wanted very much to go to Spain where I could study it. I was trying to learn to write, commencing with the simplest things, and one of the simplest things of all and the most fundamental is violent death" (Hemingway 2). Both Hemingway and Hughes, here and throughout their work, were compelled to write about "the simplest things." While Hughes aimed to describe ordinary but complex abstractions such as beauty and music, sorrow and love, Hemingway approached simplicity with concrete precision. Meanwhile, McKay's "loose manner and subjective feeling" assuredly separate his own style from Hemingway's and especially from Hughes's, but that looseness and subjectivity frequently led to broad generalizations in his non-fictional discussions of boxing matches and bullfights.

One of McKay's admirers in Harlem, the poet Albert Rice, declared his own love for bullfighting by citing it as evidence of his radicalism, illustrating the claim with similar views on nationality and ethnicity. In an autobiographical sketch appearing in *Caroling Dusk* (1927), an anthology edited by Countee Cullen, Rice began by noting that he had migrated to Harlem from Washington, D.C., where his radicalism "could not become reconciled to the conservative bourgeois ideals around me" (Rice 176). Rice had followed the unabashedly Bohemian poet and artist Richard Bruce Nugent in moving from Washington to New York, and he described his friendship with Nugent, who had illustrated Wallace Thurman's essay on Harlem for the *Haldeman-Julius Quarterly*, as "an apprenticeship in literary vagabondage with the bizarre and eccentric young vagabond poet of High Harlem" (Rice 176). Rice further depicts New York City, which he calls "an outpost of Europe," as Latinate and not Germanic. Much as McKay does in *The Negroes in America* and *A Long Way from Home*, Rice differentiates between these two strains of western culture on the basis of their tolerance for Bohemianism and, significantly, on what he sees as their characteristic sports. Although he resists translating that essence into a specific outlook on race, he includes McKay in his litany of comparisons:

> Despite my radicalism I am religious. I admire the socialist form of government, and my favorite poet is Claude McKay. And some day I hope to flee the shores of this exquisite hell. My temperament is Latin. I abhor all things Anglo-Saxon. I'd

rather live in the squalor of Mulberry Street, N. Y. (Little Italy) than at Irvington-on-the-Hudson. I love bull fights and dislike baseball games. I like dancing and dislike prayer meetings [177].

Rice's rejection of Irvington-on-the-Hudson is a reference to the location of Villa Lewaro, the mansion built by Madame C.J. Walker, the beauty-shop owner who had become a millionaire selling cosmetics, specifically "skin-whitening" products. Walker envisioned the mansion as "a showplace and inspiration to other blacks that they, too, can achieve the 'American Dream'" (Dodson et al., 160). Walker died in 1919 and bequeathed the estate to her daughter, A'Lelia, who became the best-known high-society hostess in Harlem during the Renaissance. According to Jervis Anderson, the uneducated A'Lelia was not popular with the Renaissance elite, who saw her parties as "the frivolous gatherings of a black-and-tan Bohemia" (Anderson 226). Rice's allusion is rooted in his disdain for capitalism, however; as Anderson points out, Walker was "far from Bohemian … as conspicuous and as extravagant a consumer as any in the Harlem bourgeoisie—perhaps more so, since she was richer than the rest of them" (226).

Beyond that specific social reference, Rice starts and concludes his dialectic with religious allusions, defining cultural character as inherently ritualistic and deeply embedded. Similarly, Rice considers baseball a white, Protestant game, aligned with prayer meetings and contrasted to Little Italy. More than that, the sport provokes his disdain because it is distinctly American—as contrasted to bullfighting, an entirely foreign sport—and therefore bourgeois. By contrast, Hemingway saw bullfighting and baseball as similar in their ceremonial aspects and "moral values," and he compared them in both *Death in the Afternoon* and *Dangerous Summer* (Mandel 58). As a reporter for the *Toronto Star* in 1923, he wrote of matadors entering the ring: "From their faces they might be major league ball players" (qtd. in Mandel 58).[2]

The reduction of baseball to bourgeois, Anglo-American characteristics, as intimated by Rice, has been widely advanced over the years in a variety of contexts. For instance, the conservative philosopher Michael Novak declared in *The Joy of Sports* (1976) that baseball is "as close a liturgical enactment of the white Anglo-Saxon myth as the nation has" (Novak 58).[3] Novak's essentialist analysis shows how easily the traits of any games can be ascribed to most any nation, people, or ethnic group—with awkward results. Similarly, Rice and McKay attribute inherent, defining characteristics to Anglo-Saxon language, religion, and sports. But while McKay would later admire Hemingway for liberating literature with "Anglo-Saxon words," Rice seems to see American culture—even on the ballfield—as hopelessly closed to non-whites, socialists, and Bohemians. Harlem, of course, is an exception in Rice's logic, as is New York City in general. It may be part of an "exquisite hell," where nary a bullfight can be found, but at least it offers the enclave of a black Bohemia. For Rice, the baseball games (and prayer meetings) attended by so many would seem to be part of another Harlem altogether.

McKay sketched Harlem in similar terms. In his novel *Home to Harlem* (1928), McKay depicted the lives of African Americans in the kind of blunt, startling tones he had admired in Hemingway's novel of two years before, *The Sun Also Rises*. Despite some distinct ideological differences, McKay's book owes a great deal to Hemingway's. The novels are similar in many ways, from their bluntness—McKay described Hemingway's novel as "a fist in the face of the fake romantic-realists" (*A Long Way* 251)— to the names of their rootless protagonists, McKay's Jake Brown and Hemingway's Jake Barnes. Carl Van Vechten's *Nigger Heaven*, also published in 1926, has been more frequently cited as an influence on *Home to Harlem* (Huggins 125). However, McKay says in *A Long Way from Home* that he began writing the sketches that made up *Home to Harlem* in 1925 and didn't read Van Vechten's book until late in 1927 (*Long* 282–83).

McKay considered *Home to Harlem* a proletarian novel (Cooper, "Introduction" xxii–xxiii), but despite its depictions of longshoremen and railroad workers, his celebration of nightlife and non-traditional relationships seems more insistently Bohemian than is Thurman's viewpoint in *Infants of the Spring* or "Negro Life in New York's Harlem." In *Home to Harlem*, one finds no descriptions to the sporting events and prayer meetings singled out and so despised by Albert Rice, perhaps because McKay, too, saw these as elements of bourgeois rather than working-class life. This omission stands out because McKay depicts Harlem as a diverse place, particularly in its cabarets and saloons, where gamblers and ballplayers mixed with devotees and one another.

Home to Harlem, with its portrayal of the seedy side of New York's black Bohemia, generated controversy among the Renaissance elite; Du Bois famously complained that after reading the novel, he felt "distinctly like taking a bath" (Lewis, *W.E.B. Du Bois* II 226). However, it also celebrates the humanity, optimism, and resistance to political ideology that McKay perceived in Bohemian life. Although McKay felt Prohibition and the hubbub that surrounded Van Vechten's *Nigger Heaven* had made the Harlem intelligentsia "cabaret-minded," he saw the worlds of Bohemians and intellectuals as incompatible and opposite (*A Long Way* 47). In *A Long Way from Home*, for example, he describes an evening out with members of the Renaissance literati:

> And now that I was legging limpingly along with the intellectual gang, Harlem for me did not hold quite the same thrill and glamor as before. Where formerly in saloons and cabarets and along the streets I received impressions like arrows piercing my nerves and distilled poetry from them, now I was often pointed out as an author. I lost the rare feeling of a vagabond feeding upon secret music singing in me [114].

In the world of *Home to Harlem*, cabarets and speakeasies offer not only respite from working-class existence but also an outlet for artists and intellectuals. The two do not co-exist peacefully. A series of dualisms shapes the novel's conflicts, represented by its protagonists, the hedonistic American Jake and the intellectual Caribbean Ray.

In many ways, the cabarets in *Home to Harlem* are arenas of conflict, ostensible sanctuaries where possibilities seem endless but divisions are ultimately confirmed. McKay describes the nightlife of Harlem in the same sort of detail one finds in Thurman's essay, classifying nightclubs and defining them by their clientele. McKay describes several actual nightclubs, but the fictional Baltimore cabaret figures most prominently. At the Baltimore, early in the novel, Jake meets a singer whom he considers the quintessence of his desire; when he loses track of her, he re-directs his frustration at the cabaret and stops going to the club. This foreshadowing takes on a strange significance in a later chapter, "The Raid of the Baltimore," which has little to do with the primary plot of the novel and takes place in a speakeasy rather than in the Baltimore itself; in the opinion of Robert A. Russ, many of the novel's chapters could be read independently, "for they typically contain a unity all their own" (Russ 359). McKay, the social realist, takes the opportunity to draw a sketch of Harlem and race relations as they existed in the shadowy subcultures of the Renaissance era.

McKay sets the scene in Madame Suarez's buffet flat, an exclusive gambling and drinking den that caters to wealthy patrons of both races. As with the decadent parties described by Thurman in *Infants of the Spring*, the interracial, illicit atmosphere of the flat is decidedly more Bohemian than proletarian. In fact, Jake, who gains entrance via his acquaintance with another cabaret singer, becomes "the first longshoreman, colored or white, to tread that magnificent carpet" (103). In any case, Jake's presence hardly matters. The appearance of the boss of the Baltimore, along with several white friends, carries more significance, allowing McKay an opportunity to explore the intoxicating qualities of Harlem's underworld. In the speakeasy, McKay observes, one finds both "the big men of the colored sporting world and their white friends" (106). This "sporting world" is the realm of gamblers, and, indeed, the mixture of black and white has an unreal quality, symbolized by games of chance, for most of the actual nightclubs of Harlem were segregated. This "sporting" element of black Bohemia, on the other hand, represents a "strange un-American world where colored meets and mingles freely and naturally with white in amusement basements, buffet flats, poker establishments" (106). For Bohemians such as McKay, only the unsanctioned side of American sports—that of gamblers, who had conspired to fix a World Series and infiltrate the bourgeois game of baseball less than a decade before—permits pleasure.

In the end, the white friends of the boss of the Baltimore reveal themselves as undercover policemen who raid the flat. The boss himself comes under indictment as an accessory to the crime, and the city shuts the Baltimore down. McKay's narrates the scene starkly, without irony: The "Moral Arm of the city" had superseded the boss's connections at Tammany Hall and, for a long time afterwards, black cabaret proprietors refused to admit white customers; even "near-white members of the black race ... had a difficult time proving their identity" (111). In an era of Prohibition, McKay suggests, even Bohemian enclaves could not escape bourgeois control, which served to reinforce hard and fast codes according to race.

The onset of Prohibition, coinciding in 1919 with the fixing of the World Series, was followed by a new era in baseball in which a nearly omnipotent commissioner was entrusted to purify the game. The ensuing decade would also bring an explosion in fan interest and media coverage, which in turn increased the profits reaped by the owners and the other corporate interests that McKay condemned in *The Negroes in America*. But the winter of 1919 also marked the formation of the first professional Negro baseball league, ignored by McKay in his treatise—his most direct and extensive treatment of sports, race, and capitalism. For McKay and most Bohemians in Harlem, the political implications of professional sports blinded them to the potential power of a baseball league owned and operated by African Americans.

4. The "Lost Arts"
Baseball and Boxing in the Cultural Historiography of James Weldon Johnson

In the early 1930s, James Weldon Johnson paid homage to baseball in two works that stand as the most extensive treatments of the game by a major Harlem Renaissance writer. Devoting a chapter of *Black Manhattan* (1930)—his "impressionistic history" of African American culture in New York—to the athletes, their achievements, and their fame, Johnson placed ballplayers and "sportsmen" on a par with performing artists and other cultural dignitaries. For Johnson, baseball in particular was a form of popular entertainment, and, as such, he aligned it with the Black Bohemia that accepted its subcultural status and resisted pressure to assimilate to the tastes of the growing African American middle class of the 1920s. In his autobiography, *Along This Way* (1933), as Johnson recounted his experiences as a young ballplayer, the sport became for him not a sociological subject but an art form. Like the minstrel tradition that gave rise to popular musical theatre, African American baseball in both *Black Manhattan* and *Along This Way* emerges as a unique folk art; in these sketches, Johnson defines athletic performance as creative, indigenous, and distinctively racial.

The extent to which African American athletes managed to challenge institutional racism seems to have been of primary importance to Johnson. As a committed integrationist, he measured the social impact of professional sports by their success in achieving mainstream recognition—a principle that probably explains his apparent lack of regard for Negro League baseball in the Renaissance years. Moreover, the disappearance of a distinctively African American style of play, significant in his construction of cultural history and capable of generating romantic reminiscences in his autobiography, apparently diminished Johnson's interest in the game. Instead, at the peak of his career, Johnson turned his attention to boxing—a sport that he admitted never moved him—because of its demonstrable interracial appeal. For Johnson, the prominence of sports in Harlem was something to celebrate, if only imaginatively and nostalgically. While the formation of the Negro Leagues failed to catch his fancy or attract his support, the rich history of black baseball, with its mythological aura and its intrinsic connections to the worlds of nightlife and entertainment, gave the game a central role in his sketches of Bohemian life.

Johnson's interest in athletics was evident, if not predominant, throughout his writing career. As a columnist for the *New York Age* between 1914 and 1922, he wrote periodically on sporting issues, though rarely about baseball. Frequently in those years, Johnson turned his attention to boxing—a sport he claimed never moved him—because of its demonstrable cross-cultural appeal; writing as a public intellectual, Johnson used his forum to draw on the mainstream popularity of boxing and argue for the appeal of interracial bouts. However, in his longer, more ruminative works, published after he had resigned from his official position with the NAACP in 1930, baseball displaced boxing as Johnson's topical sport of choice. Immediately upon his departure from public life, Johnson published *Black Manhattan* and traced the history of African American baseball in New York from its early roots in popular entertainments, such as vaudeville and minstrelsy, through its more serious and pragmatic manifestation in the Negro Leagues.

The African American press took notice of Johnson's attention to sports, even if most artists and intellectuals did not. Reviewing *Black Manhattan*, the *New York Age* observed: "Mr. Johnson is at his best in his description of the growth of the race along artistic, sporting, and theatrical lines" (Review 4). Meanwhile, the conservative critic George Schuyler, noting the "almost total absence" of references to labor and business in Johnson's book, complained in the *Pittsburgh Courier*: "It strikes me that Mr. Johnson has given a little too much space to the New York Negro's activities in the sporting and theatrical worlds: the realm of entertainment. ... One feels that much of the space so utilized could have been better filled with more sociological and economic information" (Schuyler 4).[1] From a contemporary perspective, it is primarily in *Black Manhattan* that one finds any evidence that the writers of the Renaissance were aware of the history being made by the pioneering ballplayers—something well-known by the press and the people of Harlem.

By the time Johnson published *Black Manhattan*, New York City had joined Chicago and Philadelphia as one of the hotbeds of Negro League baseball. The first African American league, the Negro National League, consisting entirely of clubs in Midwestern cities, was organized by Rube Foster in 1920. The Eastern Colored League formed in 1923, including teams in Harlem (the Lincoln Giants) and Brooklyn (the Royal Giants). As a testament to the popularity of Negro League ball in New York, the Bacharach Giants of Atlantic City also played occasional home games there. In addition, the Cuban Giants—still considered something of a barnstorming club at the time, despite their membership in the organized leagues—were based in New York City, with a sister operation, based in Cincinnati and competing in the Negro National League. The Cuban Giants were the first all-black professional team, organized in 1888. Although based in New York City, they were, like many independent teams of the era, a barnstorming operation. They referred to themselves as Cubans because discrimination against Latin-Americans was thought to be not so strong as it was against African Americans, while the Giants nickname seems to have been taken to align the club with the city's representative in the white National League, the New York Giants. In time, the "Giants" name became a code word that indicated to fans that a particular barnstorming team was African American; most newspapers refused to print photos of black teams (James, *Historical* 180).

Despite this flurry of activity, Johnson alludes only briefly in *Black Manhattan* to the organized clubs that achieved great popularity in the 1920s. Instead, he concentrates almost exclusively on the independent teams that played in the nineteenth century. He concedes that with the formation of the leagues, the clubs "have become better organized" and that they "play very good ball and are quite popular," but he emphasizes to a much greater extent the early barnstorming teams and "baseball comedy" (74). For Johnson, baseball is above all a form of entertainment, and, as such, it has much in common with popular theatre. Indeed, in *Black Manhattan* he discusses the history of both as interrelated, central elements of New York's "Black Bohemia."

While Johnson's interest in sports was unusual among the writers of the Renaissance, his designation of sports and popular theatre as kindred elements of black Bohemia was not. While writers such as McKay wrote of the gamblers and sportsmen who reigned in Harlem's cabarets in terms that were perceived to be shockingly realistic, Johnson's portrait of the

Bohemian subculture in *Black Manhattan* seems comparatively genteel. He describes not a teeming underworld, as W.E.B. Du Bois perceived in *Home to Harlem*, but a world of cultural achievement and racial pride, much like the Black Bohemia that Johnson had previously depicted in his anonymously published novel, *The Autobiography of an Ex-Colored Man* (1912).

In *Black Manhattan*, Johnson quotes from his novel extensively to illustrate the clubs of the early Black Bohemia, calling the description in the *Autobiography* "a fresher picture of these places and the times than anything I might now write" (75). In the *Autobiography*, Johnson describes, in particular, a night club situated above a Chinese restaurant (he later identifies the club as one owned by Ike Hines in the West Thirties). The walls are adorned with pictures of stage celebrities, jockeys, boxers, and Frederick Douglass; the illegal bar is hidden in a closet; and the clientele consists of both black and white patrons:

> No gambling was allowed, and the conduct of the place was surprisingly orderly. It was, in short, a center of colored Bohemians and sports. Here the great prize fighters were wont to come, the famous jockeys, the noted minstrels, whose names and faces were familiar on every bill-board in the country; and these drew a multitude of those who love to dwell in the shadow of greatness [*Autobiography* 76].

The "Club," as it is simply called, constitutes a world—a subculture—that brings together artists and athletes as socially significant figures, on the basis of their similar popularity. This use of "subculture" is informed by Raymond Williams, who classifies subcultures in two groups: "residual," which have been appropriated by the mainstream culture or which oppose the dominant culture only in novel or archaic ways; and "emergent," which arise as substantially alternative or oppositional to the mainstream culture (Williams 121–23). Peter Donnelly, analyzing sports within Williams's framework, points out that subcultures can be both residual and emergent, as in the case of boxing, which evolved from its leisure-class, "gentlemanly" origins into a marginalized subculture—even as it increased in popularity (Donnelly 127–29). While Williams and Donnelly focus on subcultures from a British perspective, their seemingly contradictory definitions of residual and emergent subcultures are clearly suited to the marginalization of much African American popular entertainment—particularly baseball, as it aimed for mainstream, middle-class acceptance and attempted assimilation with the dominant white major leagues, only to marginalize itself out of existence.

Therefore, this kind of popularity, as exemplified by the Club and its denizens in Johnson's novel, is not simply "subcultural." Significantly, in Johnson's depiction, the artists and athletes are popular entertainers who draw "crowds of admirers, both white and colored" (77). What marks this underworld as subcultural is not only its racial makeup, but also its ironic popularity in mainstream culture. By the 1920s, this subculture had been entirely marginalized or utterly subsumed, as wealthy, white voyeurs from midtown Manhattan and points beyond turned Harlem's nightclubs into tourist attractions. According to critics and observers such as Langston Hughes, the actual participants abandoned the scene as a result: "As for all those white folks in the speakeasies and night clubs of Harlem—well, maybe a colored man could find some place to have a drink that the tourists hadn't yet discovered" (*Big Sea* 229). Although Johnson's recollection of New York's Black Bohemia is also populated by whites, mostly theatrical performers, such inclusion did not extend in both directions. Christine Stansell notes that Johnson "hung out" in Greenwich Village in the 1910s, as a result of his theatrical connections, but was rare in that regard; as late as the 1950s, James Baldwin and Richard Wright wrote of feeling unwelcome in the Village (Stansell 104, 67).

Significantly, the unnamed narrator in Johnson's novel, an accomplished pianist, first encounters ragtime music in the subculture of the Club. He notes that the piano players at the Club "knew no more of the theory of music than they did of the theory of the universe, but were guided by natural musical instinct and talent" (*Autobiography* 73). Despite—or in light of—the narrator's own awareness of music theory, he acknowledges the "alembic genius" of ragtime, which is proven by its international appeal. However, he also notes that the popularity of an art form can relegate it to subcultural status: "Whatever new thing the *people* like is pooh-poohed; whatever is *popular* is spoken of as not worthwhile" (73; emphasis in original). Ragtime, like the Club, can thus command the respect of artists and attract a widespread audience without winning elite approval.

Similarly, the appeal of the Club for Johnson lies in its ability to attract white patrons without compromising its original character. Much as ragtime appeals to "not only the American, but the English, the French and even the German people," the Club is "well known to both white and colored people of certain classes" (73, 75). While some clubs draw patrons with gambling and dancing, the "professional clubs," as Johnson calls them, are distinguished from "gambling-clubs" and "honky-tonks" by the talents of their performers. In *Black Manhattan*, Johnson elaborates: "New York's black Bohemia constituted a part of the famous old Tenderloin; and, naturally, it nourished a number of the ever present vices; chief among them, gambling and prostitution. But it nourished other things; and one of these things was artistic effort. It is in the growth of the artistic effort that we are here interested; the rest of the manifestations are commonplaces" (74).

Even though the performers are more frequently patrons of the Club than players on its stage, their professionalism is the essence of Johnson's Bohemia. At the Club, minstrels perform scenes from Shakespeare on demand, while successful jockeys buy bottles of champagne by the dozens—and waiters are instructed to leave the empties on the table as free advertising that the celebrated athlete is drinking a particular brand (77–78). In both *Black Manhattan* and the *Autobiography*, Johnson emphasizes the ability of these professionals to draw crowds of admirers of both races. Some of the white patrons are voyeurs, while others are performers who play in blackface and come "to get their imitations first hand," but all are lured by talents that are original and distinctively African American.

Johnson's history of African American baseball in *Black Manhattan* revolves almost exclusively around the "original character" of the black game. He emphasizes the popularity it achieved and, especially, the widespread coverage it attracted in the white press. "One of the main reasons why they were such good copy," Johnson writes of the nineteenth-century Cuban Giants ball club, "was the fact that they brought something entirely new to the professional diamond; they originated and introduced baseball comedy" (*Black Manhattan* 64). Many of Johnson's ensuing descriptions may seem anachronistic to the reader of today, with references to the players' "constant banter," "pantomime," and "monkey-shines" that indicate the elements of minstrelsy that were prevalent in the early years of black baseball. Johnson notes that, with very few exceptions, this style of play "never gained much headway" with white ball clubs, which played in a manner he describes as "dignified and rather grim" (65). The Negro League teams of the 1920s, he points out, largely adapted their style of play to compete with that of the white major leagues, leading Johnson to contend that no black team since had played in the style of the early Cuban Giants. In fact, as Brian Carroll has demonstrated, this tradition persisted throughout the history of the Negro Leagues, especially among barnstorming teams;

in the 1940s and '50s, clubs such as the Indianapolis Clowns (among others) combined baseball and comedy, provoking disdain from most of the African American press (Carroll, *When to Stop* 182–186). Johnson, for his part, strikes a somewhat ambivalent tone in his recollection of the Clowns' early counterparts, observing that "it is probable that the clubs of today do not wish to be quite their equals" (65).

Unquestionably, the teams that the Negro clubs wished to "equal" were the big-league teams, and, despite the lure of celebrity in the subculture of Black Bohemia, they saw professionalism as the key to this goal. In most oral histories of the Negro Leagues, for example, the players inevitably refer to the sense of purpose they felt upon donning their uniforms, which they called "suits" (Rogosin 71). However, in their striving for equality, the ballplayers' professional approach matched that of the most successful African American entertainers. At times, the two were directly connected. When tap-dancer Bill "Bojangles" Robinson became a co-owner of the Harlem Stars in 1931, the club changed its name to the New York Black Yankees and purchased old New York Yankee uniforms to wear.

The transformation of the Stars into the Black Yankees served to revive Harlem's strongest traditional Negro League club. The Stars had operated for only one truncated, cash-strapped season after a long run as the Lincoln Giants. The Lincolns were founded in 1911 as a semi-pro team, playing "several times a week before crowds that often numbered in the thousands," sometimes against white all-star teams, at Olympic Field at 136th Street and Fifth Avenue (Peterson, *Only* 70). By the 1920s, they had become Harlem's favored team, even though the Royal Giants of Brooklyn and the Bacharach Giants of Atlantic City also had strong New York City connections. After playing in the Eastern Colored League from its inaugural season of 1923 through its folding in 1926, the Lincolns became a powerful independent team, luring star players from weaker, poorer clubs.

The Black Yankees enjoyed a successful, 15-year run with Robinson as a symbol that tied them to both mainstream entertainment and the white major leagues. Robinson was known as "an avid Yankee fan" who sometimes danced atop the dugout during their games (Lanctot 453 fn38). The connection between the Lincoln Giants and the Yankees had previously been established, however. When Johnny Beckwith of the Lincolns broke his leg while sliding in 1930, the *New York Age* pointed out that "Beckwith's bone was set by the same physician who looks after the New York Yankees."[2] Robinson's involvement with the Black Yankees was mostly ornamental; his manager, Marty Firkins, was the primary investor (Lanctot 15). In time, Robinson's involvement in baseball became more controversial. In 1943, Mayor Fiorello LaGuardia named Robinson to a subcommittee that was to study racial issues in the sport and offer recommendations to major league baseball on the possibilities of integration. Several prominent African American sportswriters, such as Rollo Wilson and Sam Lacy, objected to the inclusion of Robinson, who had come to be seen as a "largely apolitical racial symbol" (Lanctot 276).

Still, Robinson's public role in the Black Yankees' establishment underscores the multifaceted connection between Negro League baseball and popular theatre that runs throughout Johnson's cultural history in *Black Manhattan*. This association helps explain Johnson's apparent preference, throughout his writing on sports, to emphasize performance and entertainment over athletic achievements and results. Johnson's roots, like Robinson's, were in the popular theatre: He first gained fame as a writer of lyrics, sometimes in dialect, to songs composed by his brother, Rosamond. In fact, Johnson's primary sources for the sports history in *Black Manhattan* were people from the entertainment world. In his preface to the book, Johnson thanks William H. Foster, one of the earliest black filmmakers, and Irving Jones, a comedian and songwriter, for "furnishing and corroborating from their intimate knowledge many of the facts regarding the era of professional sports and of Bohemian life in the eighties and nineties" (*Black Manhattan* xix–xx).

In 1929, while Johnson was researching his book, Foster was operating the Foster Photo Play Company in Los Angeles, attempting to produce films directed by and starring African Americans. As the circulation manager of the *Chicago Defender* in the 1910s, Foster had covered the burgeoning film industry for the paper; using the pseudonym Juli Jones, he was "a theatrical impresario, critic, and actor before his sojourn in filmmaking" (Kellner 124; Everett, *Returning* 112). Johnson wrote to Foster, asking primarily for Foster's recollections of the nineteenth-century vaudeville scene, adding: "You might also give me some information in another line that is related, and that is in the line of sports." Explaining his combination of the entertainment and sports worlds through their shared social relevance, Johnson asked Foster particularly about the athletes who "hung around the New York places in the old days." Foster apparently hoped to trade his reminiscences for help from Johnson in attracting investors for his budding film company, but Johnson declined and sent him ten dollars instead.[3]

Johnson's interest in the history of baseball seems to have stemmed from his respect for the game's status as a broadly popular form of entertainment, a social position that its system of apartheid severely compromised in the first half of the twentieth century. In the Renaissance years, Johnson kept scrapbooks of clippings dealing with some sports subjects, including Jesse Owens's triumphs in the 1936 Berlin Olympics and the heavyweight championship fights of Joe Louis. In writing *Black Manhattan*, Johnson seems to have relied entirely on his personal recollections when describing the exploits of the early African American game. In his correspondence with William H. Foster, for example, Johnson asked about baseball, but Foster's replies include only recollections of boxers and jockeys (JWJP, Box 7). No scrapbooks devoted to baseball exist in his collected papers; perhaps Negro League baseball's failure to reach a similar level of widespread popularity explains this absence.

While Johnson suggests in *Black Manhattan* that baseball's prominence in African American culture had faded by the 1920s, he invests the game with more lasting sheen in his memoir *Along This Way*. Elevating it among even his academic boyhood pursuits, he declares: "Baseball was my game. I not only practiced steadily but studied assiduously" (36). Growing up in Florida, Johnson followed the major leagues by reading *Sporting Life*, a popular paper of the 1880s that was a forerunner to *The Sporting News*, the weekly baseball "bible," and he recounts learning to pitch under the tutelage of one of the Cuban Giants (whom he declines to name).

Johnson selectively describes his own exploits on the diamond—confined to a single game—in the same mythic tones that characterize much writing about baseball, especially the largely undocumented Negro Leagues. As a teenager, after garnering something of a reputation locally for his mastery of several trick pitches, Johnson is asked to pitch for the local semi-pro team, known as The Roman Cities, "in a big game with a formidable team from Savannah" (*Along* 37). The opposing pitcher throws with an elaborate motion, turning his back to the hitter and twirling his arm in a figure 8 as he delivers the ball. "It was an exhibition of the perfection of masculine grace," Johnson recalls. "Beautiful pitching like that is among the lost arts" (38). Despite this grace and artistry, however, this pitcher turns out to be no match for Johnson, who compares himself first to David facing Goliath and then to a "medicine man," dazzling the tribe with his conjures: "David used long-range artillery against a short sword, and I had up my sleeve what was practically a magic power, the power to make the ball suddenly change its course and dart out of the path of the oncoming bat" (38). Johnson's Jacksonville club wins easily as he strikes out sixteen batters, but most noteworthy in Johnson's description is the effect his performance has on the crowd, which is big, vociferous, and biracial. In Johnson's description, the "lost arts" on display are easily understood and appreciated by fans of both races.

Such brief moments of racial harmony are commonly invoked in appreciative sportswriting and memoirs, as geographical rivalries temporarily supersede the racial divide. Johnson notes that white fans in Jacksonville were ardent boosters of the Roman Cities, especially when they played a club from Georgia (37). In both *Along This Way* and *Black Manhattan*, he recalls that in the nineteenth century, African American teams in the South often drew as many white fans as black to their games; white southerners, he notes approvingly, were often "fierce partisans and strong supporters" of their local black teams (*Black Manhattan* 63). Lester Walton, a sportswriter and colleague of Johnson's during his tenure with the *New York Age*, held a similar opinion on the interracial support of African American baseball in the years before the organized Negro Leagues: "Just as the public like colored shows and acts, so it is fond of colored baseball players, which fact is borne out by the local and consistent manner in which white fans patronize colored semi-professional clubs" (Walton 6).

Johnson's description similarly appropriates not only the rhetoric of sport and its transformative effect on fans, but also that of popular entertainment, characterizing the hero's enchantment of the crowd in many of the same terms he uses to describe the culture of New York City's Bohemian clubs. Fans of both races are spellbound by his performance, and, in turn, the ballfield is transformed into a vaudevillian amphitheater:

> As the game went on it assumed a humorous aspect. As many spectators as could do so crowded behind the catcher to watch the vagaries of the ball, and yells of derision greeted bewildered batters, especially when they lunged at the elusive wide-breaking out-curves.... My reward was a pretty full cup of the sensation of being a popular hero [38–39].

Johnson has become more than a baseball star. As the game assumes a "humorous aspect," its result becomes secondary to the entertainment that produces a protagonist with wide-ranging appeal. Johnson then goes one step further, conflating theatrical performance and sport, concluding his reminiscence by noting that after the game, a "colored sport ... said to be the best-dressed man in Jacksonville," challenges the validity of the performance by suggesting that Johnson's pitching depends on an optical illusion. Johnson declines to bet, but he demonstrates for free that his magic is the real thing: He throws the ball so that it moves around one tree and back out behind another (39). The magical realism creates the atmosphere of a traveling carnival, folkloric and fabulous.

Like the impromptu challenge between unknown *wunderkind* and Ruthian hero that Bernard Malamud stages in *The Natural*, the sideshow recalls contests of strength and skill: It may be mythic and unreal, but it is not a hoax in the Barnum tradition. In Malamud's novel, soon after the heroic Roy Hobbs boards a train to Chicago for his major-league tryout, he encounters the mythic Walter "The Whammer" Wambold, a star slugger reminiscent of Babe Ruth. At the next station stop, a contest of skill is staged in which Roy uses an unusual motion ("a little like a dancer") to strike out his rival. The carnivalesque nature of the event upsets the vanquished star as much as the simple athletic contest does:

> Though he did not show it, the pitch had bothered the Whammer no end. Not just the speed of it but the sensation of surprise and strangeness that went with it—him batting here on the railroad tracks, the crazy carnival, the drunk catching and a clown pitching, and that queer dame Harriet, who had five minutes ago been patting him on the back for his skill in the batting cage, now eyeing him coldly for letting one pitch go by [Malamud 21–22].

Similarly, Johnson's baseball reminiscence, which begins with his reminding the reader that he had begun as a student of the sports pages, concludes firmly in the tradition of baseball lore. While affirming his appreciation for the basic skills of the game, Johnson adds elements of theatre to the athletic performance. The significance lies in the interplay between theatre and sports, in their broad-based popular appeal; Johnson draws on the black and white traditions of each.

Performance, Protest and the Social Significance of Boxing

Despite the apparent pre-eminence of baseball in Johnson's adolescence, the game did not make its way into many of his earliest writings. As editor of the Jacksonville *Daily American*, which he founded in 1895,

Johnson argued the importance of achievements in horse racing and boxing, sports in which African Americans had achieved cross-cultural fame. There is no evidence, however, that he wrote about baseball in the newspaper. Johnson began publishing the *Daily American*—the only daily African American newspaper of its time—in May 1895 and folded it in early 1896. No copies of the paper survive (Levy 53–60). Johnson kept two scrapbooks of clippings from the paper, however, consisting primarily of his editorials. None of the extant clippings in the scrapbooks deals with baseball (JWJP). In his editorials for the *Daily American*, Johnson asserted the social significance of sports generally and complained that the public did not take sports seriously enough. On one occasion, he deplored the fact that a proposed Corbett-Fitzsimmons fight was not likely to be held in Florida. (The fight, in which Bob Fitzsimmons defeated James J. Corbett for the heavyweight title, was held in Carson City, Nevada, in 1897.) In another instance, criticizing the failure of the Jockey Club Bill, Johnson lamented, "Florida is getting to be a hard place for sports" (JWJP).

By the time he began writing columns for the *New York Age* in 1914, Johnson's primary interest in sports lay in their significance to the fight for equality. Of boxing, he wrote in detached terms: "The writer is not particularly interested in prize fights, and would not go across the river to see one, but he contends that so long as there are these contests in physical strength, stamina and skill, the colored men in the game should have fair play."[4] But while a prizefight could not incite him to ferry across the Hudson, boxing carried enough social weight to compel Johnson to write about it at least twelve times in his eight-year residence at the *Age*. Significantly, this tenure began not long after the first African American heavyweight champion, Jack Johnson, fled the country following charges that he had violated the Mann Act by "transporting" his white girlfriend across state lines. In 1915, less than six months after Weldon Johnson's first column appeared in the *Age*, Jack Johnson lost the title to Jess Willard in Havana.[5] The infamous fight, presumed by many to have been fixed, prompted Weldon Johnson to compose a "eulogy" for the fallen fighter.[6] Four years later, assessing Jack Dempsey's fourth-round knockout of Willard, Weldon Johnson asserted that the lopsided nature of Willard's defeat was proof that the bout in Havana could not have been on the level.[7]

The fight in Cuba, along with Jack Johnson's continued exile, enflamed racial passions, while African Americans raised questions about the legitimacy of his defeat. Although the film of Johnson's knockout of James J.

Jeffries had been banned in fifteen states, the photograph of the vanquished Johnson lying on the canvas in Cuba, shielding his eyes from the sun, would remain a fixture in white-patronized taverns for years. The furor over the Johnson-Jeffries film in 1910 led to laws that banned all motion pictures depicting prizefights, though a pirated version of the film of the Johnson-Willard fight was widely distributed. Opposition to one law went as far as the U.S. Supreme Court, which declined to hear the case; by 1924, attempts to strengthen the law on a national basis had failed in Congress. By then, however, interracial bouts were either banned or severely restricted in most states (Sammons 40–46). Willard, without a serious rival after Johnson, wrote a series of articles that appeared in several newspapers in 1915, vowing never to fight another African American. Part of Willard's reasoning was self-congratulatory—he declared there were no worthy contenders—but he claimed his primary reason was socially motivated, charging that "a championship fight between a black man and a white man makes bad blood between the races."[8] Distancing himself from the racial conflagration, Willard criticized "white men for feeling that way," concluding that "everything depends upon the man."

In his own column, Johnson quoted Willard extensively and praised him unequivocally.[9] What he found significant about Willard's views, however, was not so much the logic driving them (Willard, of course, had everything to lose by fighting a black challenger), but rather the audience they might reach. "If they had been said by a college president," Johnson wrote of Willard's words, "they would not be so important.... But what the champion prize fighter of the world says in a widely circulated newspaper will reach a great mass of people who not only have racial prejudices, but boast of the fact." The social potential of sports, for Johnson, lay not only in their potential to advocate and demonstrate equality, but also in their ability to speak to the great masses of people that intellectuals could not or would not reach.

A similar furor surrounding the Wills-Fulton fight in 1920, which Johnson would not deign to cross the river to see, while the *Age* covered it on the front page, became a case in point. The bout between Harry Wills, an African American contender for the heavyweight crown, and Frank Fulton, his white opponent, had been fought in Newark because Tex Rickard, who promoted most of the fights in New York City, refused to stage mixed-race contests. Rickard had promoted the Johnson-Jeffries fight, and, claiming concern for public safety in much the same manner that

Willard had, never allowed another interracial bout to take place under his purview. Rickard, who ran Madison Square Garden (and gave the New York Rangers hockey club their incongruous nickname), wielded his influence over contests throughout the city that involved any fighter who hoped to end up in its largest arena (Roberts and Skutt 495–96). In spite of Rickard's position, the New York newspapers, both black and white, covered the fight and its aftermath with gusto. The popularity of boxing, particularly in Harlem, held a larger meaning for Johnson: As calls grew louder for a championship fight between the victorious Wills and Jack Dempsey, who had won the crown from Willard the year before, Johnson argued that the color line itself provoked the controversy, as well as the size of the crowd. The line, he argued, could not hold; its very existence created interest in fights between the races.[10]

Johnson took a pragmatic position. Economic pressure, he believed, would be more effective in breaking the color line than faith in "the spirit of sportsmanship and fairness."[11] Nearly three years later, however, Wills's promoters had failed to convince Rickard, Dempsey's promoter, to fight. Even the creation of a state boxing commission could not budge Rickard. Johnson noted in another column that some white newspapers had supported Mayor Jimmy Walker's call for a bill that would erase the color line. (As a state senator, Walker had been responsible for the "Walker Law," legalizing prizefighting in New York, and for creating the New York State Athletic Commission in 1920.) Nonetheless, Johnson noted, "a strong, united and determined protest from colored people is yet lacking."[12] In this regard, Johnson's rhetoric could be assertive and provocative, endorsing self-sufficiency within the African American community and appealing for fair treatment by the dominant culture.

In 1924, the State Athletic Commission insisted that Dempsey fight Wills for the title and refused to grant a license to Gene Tunney, Rickard's preferred opponent (Sammons 77). After the commission ordered Dempsey's license withheld, Rickard moved the fight to Philadelphia, while Wills never gained his title shot. Court records later showed that Rickard had attempted to reduce Wills' share of the gate drastically if the fight had gone off.[13] Wills, who never accused Dempsey of ducking him, has since been called "one of the greatest heavyweights to never fight for the championship" (Roberts and Skutt 178–79). It would be fourteen years before another African American, Joe Louis, would have a chance at boxing's biggest prize.

Johnson regularly appealed to the fairness and intelligence he saw in the larger culture, mirroring the "ambivalences" that ran through the New Negro movement (Lewis, *When Harlem* 147). David Levering Lewis elaborates: "Mistakenly, many of Johnson's critics perceived the ambivalences as uniquely Johnson's own; in fact, they ran through the community" (147). In another column written at the height of the Dempsey-Wills controversy, appearing in the same issue of the *Age* that carried the news of Jack Johnson's surrender to authorities at the Mexican border, Weldon Johnson analyzed the color line as it then stood in different sports.[14] Boxing and track, he said, seemed headed in the right direction. Baseball, meanwhile, had shown no inclination to open its doors to African Americans, though Johnson considered its increasing popularity a promising sign. Referring to the fact that the major leagues had not always been segregated, Johnson surmised that "the time may return when the keen rivalry between clubs will induce managers to discard an inferior white player when he can easily secure a superior colored one." In the midst of the first season of organized Negro League baseball, however, Johnson paid no attention to the pressure that major-league owners might feel from African Americans organizing their own game. Instead, he saw in the growth of the white game—Babe Ruth was just rising to prominence in his second season with the New York Yankees—the possibility that an increased need to compete on the part of the other white clubs would produce a newfound opportunity for black players with undeniable ability. Rooting his argument in the logic of rational analysis, Johnson suggested that "perhaps color prejudice has been relatively weak in sports and athletics"—presumably he was referring to the *onetime* integration of baseball, or the *possibility* of Harry Wills gaining a title fight—"because it is more obviously absurd there than any where else." While he had previously argued for the pragmatism of economic pressure in arranging mixed-race fights, Johnson here expressed faith in the rationality, if not the good will, of white fans and owners. "Fair play," Johnson was willing to concede, might be a dream, but the desire to win and fill seats were something solid to rest one's hopes on.

Despite this faith in reason, Johnson acknowledged that the "absurdity" of racism in sports assuredly existed, specifically attacking those who tried to defend it in rational terms. After Jack Johnson's return to the United States, William Randolph Hearst's *Evening Journal* argued that Jack Johnson would be likely to defeat Dempsey, because Johnson was "closer to the gorilla." Weldon Johnson pointed out that before Jack Johnson had beaten Jim Jeffries to win the title, the *Evening Journal* had used the same argument in predicting that an African American lacked the intelligence to win.[15] "It is a wonder," he wrote in another column, "that somebody didn't try to prove, after he licked Jim Jeffries, that Jack Johnson was a white man."[16] Weldon Johnson reserved his bitterest critiques for white observers who objected when African American athletes were given even limited opportunities. After Harper Leech, a white writer for the *Memphis Press*, criticized the "intellectuals" at Northwestern University for placing two African Americans on the school's football team, Johnson observed: "If they had been only as good as some other white players they never would have made the team. The correspondent of the Memphis Press knows this, if any white man knows it, and he ought to be man enough to admit it."[17]

For the most part, however, Johnson's columns on the color line in sports reflect the moderate, pragmatic views concerning racial protest that were generally associated with the NAACP. In his pamphlet *Negro Americans, What Now?* (1934), he explained his viewpoints on the racial situation as he saw it and pointed to "the ways which, I believe, lead out" (*Negro Americans* vi). Johnson argued for increased, coordinated protests but took an ambivalent position on racial unity. He defended the political independence of the African American voter but cautioned against "voluntary isolation," which could only lead to "a permanent secondary status" (15). Taking on Du Bois specifically, Johnson dismissed the idea that segregation had already caused African Americans to be isolated from society at large, and that closing ranks was thus the only practical response. The effects of years of segregation, he contended, had been "more apparent than real" (*Negro Americans* 15). Johnson further argued that even the achievements that had contributed the most to racial pride had been realized within the broader context of the dominant culture: "Our separate schools and some of our other race institutions, many of our race enterprises, the greater part of our employment, and most of our fundamental activities are contingent upon our relationship with the country as a whole" (15).[18]

This emphasis on activities that are directly related to the "country as a whole" apparently left the Negro Leagues out of Johnson's protest writings that deal with sports. By the 1920s, most of the African American athletes who had gained mainstream acclaim were boxers and jockeys; few of them played a team sport. (The conspicuous exception was Paul Robeson, who was a football star at Rutgers before becoming more widely known as a singer, actor, and political activist.) Indeed, in *Black Manhattan*, Johnson attributes the success of African Americans in horse racing and boxing to the individualist natures of those sports. The African American, he wrote, "never gets so fair a chance in those forms of sport or athletics where he must be a member of a team as in those where he may stand upon his own ability as an individual" (*Black Manhattan* 62–63). Although those athletes, like minstrel performers, were dangerously susceptible to marginalization and the demands or whims of popular opinion, they had singular opportunities to achieve mainstream popularity and reap financial rewards. For Johnson, such popularity and rewards carried demonstrable importance in the pragmatic project of forcing change in American culture.

Johnson's emphasis on integrated cultural institutions, even as he argued for the historical significance of the early, distinctive arts in sports and theatre, left him open to criticism, especially by the more radical critics of the 1960s and '70s. Harold Cruse found Johnson's two strains of argument incompatible, even incoherent. Cruse contended, however, that the source of the problem was an out-of-touch intelligentsia rather than a deeply embedded conservatism. "The analytical flaws in James Weldon Johnson's treatment of the Harlem Renaissance developments," Cruse argued, "reflected the lack of a definitive cultural philosophy characteristic of the other Harlem intellectuals" (Cruse 37). Cruse specifically blames Johnson and other leading intellectuals for failing to support the cause of the African American theatre in Harlem. His provocative questioning—"Without an ethnic theatre how can there be a cultural renaissance? Or better—what is the cultural renaissance for?"—could easily be expanded to include baseball and other sports (Cruse 36).

Professional team sports helped to define the character of Harlem and other black population centers within the context of African American culture and with little or no outside capital. Team sports and organizations became influential, popular, and prevalent in African American society, although the forces of institutionalized racism, segregation, and economic discrimination stifled their roles as community-builders (Riess, *Sport* 109–10). Slowly and fitfully, however, Negro League baseball undoubtedly became one of the "race institutions" cited by Johnson, working within the framework of segregation in hopes of forcing major-league baseball to integrate, whether by pragmatic or idealistic means. Moreover, the organized leagues clearly acted as "social institutions," which have been defined in the context of sports as bodies that are distinctive organizations, provide unique social activities, construct social identity, offer links to other social structures, and are agents of social control (McPherson, Curtis, and Loy 1). And yet, just as the game failed to capture Johnson's interest in nine years of writing columns for the *Age*, baseball found no place in *Negro Americans, What Now?* Perhaps, amid the heady days of the early Renaissance, it carried for Johnson the taint of isolationism; perhaps, in the early days of the Depression, the temporary financial disintegration of the leagues had convinced him of their inefficacy. While the game remained ever capable of stirring his sense of nostalgia, in the end organized Negro League baseball failed to move Johnson—as it also failed to move Hughes, Thurman, McKay, and the other artists of Harlem's Black Bohemia—to recognize its potential and rally to its cause.

PART II

Sportswriting
and the Harlem Press

5. "Jazz Journalism"
Sportswriting and Popular Culture in the Black Press

On the Saturday before Thanksgiving in 1922, William H. Ferris paused on Whalley Avenue in New Haven on his way to the annual football game between Harvard and Yale. Observing the crowd, which would exceed 70,000 that day, Ferris took note of the "hundreds of automobiles of every description, with women occupants clad in the most gorgeous and expensive furs" and concluded that "The Game," as it was already known, had become something more than just a game. Ferris, a Yale graduate (Class of '95), could claim some historical perspective. He had attended the 1894 contest between the two schools, played in Springfield, Massachusetts, before a substantially smaller crowd, when "the game itself was the main attraction" (Ferris, "Impressions" 4). Twenty-eight years later, writing in Marcus Garvey's weekly newspaper, *Negro World*, Ferris observed that "The Game" had become "a presentation of American civilization in its meridian splendor."

Five days after that Harvard-Yale contest in 1922, on Thanksgiving Day, Ferris attended another college football game, this time between Howard and Lincoln universities in Washington, D.C. To Ferris, the literary editor of Garvey's newspaper and an officer in his United Negro Improvement Association, the Howard-Lincoln rivalry emitted the same aura as that between Harvard and Yale: the game seemed less significant than did the fans in attendance. "They, too," he wrote of the well-attired crowd, "represented the civilization of the American Negro at its highest water mark. They represented colored society at its best, the men and women who have gone out into the world and won their spurs and the youth who will be the future leaders of the race" (4). Such was the social significance of sporting events during the Harlem Renaissance, when the popularity of a college football game could be seen as just another indicator that the cultural life of America—in which spectator sports played such a prominent part—had expanded to include the African American community. Harlem's leading newspaper, the *Amsterdam News,* gave the 1922 Howard-Lincoln game front-page coverage, with a sub-headline reading: "Game Witnessed by Prominent Men and Women from All Over Country; Social Functions Give Washington a Week's Holiday" (Dougherty, "Thousands" 1). Meanwhile, the even lengthier sub-heading above Ferris's story in the *Negro World,* which took a socially-conscious, internationalist approach in its intermittent sports coverage, provided a bevy of details: "Nearly Twenty Thousand People, Some Clad in Furs, Witness the Game— Eight Hundred Automobiles, Including a Royal Benz, a Mercedes and a Rolls-Royce, Are Parked in the Field and in Adjacent Streets." For both Ferris and Romeo Dougherty, the sports editor of the *Amsterdam News,* the opulence on display in Washington that weekend exemplified not so much conspicuous consumption as cultural achievement and social progress.

In many ways, Ferris's comparison of the two football games encapsulates American culture in the Roaring Twenties. Along with the stylish dress and high-society gatherings, large-scale spectator sports and the Harlem Renaissance are now considered symbols of the decade. At the time, however, only the African American press considered these intrinsic elements of the era in the context of each other. Just as sports became a pervasive, influential aspect of American culture in the 1920s, they reached new levels of popularity and significance in the African American community as well. The African American press took seriously the cultural influence of sports, and it also used the platform that sports provided to speak to an especially wide audience about political and economic issues that white sportswriters ignored throughout the era (and for decades to come). The annual Thanksgiving game between Howard and Lincoln, for example, became more than the quintessential social gathering of the Renaissance; it also became the event that established the central role of the press in African American life. In 1926, Eugene Gordon described the spectacle in the *American Mercury*:

> Hundreds of photographs are made by staff photographers, and since the game is important in the social calendar, "society" reporters mingle with the scribes from the sporting departments. The city at which the game is played becomes temporarily the social capital of Aframerica. No other event draws together so many of the educated and wealthy colored folk [Gordon, "Negro Press" 212].

5. "Jazz Journalism"

The power of sports to bring people of different classes together meant a great deal many writers in the African American press, but the chance to break down barriers of education and class carried extraordinary significance for those who wrote about sports. For the sportswriters, many of whom did double-duty as theatre critics, access to such an event led to social contacts, a wider reading audience, and an opportunity to demonstrate their talent, knowledge, and political acumen.

Political debates and cultural critiques regularly overlapped in the Renaissance press, even in the sports pages. The feuds between the devotees of Booker T. Washington and W.E.B. Du Bois—complicated in the 1920s by alternative forces such as the black nationalism of Garvey—simmered beneath most of the debates that raged among the sportswriters in Harlem's weekly newspapers. Whatever their political leanings, however, nearly all the sportswriters in the African American press promoted sports as a vehicle for social change rather than as a pleasant diversion. In New York City, these papers covered the political spectrum, from the Garvey-influenced *Interstate-Tattler* to the Washington-supported *New York Age*. Even the ideologically driven *Crusader*, representing the radical left, carried features on the Renaissance Five basketball team. The *Messenger*, a socialist magazine that supported the Industrial Workers of the World and eventually became the publicity organ of the Brotherhood of Sleeping Car Porters, also featured a monthly column on sports. Among the major publications of the era, only Charles S. Johnson's *Opportunity* and *The Crisis*, under Du Bois, took a more traditional intellectual approach, ignoring sports almost entirely. Sports coverage, for many Renaissance journalists, served a dual purpose: the popularity of sports helped sell newspapers, to be sure; but more important, the status of teams and other athletic organizations as social institutions allowed the papers to solidify their own status as unique chroniclers of a marginalized community. For sportswriters in particular, this coverage became their means of participating in the pressing debates of the day.

Sports, Sensationalism and the Popularity of the Press

At the height of the Renaissance in the mid–1920s, two major African American weekly newspapers called Harlem home: the *New York Age* and the *Amsterdam News*. In addition, among several other weeklies that appeared for short periods of time, the *Interstate-Tattler* reached a significant and spirited readership. The nationally distributed *Negro World*, published by Marcus Garvey's Universal Negro Improvement Association, also came out of Harlem. Other competition came from newspapers with national editions, primarily the *Chicago Defender*; the *Pittsburgh Courier*; and the *Afro-American*, which was based in Baltimore but published editions in several cities along the eastern seaboard. Most of these papers rose to prominence immediately following World War I, in a period that saw the founding of myriad African American magazines and newspapers. Spurred by the migration of African Americans from the South to northern cities during the war, and in many cases by the racially divisive, often violent backlash that those migrants felt when white soldiers returned after the Armistice, these periodicals exhibited the assertive, initial fervor of the New Negro movement.

The newspapers expressed this assertiveness in sensational exposés of the era's pervasive racism, usually trumpeted in a banner headline, a device African American editors used "to carry on a cold, bloodless war with the general press" (Pride and Wilson 217). Of course, the 96-point headline also helped sell papers. However, the increased popularity of African American newspapers in the postwar period stemmed more directly from the papers' increased attention to the popular pursuits we now associate with the Roaring Twenties, such as speakeasies, jazz, and sports. Politics and popular culture, traditionally treated as disparate entities in the white press, came together in the African American newspapers, where they co-existed in a manner that many high-minded readers dismissed as outlandish.

The combination of sensationalism and pop culture drew the ire of Harlem's leading intellectuals, who considered the two trends part of an entrenched lowbrow conservatism emanating from the influence of Booker T. Washington. In New York, particularly, Washington's longstanding support of the *New York Age* strengthened this perception: while the *Age* stuck with a staid approach in the Renaissance years, its rivals—especially the *Amsterdam News*—followed the trend of tabloid journalism and set a contentious tone in the Harlem press. The sensationalistic nature of the African American newspapers, however, can be placed in a larger context, amid the rise of the tabloid in the mainstream white press. The African American papers that achieved the greatest popularity in the Renaissance—namely, the *Amsterdam News*, the *Chicago Defender* and the *Pittsburgh*

Courier—all began publication just after the turn of the century, as the newspaper wars waged by Hearst and Pulitzer gave rise to "yellow journalism" and sent ripples of change through the industry. The *Amsterdam* and its even more sensationalistic followers, the *New York News* and the *Interstate-Tattler*, appeared alongside and were undoubtedly influenced by New York's "picture newspaper," the *Daily News*. The Harlem papers, though never so lavishly illustrated (for economic and technological reasons) as the top-selling white tabloids, followed the tabloid formula of emphasizing crime stories and features, especially society news and sports.

As early as 1938, historian Simon Michael Bessie defined the tabloid trend, which he called "Jazz Journalism," as an integral aspect of the Renaissance era. Self-consciously looking back at the "gay years" of the 1920s from the perspective of the "grim years" of the Depression, Bessie called the tabloid "part of a pattern which included speakeasies, jazz, collegiate whoopee, bathing beauties, movie-star worship, big-time sports and many other gigantic exaggerations" (Bessie 24). Bessie specifically aligned the tabloid with jazz, though he never mentioned the African American press in his 240-page study:

> There is an interesting parallel between the tabloid and another great symbol of the twenties, jazz. It too was denounced as vulgar, depraved and vicious and learned opinion was agreed that it could not last long. People no longer regard the continued existence of jazz as a subject for wonder. There is a growing realization that jazz is the true rhythm for the American songs of our times, a musical development with a respectable ancestry and a sound basis in popular needs and desires [Bessie 25].

His awkward attempt at legitimization notwithstanding, Bessie's affirmation of "popular needs and desires" demonstrates the social significance of jazz, sports, and other entertainments, which the tabloid press recognized and the mainstream press—like the intelligentsia—largely ignored. The *New York Times* of March 1, 1920, for example, contained no pictures and less than one page each of sports and features (Bessie 230–31).

The more traditional papers in the mainstream press, such as the *Times*, gradually increased their sports coverage in the 1920s. According to historian Brian Carroll, sports coverage constituted forty to sixty percent of the local sections of daily newspapers in the decade, while the wire service United Press increased its sports coverage by 300 percent between 1925 and 1928 (Carroll 27). The much-ballyhooed age of sportswriting that resulted, however, isolated its most prominent practitioners at the same time it expanded their forum. Aside from a few conspicuous exceptions—

especially Damon Runyon and Heywood Broun—sportswriters wrote only about sports. *New York Herald-Tribune* sports editor Stanley Woodward, in one of the first books exclusively devoted to sportswriting, lamented in 1949: "[T]he 'Golden Era' represented a setback to sports writing. Had the sports page as such started in the Nineties, when city staff writers were detached to cover the principal sports events, we could perhaps have made greater progress" (Woodward 49). The African American sportswriters, on the other hand, lacked the luxury of specialization and continued to handle multiple assignments throughout the Renaissance. Woodward, however, never mentions the African American press in his analysis; neither does he address the issue of race, even though he is best known today for breaking the story when the St. Louis Cardinals threatened to strike rather than play the Brooklyn Dodgers and Jackie Robinson in 1947. (Woodward reported in the New York *Herald-Tribune* that the National League President, Ford Frick, had gotten wind of the planned strike and averted it by threatening to suspend for life any participating player. Although the story has since been confirmed, Woodward named no sources in the story.)

In the early years of the twentieth century, such wide-ranging capability among sportswriters was neither new nor unusual—in either press. As Woodward pointed out, sportswriters at all papers tended to start out in news before "escaping" to sports, where

> they find that the field of sports is less cramped than it is supposed to be; that coverage of sports involves all the things that come up in general newspaper work, such as law, politics, economics, domestic relations, genealogy, dramatics, police, female fashions and war. When a man goes out on a sports assignment he may become involved in any or all of these before he gets home [Woodward 62].

The sportswriters in the African American press, however, developed their wide range as much as a matter of priority than practicality. The sports editors typically handled the theatrical coverage and were likely to appear on the front of the paper or the editorial page as well. The Harlem papers gave prominent play to sports and entertainment coverage not only because it widened the reach of the press; it also gave the journalists a leg up on the intelligentsia, an edge that the reading public largely found wanting in the writing of intellectuals, undercutting the putative conservatism of the press.

Meanwhile, the artists of the Renaissance, many of them members of a Bohemian community that was often at odds with the established intelligentsia, embraced jazz but neither sports nor the press. They considered both unsophisticated and bourgeois. Wallace Thurman, for example, spoofed the newspapers' queasiness concerning the Renaissance and its milieu in *Infants of the Spring*. In Thurman's novel, the fictional *New York Call* runs an anti–Bohemian editorial, arguing that the young generation of writers and artists were "pandering to a current demand for the sensational, libeling their own people, injuring them, insulting them by being concerned only with Jezebels, pimps and other underworld fauna" (*Infants* 197–98). When the paternalistic Dr. Parkes (modeled on Alain Locke) suggests to Thurman's protagonist, Ray, that he should take care to avoid such publicity, Ray replies: "I intend to live just as I please, regardless of yellow journalism, or a public which might offer me material aid should I, in their opinion, prove myself worthy" (198).

Thurman's novel failed to represent the range of views that were expressed in the press; elsewhere, he strove more for balance. Considering the Harlem newspapers in his essay "Negro Life in New York's Harlem" (1927), Thurman ranked the *Amsterdam News* the "most progressive Negro weekly published in Harlem," begrudgingly conceding that the paper "does feature the work of many of the leading Negro journalists and has the most forceful editorial page of the group, even if it does believe that most of the younger Negro artists are 'bad New Negroes'" (144). Thurman's satire took many targets—*Infants of the Spring* itself is a bitter send-up of the Renaissance and its excesses—but he measured his ire somewhat when aiming it at the Harlem papers. Ultimately, he complained most loudly about the papers' sensationalism, charging that for years the African American press was interested only in "gossip and scandal" (144). Even so, Thurman admitted that the Harlem papers occupied a significant role in and paid unique attention to the community. "Now," he continued reluctantly, "some of them have actually begun to support certain issues for the benefit of the community and to cry out for reforms in the regulation journalistic manner" (144).

As the charges of sensationalism drove a wedge between the press and the intellectuals of the Renaissance, the journalists began to defend themselves. In the December 1928 number of *Opportunity*, Roy Wilkins, then the news editor of the *Kansas City Call*, suggested that the African American press was no more sensationalistic than were white newspapers (Wilkins, "Negro Press" 362–63). In a more systematic analysis that appeared in *Opportunity* the following year, P.B. Young, Jr., examined the content of seven leading African American newspapers to determine the percentage of "sensational" news in their pages. (Perhaps reflecting the perception that the Harlem newspapers were more provincial than the national weeklies, Young failed to include any of them in his list of seven "representative" publications.) After reading through 112,198 column inches, Young labeled every article according to ten classifications, with "sensational news" being one. Others included "sports news," "cultural news," "personal news," "human interest stories," and "magazine (feature) material," all of which he called "socially significant content" (Young 370–71). Overall, Young found less than ten percent of the collected newspapers' content to be sensational in nature. The Baltimore *Afro-American* was found to have the greatest percentage of sensational news in Young's evaluations, while the Norfolk *Journal and Guide* had the smallest (Young's father was the editor of the *Journal and Guide*). The Chicago *Defender* ranked third-to-last in its percentage of sensational news, despite its reputation for being the most notorious transgressor in this regard; Young attributed that to the prominence of sensational headlines on the *Defender*'s front page (Young 371). Still, editors quickly admitted that sensational news figured prominently in their newspapers. According to E. Washington Rhodes, the editor of the *Washington Tribune*, "scandal, especially when implicating preachers, has the greatest news value," while Young added: "Social, sport, and church news come next" (372).

In Young's estimation, the *Pittsburgh Courier*, by then the most popular African American paper in the country, carried the greatest percentage of sports stories in its sections. Not coincidentally, the *Courier* surpassed the *Defender* in the late 1920s as the leading black weekly in the nation, with a circulation of about 250,000. The *Courier* rose to prominence by taking a decidedly middle-of-the-road stance on "economic issues, racial accommodation, and the loyalty of blacks to the United States," attacking both the activist left and "Bookerite" conservatism; similarly, editor Robert L. Vann found both W.E.B. Du Bois and James Weldon Johnson—the most visible leaders of the NAACP—excessively radical (Kellner 284). Much of the *Courier*'s popularity, however, came from its emphasis on features such as sports. Eugene Gordon, who critiqued the African American press for several magazines in the 1920s, concluded that these elements, rather than the newspaper's bourgeois editorial position, drove the *Courier*'s increasing popularity: "A few persons, I am sure, buy the paper solely because of these features" ("Outstanding," December 1927, 359).

Gordon generally praised the *Courier*'s special features, such as Geraldyn Dismond's gossip column devoted to Harlem society and the "excellent sports pages" edited by Rollo Wilson (Gordon, "Outstanding," December 1927, 359). The *Courier* paid attention to Harlem in its sports pages as well, featuring "On the Eastern Sport Trail," a column by the *Amsterdam News* sports editor, Romeo Dougherty. Specifically citing the *Courier*'s featured writers, Gordon wrote: "When one is unable to predict with assurance from week to week just whom [George] Schuyler is going to shoot a spitball, or whom Mrs. Dismond is going to regard critically through her lorgnette, or Floyd Calvin interview, or Rollo W. Wilson discuss from the sportsman's point of view, there is, naturally, a vigorous and expectant curiosity" (359). In the *American Mercury*, Gordon similarly singled out Wilson for praise: "Not only does he know sports, but he can write of them. Most of the others know the subject but cannot write" (Gordon, "Negro Press" 212). Later, in the Depression years, the *Courier*'s reliance on sports grew so extensive that it referred to itself as "the Joe Louis paper" because of its devoted attention to the African American heavyweight champion (Washburn 134). Still, amid its rise to prominence in the Renaissance, Gordon ranked the *Courier*'s sports coverage as the best in the black press.

Sports, Radicalism and the Social Carnival

Gordon, who served as the features and story editor for the *Boston Post* from 1919 through 1940, contributed to the communist *Daily Worker* and co-authored *The Position of Negro Women* (1935) with the radical leftist Cyril Briggs (Wolseley 204). Still, many critics consider him conservative, largely because of his traditionalist, sometimes cantankerous literary ethos. Between 1928 and 1930, Gordon edited the *Saturday Evening Quill*, publishing work by Waring Cuning, Helene Johnson, Dorothy West, and others who "had no interest in participating in a revolution in Afro-American letters," in the words of historian Walter C. Daniel (342). W.E.B. Du Bois and Charles S. Johnson—both members of the "old guard" that sometimes clashed with those on the younger generation of the New Negro movement—thought highly of the *Saturday Evening Quill* (Daniel 343). Daniel notes that Johnson, as the editor of *Opportunity*, would have been especially well-acquainted with Gordon and his assessments of African American journalism.

Gordon's lack of interest in literary revolt might have had more to do with his disinclination to join the crowd, however. In an autobiographical note, written for *Opportunity* after he won two prizes for short-story writing in 1927, he remarked: "I abominate Negro literature because of the limited scope of its appeal; I like literature which takes cognizance of the Negro's place in the national life because it is usually freshly original and is universal in its appeal" (Gordon, "Contest Spotlight" 204). Gordon's iconoclasm echoed the firebrand contrariness that characterized two writers he particularly admired: George Schuyler and H.L. Mencken.

Mencken's harsh critiques of mainstream American culture made him a popular figure in Harlem, and he influenced many Renaissance writers directly by publishing them in his magazine, the *American Mercury*. Discussing Mencken's influence on Schuyler particularly, Charles Scruggs points out that Schuyler wrote nine cover stories for the *Mercury* between 1927 and 1934 and appeared in the magazine more often than any other writer during Mencken's editorship (77). In particular, Mencken urged African American writers "to satirize black life as well as white" (Scruggs 76). According to Scruggs, Mencken's influence loomed larger than his followers admitted or even knew:

> Which came first, Mencken or the black Menckenites? As Schuyler pointed out, he had himself been skeptical of the accomplishments of the literary movement long before Mencken had challenged them. Yet it is also clear that Schuyler, Theophilus Lewis, Wallace Thurman, and Eugene Gordon, the Young Wits who were dissatisfied with the bombast attached to Negro literature, had all learned their muck-raking from Mencken [Scruggs 132].

While Gordon often used a "light touch" in his satire, in Scruggs's estimation, Schuyler followed Mencken's lead more closely and certainly did not satirize lightly. Mencken's "astringency" made him an unpopular figure in the broader ranks of the African American press (Scruggs 77). Both of the major Harlem newspapers, for example, attacked Mencken's analyses of the Renaissance. The *Age* accused him of sophistry, while the *Amsterdam News* called Mencken "sincere" but "naïve," lampooning his assertion that the New Negro movement suffered from "self-satisfaction." In a column that appeared in the *New York World*, Mencken had called many of the Renaissance achievements "artistic failures," marred by too much attention to propaganda and "the self-satisfaction which now afflicts the race not only in the aesthetic department but all along the line" (qtd. by Scruggs 126). If anything, the *Amsterdam* countered, African Americans could have stood to satisfy themselves much more (Scruggs 128–29).

However "light" Gordon's satirical touch was generally, he laced his critiques of the African American press with pointed language and Menckenian invective. Dismissing the quality of the features that appeared in the *Chicago Defender* in 1926, he sneered that they were "evidently written for the *lowbrow* of the *moron* contingent" (Gordon, "Survey," January 1927, 10; emphasis in original). Pre-emptively defending himself, Gordon argued that "destructive criticism" serves the same purpose as a forest fire, clearing away dead brush. His rankings generally assessed what he considered to be the best ten or twelve newspapers in the country, and he deemed only those to be worth reading at all. Explaining his reasons for discussing just thirteen papers in his essay for the *American Mercury*, he wrote: "From a pile of 220 Aframerican weeklies one may drop 197 as little more than waste paper. Of the remaining twenty-three, ten are mediocrities" (Gordon, "Negro Press" 208). Even his praise is striking in its acidity. Commenting on the improvement he had seen in several papers in 1927, Gordon declared: "The Negro press has arisen from that pitiable state of ludicrous imitation which once made it ridiculous" (Gordon, "Survey," December 1927, 358).

Gordon argued that the increased attention papers were paying to sports and other popular entertainments had propelled this ascendance. In 1927, the *Courier*, buoyed by its sports coverage and other features, rose to the top of Gordon's annual rankings for the first time (previously, either the *Defender* or the *Afro-American* had been rated number one). Gordon's approval of the sports and entertainment coverage in the African American press hardly indicates a counter-revolutionary bias; rather, the absence of substantive radicalism he saw in the press caused him to consider the papers' willingness to treat popular culture as a serious subject their most daring, innovative maneuver. For example, Garvey's *Negro World*—radical by any measure but rarely interested in sports or entertainment—made Gordon's list only once, ranking ninth overall in 1924. The next year Gordon dropped it, dismissing the paper as "a jumble of 'back to Africa' rubbish'" (Gordon, "Negro Press," 1926, 215). Perhaps Gordon did not take Garvey's nationalism as seriously as did others (for example, the U.S. government, which deported him in 1927), for he summarized the political leanings of the press in the same article by concluding, "A 'radical' Negro press simply doesn't exist" (213).

Despite this kind of dismissal, common among Renaissance writers of both the new and old guards, the *Negro World* in the early 1920s became the first African American newspaper to surpass 200,000 in circulation (Vincent, *Voices* 29). The *Courier, Defender,* and *Afro-American* followed later in the decade, and critics have attributed their increased popularity to a more militant editorial stance. Historian Theodore Vincent, for example, disputes Gordon's explanation—that people were reading the paper primarily for its sports coverage and other features—for the *Courier's* broadening influence. Instead, Vincent argues, "the rise of the Pittsburgh *Courier* in the mid-1920s can be attributed to editor Vann's adoption of a more militant editorial policy and his hiring of two columnists from the staff of the socialist *Messenger* magazine" (*Voices* 30). One of the columnists the *Courier* hired away from the *Messenger* was Schuyler, whose contrariness was then novel enough to excite critics on both sides of the political divide; in time, he became known as the foremost conservative columnist in the African American press. What Vincent praises as militancy, Gordon also admired, but in terms of original thinking and iconoclasm. Gordon had acknowledged this shift as well: In his list of "notable achievements in Aframerican journalism in 1926," he cited the *Courier's* "more trenchant editorials" (Gordon, "Survey," January 1927, 9). Even Gordon's use of the soon-outdated term "Aframerican" speaks to his influences and, ultimately, his ideology. (As Roi Ottley noted in 1943, "For years many literary folk liked 'Aframerican,' which has a melodious tilt, but this term has a derisive meaning to Negroes. H.L. Mencken and George S. Schuyler, the Negro satirist and *Courier* columnist, did much to give it this bad reputation, and today they are practically the only writers who use it" [Ottley 279].)

Despite the bourgeois appeal of the black newspapers overall, a range of viewpoints distinguished the Harlem press. The papers' funding sources, politically motivated and drawn to Harlem from around the country, created a battleground for a decade of editorial warfare. While Washington's Tuskegee organization secretly supported the *Age*, many of the papers that emerged in Harlem during the Renaissance openly identified themselves with radical organizations such as Garvey's. Despite their affiliations with specific nationalist, socialist, or communist causes, these organs made general coverage of the African American community part of their mission and aimed for a mass audience (Vincent, *Voices* 36). Their success forced the comparatively moderate African American papers, such as the *Age* and the *Amsterdam*, to follow suit or fade from the scene. The *Amsterdam*, for example, finally rose to national prominence in the 1930s when it associated itself with more aggressively left-wing writers; meanwhile, the steady decline of the *Age*, just as the African American press enjoyed years of growth, has been attributed to its habit of "playing down" the news of black radicals in the Renaissance and Depression years (Vincent, *Voices* 30).

In the 1920s, Harlem enjoyed a far wider range of voices than that of any other African American community with the possible exception of Chicago, which had nine African American newspapers in 1921 (Vincent, *Voices* 23). While the rivalry between the *Age* and the *Amsterdam*—and thus between devotees of Washington and Du Bois—played out from city to city, only Harlem supported multiple papers aligned with Garvey's movement (narrowly focused, perhaps, but certainly not provincial). In addition, socialist publications produced in Harlem, such as the *Crusader* and the *Messenger*, included not only polemical pieces but also features on cultural topics such as sports. For a brief period, especially in 1922, when Garvey published the *Negro Daily Times*, the African American press in Harlem glaringly contradicted E. Franklin Frazier's claim that "although the Negro press declares itself to be the spokesman for the Negro group as a whole, it represents essentially the interests and outlook of the black bourgeoisie" (Frazier, *Black Bourgeoisie* 146). Vincent notes that several scholars have followed Frazier's lead in criticizing the African American press for catering excessively to the middle class. However, Vincent cautions that "this criticism should not obscure the radical side of the press and the special problems facing blacks in producing *any* type of journal" (Vincent, *Voices* 28).

Prominent figures of the Renaissance era leveled similar charges at the Harlem press, however. Compared to papers such as the *Courier* and the *Defender*, Claude McKay noted, "the Harlem weeklies are provincial" (*Harlem* 15). Indeed, even at the height of the Renaissance—when James Weldon Johnson declared that Harlem had become synonymous with "Negro metropolis"—only Garvey's *Negro World* showed any interest in distributing nationally. (Indeed, the *Negro World* distributed internationally, with a Spanish-language edition circulating in the Caribbean islands.) "Harlem *is* lacking in group solidarity and the high seriousness of other Aframerican communities," McKay contended. "Even intellectually, Harlem is backward, some contend, although it has more well-paid teachers and excellent schools, libraries and librarians than any other black belt" (*Harlem* 15; emphasis in original). This paradox could be seen most acutely in the press, where the emphasis on popular culture seemed to have subsumed "high seriousness" to such an extent that some African American intellectuals refused to read the papers. "Indeed," McKay wrote, "I have heard individuals say they are ashamed to carry a Negro newspaper in public!" (96).

McKay's contention might have been exaggerated. In the 1920s, according to Charles Scruggs, "both highbrow and lowbrow read [African American newspapers] eagerly, the lowlifers fixing their eyes on the tabloid murders and baseball scores and the sophisticates turning their attention to the theatre section and editorial pages" (Scruggs 77). Of course, the same could be said of newspapers of many stripes and of their readers, with one primary difference: In the African American press, the same editors produced both the baseball and theatre news. Gordon offered a similar observation in one of his *Opportunity* surveys, but with a more optimistic slant:

> There still remains ... a few colored folk who declare boastfully that they never read a Negro newspaper; the number of these, happily, is diminishing. Most colored folk not only read these papers but prove their interest in, and, often, their partiality for, a particular journal, by quoting from it to uphold an opinion or a view ["Outstanding," December 1927, 358].

The apparent disagreement between Gordon and McKay represents two shades of a shared viewpoint. McKay, almost two decades removed from his most intense period of leftist activism and direct participation in the Harlem press, remained focused on the attitude of the intellectual outsider. In his view, the celebration of popular entertainments in the Harlem press lacked international perspective and, by implication, sophisticated analysis. Gordon, in contrast, consistently defended the cultural contributions of the African American papers; however acerbic his critiques of the press, they always affirmed the papers' importance in the community.

Still, the line between the intellectual elite, a group that saw itself aligned in spirit (if not in day-to-day comforts) with the working class, and the bourgeoisie cannot be drawn so easily. For example, according to Adam McKible, the radical *Messenger* was intermittently edited in the 1920s by Schuyler, Thurman, and drama critic Theophilus Lewis, who collectively "intensified *The Messenger*'s interest in the black bourgeoisie and also made the magazine more 'literary'" (McKible 124). In Harlem, the *Amsterdam News* aimed to align itself with the more radical intellectuals, while the *Age* faded into obscurity with the less fashionable old guard. In 1939, a study conducted by the Federal Writers Project described the division:

> While the *Age* appeals to the members of the hundreds of smaller clubs and fraternal organizations by giving them a great deal of space, the *Amsterdam News*, with its full pages of photographs and articles, society gossip, fashions, art, music, the theatre, sports, and cocktail parties of the wealthy groups, sororities and exclusive young people's circles appeals directly to the "upper tenth," as Dr. Du Bois might say [Gross 4].

This association of sports with the wealthy and their social events indicates not so much the status of athletics in Harlem society as their appeal to all classes. In a sense, sports gave the Harlem journalists an entry point into a sphere of society that most cultures and communities keep closed to the press. Similarly, as sporting events such as the Thanksgiving football game between Howard and Lincoln became social events, the presence of the press brought other sectors of society into contact with the upper class. Gordon, in another *Opportunity* analysis, compared the African American papers favorably to other "class sheets"—specifically, German, Jewish, and Catholic publications (Gordon, "Survey" 8).

Such allegiance to social standing must have seemed small-minded to the cosmopolitan leaders of the New Negro movement. Indeed, the newspapers' emphasis on seemingly mundane concerns such as scandal, society, and sports only aggravated the disdain that African American intellectuals and artists had for the press. Those who ran newspapers, meanwhile, embraced their specialized status in practical terms, understanding it as their primary source of financial support. Roy Wilkins dismissed the standards of the Renaissance elite as all but irrelevant to working editors, who needed to keep in mind the interests of their papers' readership. "The Negro newspaper," Wilkins concluded, "is of necessity a class newspaper" (Wilkins, "Negro Press" 363). Wilkins' description of the African American newspaper as one inevitably rooted in a specific social class failed to resonate with the Renaissance elite until after the movement had waned and the Depression had set in. By then, the press was already ahead of the game, communicating its readership's concerns and giving them a collective voice. In 1927, for example, Gordon identified "a distinctive journalistic genre emerging" (Gordon, "Survey," 1927, 7). The same critic who despised the phrase "Negro literature" detected and praised a growing awareness of the relationship between African American culture and American culture at large. Arguing that this awareness had sprung from the newspapers of the Renaissance in particular, Gordon asserted: "the Negro press is religiously, almost fanatically, race conscious, and, hence, is doing more than any other agency to develop and sustain this consciousness in its readers" (Gordon, "Survey," 1927, 8). Echoing Gordon, Walter White called the establishment of the African American press as a community institution, despite its lack of capital and formal training, "a miracle of journalism" (qtd. by Everett, *Returning* 6). In a study of the criticism that appeared in the African American newspapers of the era, Anna Everett similarly asserts that the press "became African Americans' voice with which to 'talk back' to mainstream American society, but more importantly, to communicate with itself at this crucial moment of self-invention" (Everett, *Returning* 6).

White, who succeeded Du Bois as the executive secretary of the NAACP, tempered his declaration of this miraculous occurrence by noting the perpetuation in the African American press of a brand of "personal journalism," the result of the newspapers' unusual reliance on its readers, rather than advertisers, for most of their financial support. The African American newspaper, White concluded, "has therefore of necessity remained more responsive to its readers' wishes than has any other" (White 209). The Renaissance elite widely dismissed this brand of journalism, reminiscent as it was of small-town papers and school yearbooks. But while Renaissance writers experimented with stylized versions of vernacular in their poetry and prose, the press fashioned a new discourse in increasingly literate and urbane African American communities; the writers in the African American press emerged as "organic intellectuals," in contrast to the formally trained intelligentsia of the Renaissance (Everett 53). Beneath this emergent discourse, Everett notes, lay the "fundamental antimonies that existed between the black bourgeoisie and its often tolerated other" (5). According to Theodore Vincent, the "organic" nature of the intellectualism in the press invested its writers with a special kind of freedom: "There were reasons black journalism was the most liberated of black institutions involved in political expression. The press, like the comparatively non-political church and fraternal orders, was created by blacks to serve black society" (Vincent, *Voices* 23).

While most of newspapers embraced the direct responsiveness of this discourse, however, this undeniably insular quality left the Harlem newspapers paradoxically boxed in. On the one hand, the prevalence of "personal journalism," along with its emphasis on scandal, society, and sports, seemed to Renaissance intellectuals and artists hopelessly narrow-minded and bourgeois. On the other hand, the wide range of discourses in the Harlem press—enlivened by the carnival of scandals, societies and sporting events—separated it from that of the more monolithic African American communities in the rest of the country. Celebrating this carnival in spite of its "provincialism," McKay contrasted the attitudes that appeared in the national weeklies with those represented in Harlem:

> Some jeer at Harlem as the capital of clowns whose fame rests upon cults and cabarets. They say that Harlem is a vast circus in which the people seem satisfied with an array of noise makers who swing in the dance halls and sing wildly in peace kingdoms; that they love spectacular parades of drums and uniforms, and prancing on the pavements by days and jiving in the honkey-tonks by night [*Harlem* 15].

As McKay's own critiques demonstrate, not all of the jeering came from outside of Harlem: the range of viewpoints and sheer vitality of the Harlem newspapers in the Renaissance somehow struck intellectuals, Bohemians, and proletarians alike as lacking in high and common purpose.

A generation later, the circus had been completely shut down, to the dismay of some members of the press. Al Monroe, the theatrical editor of the *Chicago Defender* and a former sportswriter for the *Chicago Whip*, remarked in 1960: "I think the Negro press is entirely too serious. In brief, there is hardly a laugh in any of the pages, and many a would-be reader is lost for this reason" (qtd. in Hill 50). The Harlem press could be self-serving and sensationalistic, occasionally obscuring its celebration of popular entertainments and muffling the voice it gave to the masses. Nonetheless, the journalists preceded most Renaissance artists and intellectuals by a decade in recognizing the importance of the popular culture that emerged from the community they served.

6. "A Course in the Curriculum of the Institution"

Sports and Politics in the Harlem Press

In late October 1929, as New Yorkers and the rest of nation began to absorb the initial shock of the stock market crash, *Amsterdam News* sports editor Romeo Dougherty wrote a column bemoaning the end of the Negro League baseball season. Apparently, he knew not all of his readers would share his sentiments, but that had nothing to do with the crash. Dougherty predicted—even dreaded—that the popularity of college football would bring an influx of mail from the southern schools. Dougherty noted somewhat sardonically, however, that the Tuskegee Institute stood out in this regard. "Let those who decry the work of the late Booker T. Washington," Dougherty wrote, "stop and give a thought to a mind that must have been brilliant, for Tuskegee not only sends her matter where it can do the most good, but it comes in printed envelopes correctly addressed to the department where they know it should be sent."[1] This faint praise of Washington's legacy is significant, not only because of its seemingly incongruous appearance in the midst of a sports column in the waning days of the Harlem Renaissance. The backhanded compliment also demonstrates the complex political viewpoints regularly expressed in the African American press of the era: the *Amsterdam*, for example, made its name by countering Washington's influence, which was embodied in Harlem by the *New York Age*.

In a nascent way, later debates over the social significance of popular culture and sports in particular—largely emanating from the overarching battles among the followers of Washington, Du Bois, and Garvey—were sketched out on the pages of the Harlem press. The *Amsterdam News*, for example, was founded in 1909 and gradually became the dominant paper in Harlem not only by challenging the *Age*, but also by arguing for equality and social change in the manner of Du Bois and the NAACP; more than a century later, the *Amsterdam* continues to publish weekly and retains its status as Harlem's community newspaper. In the Renaissance years, Dougherty played a prominent role as the *Amsterdam* asserted its prominence at the expense of the *Age*, aligning himself with more progressive movements and continually pointing out the anachronistic methods and lesser influence of his rivals. However, the *Age* commanded a certain respect throughout the 1920s, from the younger generation as well as either side of the Washington–Du Bois divide.

Between Accommodation and Integration: The New York Age

The *New York Age* represented and promoted Washington's "accommodationist" approach to race relations in New York City. Washington secretly supported the *Age*, which was founded in 1881 as the *Rumor* (it changed its name to the *Freeman* in 1884 before settling on its longstanding name in 1888), until 1907, when he purchased the paper outright and installed Fred R. Moore as editor (Wolseley 31–32). The *Age* responded to the founding of the *Amsterdam News* in 1909 by growing somewhat less stodgy—Moore hired James Weldon Johnson to write editorials for the paper in 1914—though it generally retained its conservative stance (Osofsky 120). In 1926, Eugene Gordon described the paper: "The *New York Age* is the ancient harridan of black newspaperdom, and Fred R. Moore is her old man. He has lived with and been faithful to her for nineteen years. She is a fine brain in a somewhat passé body" (Gordon, "Negro Press," 214). The sports coverage in the *Age* established the form for its rival papers, but its adherence to Washington's theory left it vulnerable to the paradoxes inherent in that approach. As a result, the newspaper's attempts to promote the importance of sports, and of the Negro Leagues in particular, suffered under the weight of moralistic argumentation and conflicted allegiances.

Until the mid-1910s, the *Age* covered sports intermittently and perfunctorily. Managing editor Lester A. Walton, Moore's son-in-law, handled both the sporting and theatrical news, although his interest moved gradually toward the latter. Walton had started his newspaper career in the 1890s as a sportswriter with the African American *St. Louis Star-Sayings*. Upon moving to New York and the *Age*, he joined a jazz group, The Frogs (the name referred to both Aesop and Aristophanes), singing and acting in musical revues (Morgan 1). Other members of the Frogs included the comedy team of George Walker and Bert Williams; the songwriters Bob Cole and James Weldon Johnson's brother, Rosamond; the conductor James Reese Europe; and the actor/playwright Jesse Shipp, who also worked as an umpire in the Negro Leagues. After several years with the *Age*, Walton worked in the 1920s and '30s as a drama critic for the integrated *New York World*. Walton later served as the U.S. envoy to Liberia from 1933 to 1946, sat on the New York City Commission on Civil Rights from 1955 to 1964, and helped convince *The New York Times* to capitalize "Negro" in its pages ("Lester A. Walton" 43).

Walton's sportswriting for the *Age* emphasized events of wide social interest or significance, such as the major college football games and boxing controversies. He usually restricted the baseball coverage on his "Dramatics and Athletics" page to game stories, filled with detail. In October of 1914, for example, the paper ran full-season statistics for the Lincoln Giants and the Lincoln Stars—information that is especially hard to find from the period preceding the organized Negro Leagues. When Walton did give his full attention to baseball, he focused on the color line and, in the conservative manner characteristic of the *Age*, argued against it in moral terms. Comparing the "ungentlemanly conduct" of many white ballplayers to the exemplary but unrewarded behavior of their African American counterparts, he asked in 1915: "Do we ever hear of members of the Lincoln Stars, Lincoln Giants, Royal Giants, St. Louis Giants or American Giants fighting and making themselves obnoxious as the Ty Cobbs and Larry McLeans of the big leagues?" ("Unwritten" 6).

In a 1916 column in the *Age* about Cobb's violent tendencies, James Weldon Johnson made the same point more subtly. Describing Cobb somewhat wryly as a "hot-blooded Southern gentleman, one who brooks not the slightest indignity," Johnson offered this prediction: "Some of these days, the police, the umpires, and his fellow-players are not going to prevent Mr. Cobb from climbing into the grandstand, and the result will be that he will come out of the grandstand in a condition which will make necessary his permanent retirement from active participation in the national game" (Johnson, "The 'Georgia Peach'" 4). Cobb avoided this fate, but McLean, who had hit .500 for the Giants in the 1913 World Series, was released because of his bad temper and fondness for liquor (James, *Historical* 112). In 1921, he was shot and killed in a bar brawl in Boston.

On its editorial page, the *Age* used athletics as a moral example in other contexts. In "Athletics and the Church," probably written by Walton, the paper asked why track meets in New York City were more frequently integrated than church meetings. "Athletics are never directly associated with religion, while the church is," the editorial observed. "And yet the Golden Rule is at times more religiously observed in athletics than in the church" ("Athletics and the Church" 4). Here, however, the *Age* restrained from a moralistic appeal for fair play—perhaps it was implied by the subject matter—and pursued a strictly logical course instead. "There is much practical Christianity in giving the colored man an opportunity to match his brain and brawn against that of the white man," the editorial continued, conflating theories of competition and salvation. "To preach Christianity and to fail to practice it as some of our white brethren do in white churches is becoming farcical. Such incongruities do Christianity no good."

Moore, the editor and publisher of the *Age*, struggled to maintain "deference to middle-class virtues, in what he considered Harlem's best society, never fully comprehending the 'New Negro' of the twenties" (Kellner 248). This balancing act became increasingly difficult to negotiate in the Renaissance years; the supposedly conservative George Schuyler declared with his customary ire, "Mr. Moore can fool some Negroes by posing as a Race Man, but along side of him, Uncle Tom was militant beyond description" ("Shafts" 4). Under Moore's stewardship, the *Age* regularly lurched between preaching and pragmatism, sometimes with contradictory effects. In one case, the paper's attempts to rid Harlem of gangsters and gamblers gave way to its support of the Negro Leagues and their proprietors. Moore, who also served as Harlem's alderman, fervently supported Prohibition and other "anti-vice" laws, and the *Age* published rumored Harlem "hootch" addresses weekly. Barron D. Wilkins, a former owner of the Bacharach Giants ballclub, had been widely known as the creator of the black cabaret culture in the mid–1910s, when he owned a self-named club on 35th Street, by transforming popular afternoon teas into "tango teas" that offered dancing and liquor (Watson 13). By the 1920s, Wilkins had gained greater notoriety as a bootlegger and the proprietor of the Exclusive Club on West 134th Street, which Moore's anti-liquor Committee of Fourteen had tried to close down. In 1924, Wilkins was murdered; nonetheless, the *Age* praised Wilkins after the murder as a communitarian, and in its funeral coverage, pictured Moore on the front page as an honorary pallbearer.

The *Age* covered Wilkins's ball club, the Bacharach Giants, as if it were Harlem's favored team. Wilkins had purchased an interest in the Bacharachs in 1919, and the club played its home games at Dyckman Oval in upper Manhattan for one year before moving back to its base in Atlantic City. The newspaper's appropriation of the team was complex: In its coverage of the team's 1920 season opener, sporting editor Ted Hooks's story began: "The Bacharach Giants, personal property of Baron Wilkins, 'Uncle Jawn' Connor, Harlem and Atlantic City, opened their season in New York last Sunday by dropping two games to the hard hitting Tesreau's Bears outfit" (Hooks, "Bacharach Giants" 7). "Uncle Jawn" was the Bacharachs' primary owner, John W. Connor, who had previously run the Brooklyn Royal Giants, named for his Royal Café on 135th Street, between 1905 and 1914. Connor, like Wilkins, had made his name running nightclubs that the *Age* opposed in theory, although it often praised them as examples of African American entrepreneurship. In 1914, for example, the *Age* had cited Connor's Rathskeller on 135th Street in a story that proclaimed, perhaps naively, "Afternoon Teas Now the Rage in Harlem."

Hooks began calling the club "Harlem's Pride," emphasizing its African American ownership. In 1916, the Bacharachs had moved north from Jacksonville, Florida, where they had been known as the Duval Giants. Two African American politicians from Atlantic City, Tom Jackson and Henry Tucker, had purchased the team and named it after the city's mayor, Harry Bacharach. The team became one of the more powerful independent clubs in the East and was a charter member of the Eastern Colored League when it was formed in 1923. The Bacharachs won the ECL's final two pennants before the league folded in 1928. The team was then part of the American Negro League's only season in 1929. After several more seasons as an independent, the Bacharachs played in the Negro National League for a half-season and folded in 1934 (Riley 43).

The Lincoln Giants, once "Harlem's Pride," were owned by white promoters; in a further transgression, the Lincolns had moved their games for 1920 out of Harlem, to the New York Catholic Protectory Oval in the Bronx. Although many Harlem fans still favored the Lincolns—playing on the same day as the Bacharachs opened their season, the Lincolns drew "hundreds of fans from Harlem"—the *Age* unambiguously gave its support to the Bacharachs, casting them as the more community-minded of the two teams. In an article announcing the changing of the guard, Hooks praised the wealth of Connor and Wilkins and compared them unfavorably to the

Lincolns' white owners. Although it had become common practice for owners to lure star players from other clubs in spite of their contract status—this was one of the reasons for the formation of the first Negro League, earlier the same year—Hooks described the Bacharachs as the primary targets in other teams' raiding sprees. "It is claimed," he wrote, "that white interests behind the other teams spend much of their time in trying to steal players from the all-colored team by offering them a few dollars more than they are getting" (Hooks, "Cyclone" 7). The Bacharachs were no more honorable in this regard than any other club; their star shortstop, Dick Lundy, had played with the black-owned Hilldale club of Philadelphia the previous year, and signed contracts with three clubs for the 1920 season (Riley 497). Connor and Wilkins made little effort to hide their lavish spending, and Hooks saw that as a sign that the community could hold its own. "It is said to be the highest salaried colored team in the game," he wrote of the Bacharachs, "and is undoubtedly the best dressed. … [Connor and Wilkins] swear that no big league team will have anything that their boys won't get" (Hooks, "Cyclone" 7).

Ultimately, though, the Bacharachs distinguished themselves from the Lincolns with their involvement in Harlem. While Connor and Wilkins had lavishly costumed their club, Hooks pointed out that they had also attended to the community:

> Something like one thousand dollars was spent to uniform these stars. Each player, aside from being presented with a big sweater which now retails at twenty-five dollars, is provided also with a leather coat of good quality. The Bacharach Giants' old outfits have been given (not sold) to the West 135th street Y.M.C.A. to encourage that organization in working up a team. This, to our way of thinking, sets a wonderful precedent in local interest for all of the baseball teams that depend for their existence upon their Harlem following [Hooks, "Cyclone" 7].

These gestures, of course, carried more symbolism than substance. The ballplayers, while not nearly so well paid as their white counterparts, earned substantially more than the average Harlem resident, even if they found themselves moving from city to city every year to sustain or improve their income. Moreover, the donation of old uniforms would have meant little to successful entrepreneurs, especially two as concerned with appearances as were Wilkins and Connor. But the extent to which Hooks went to emphasize the Bacharachs and their opulent image underscores the paper's interest in economic independence—even if its sources had raised their capital by selling something disreputable and, suddenly, illegal.

When the Lincolns and the Bacharachs faced each other that year, they drew a reported 16,000 fans to Ebbets Field in Brooklyn; it was the first time an African American team on the East Coast had used a major league stadium (Holway 143). Although the teams split a doubleheader, the page-one headline and Hooks's story in the *Age* were heavily slanted: "Bacharachs Put Whitewash on Lincolns in First Game." The *Age* continued to emphasize sartorial styles, contrasting the clubs in a sidebar devoted to the topic: "The Lincolns, while not so well-garbed, stood confident in their somewhat faded uniforms—seemingly poor but proud..." (Hooks, "For Championship" 7). As the season wore on, however, Hooks seemed to find it hard to sustain such high-pitched argumentation. In fact, according to baseball historian John Holway, the statistical records of the Eastern black ball clubs are especially sketchy for that season "partly because the New York black press lost interest in baseball coverage" (Holway 143).

At the end of the season, the *Age* dusted off its moral compass in its coverage of the scandal that had emanated from the 1919 World Series. After eight Chicago White Sox players were indicted on charges of fixing the series, Hooks reasoned, the major leagues could not refuse to admit African American players into the game for much longer. Hooks's attempt to argue his case logically begins with simple economics: Scouts for white teams had been looking for players to replace those who had been banned, but they "fell short of supplying the demand" (Hooks, "Why Do Big Leagues" 6). As Hooks points out, the scandal had included other players, such as the New York Giants' Heinie Zimmerman, even before the "Black Sox" were implicated. Zimmerman, who had led the National League in home runs and batting in 1912, had not been formally banned from baseball, but the New York Giants manager John McGraw had released Zimmerman in 1919 after hearing rumors that he was throwing games (James, *Historical* 568–69). Playing against African American clubs at the Catholic Protectory Field in 1920, Zimmerman had "produced as sensational a game as any player on the diamond," according to Hooks, and "served to make the fans wonder more than ever why he was denied his old berth with the Giants" ("Why Do Big Leagues" 6). Hooks recounts one version of Zimmerman's release—there are several—with the acknowledgment that "were it not for telling the whole story which we wish to tell, we would not mention it here." Zimmerman was later implicated in the World Series scandal as well and was formally banned from the game.

The foray into Zimmerman's travails allows Hooks to pivot from economics and logical analysis to a moralistic, even emotional appeal, as he cites for contrast the service of several ballplayers in World War I, along with their generally good citizenship. "How long is this state of affairs going to continue to exist?" he asks. "Are our star ballplayers—despite the active part they took in the war for Democracy, despite their gentlemanly behavior on the diamond and in civil life—to be forever confronted with this insurmountable color barrier? Is there no conscience in the white solons' hearts?" Indeed, several African American ballplayers enlisted or were drafted into the war—proportionately, in fact, many more than served from the major leagues, though Eddie Grant of the New York Giants was killed in action (Holway 123). The Lincoln Giants, for example, lost two of their best players—catcher Louis Santop and center fielder Spotswood Poles—for most of the 1918 season. (Upon returning the next year, Santop jumped to the Royal Giants, while Poles signed with the Bacharachs.) Hooks's ethical but non-confrontational appeal asks, in the tradition of Booker T. Washington, what more must be done to earn the faith of the major-league owners. As he turns to archaic language, giving his plea an almost Biblical fervor, it seems clear that he cannot see a solution outside of the racial and economic system that is already in place. Indeed, he concludes his column by urging the reader to appeal to a white sportswriter—"a writer on whatever daily he reads"—asking for "fair play" and "common sense."

Following the tumult of the 1920 season, William E. Clarke succeeded Hooks as the paper's sporting and theatrical editor. Clarke took a more conservative approach than most African American newspapers did in covering the booming sports scene of the Renaissance years. While most papers followed the lead of the *Defender* and the *Courier*, recognizing the popularity and social significance of the Negro Leagues, the *Age* largely restricted itself to accounts of games. (The attention to detail also continued: Clarke usually ran box scores, even in out-of-town stories, a feature that remained a rarity in the Harlem press.) When Clarke did extend the baseball coverage in the *Age* beyond game accounts, he stressed Bookerite values. His sports section endlessly praised the Negro League ballplayers for their traditional virtues, such as sportsmanship, and criticized such seemingly commonplace sports institutions such as drinking, gambling, improper dress and foul language (all of which went unreported in the white papers' coverage of the major leagues). At the end of the 1930 season, for example, Lincoln Giants manager John Henry Lloyd resigned after owner James J. Keenan criticized the team's performance in losing the championship series to the Homestead Grays. "The following Sunday," according to Clarke, "Mr. Keenan and [second baseman] Walter Cannady almost came to blows when Cannady remarked that Keenan was a poor sport."[2]

The *Age*'s reserved approach puzzled even its more sympathetic critics. Gordon, observing that the paper adhered to traditional approaches and arguments even at the risk of appearing outmoded, rated its editorials as "splendid, though tamely conservative," (Gordon, "Survey" 9). "This is odd," he concluded, "in view of the fact that the most successful papers recognize features as essential." While the *Age*, like many of Washington's followers, often lent a sure and steady voice to the debates of the era, its intransigent refusal to acknowledge its rivals—much less adjust to them—rendered the paper noticeably irrelevant as sports commanded greater attention from the press.

Garveyism Comes to Sports: The Interstate-Tattler

While papers such as the *Age* and the *Amsterdam* took sides and found connections to sports in the Washington–Du Bois debate, they agreed on one point: their distaste for Marcus Garvey and his theory of black separatism. The *Interstate-Tattler*, on the other hand, openly declared itself sympathetic to the separatist cause. Historian Theodore Vincent, who cites the *Tattler* as one of the few Renaissance-era newspapers (along with the *Boston Guardian*, the Oklahoma City *Black Dispatch*, and the *California Eagle* in Los Angeles) that consistently supported such radical causes, suggests that this position cost it popularity among intellectuals and, eventually, the public (Vincent, *Voices* 29–30). This radicalism emerged intermittently on the *Tattler*'s sports pages, particularly in those edited by Bennie Butler, a former comedian and occasional political operative who rarely identified integration as a goal in his discussions of sports. Butler's partner and successor, Al Moses, took a more conciliatory view but brought an Afrocentric historian's approach. After the *Tattler* folded under the weight of the Great Depression, both writers turned their full attention to creating a record of African American sports history as contributors to the Federal Writers Project, but by then an unmistakable sense of disillusionment had crept into their work. For Garveyite sportswriters in particular, the early promise of the Renaissance crumbled quickly and completely.

Floyd Snelson, a waiter at the Royal Poinciana Hotel in Palm Beach, founded the *Tattler* in 1922 as the "Hotel Tattler." The original *Tattler* described itself as a "snappy, society journal" circulating in New York and several resort cities. From the beginning, the paper interspersed sports and society news, though it also ran serious opinion pieces, such as its open letter to Congress endorsing the Dyer Anti-Lynching Bill. The editorial page provided strong contrast to gossipy, unsigned tidbits such as the one that appeared in the issue of October 22, 1922: "Say, D. Coleman of 221 W. 140th St., who was the new vamp you were with and took home from the Camp Fire Girls Dance on Monday night. Give a single boy a chance, old sheik." In his gossip column, Snelson used the pseudonym "I. Telonyou."

By 1924, the paper began calling itself simply *The Tattler*, with several cities and a sketch of a crackling radio console on its masthead. A year later, it had changed its name to the *Interstate-Tattler*. Previously a broadsheet, the paper became a tabloid with a stylish cover photograph (usually of a young woman), more in the manner of a magazine. The back cover featured a collage of "Interesting Pictures of Interesting People," such as Joe Williams, who had been a star pitcher for the Lincoln Giants. In the winter of 1924–25, Williams captained a team sponsored by the Royal Poinciana; he was shown in the Tattler posing with George Briton, "the star pitcher of the Poncianna baseball team," and the hotel's head waiter, who apparently didn't play ball (he was left unidentified).

Although the *Tattler*'s masthead named "sports, theatricals and social events" as its primary subjects, the paper continued to carry more serious features, such as a column by T. Thomas Fortune, the former editor of the *Age* who had recently refurbished his radical credentials by editing newspapers for Garvey. In a more intellectual if mainstream vein, the paper also carried literary criticism by NAACP co-founder Mary White Ovington. However, the paper's devotion to gossip probably held it back. In 1927, for example, the paper apologized for printing a rumor that the pastor of the Mount Zion Church had received a huge fee for delivering the sermon at Florence Mills' funeral. But even in retraction, the *Tattler* remained "snappy" and self-congratulatory. The *Tattler* staff had dismissed the rumor, it said, but a correspondent wrote about it anyway, and "The *Tattler* is liberal almost to a fault in the direction of free speech."[3]

The newspaper's sports coverage, like its political radicalism, was often subsumed by its devotion to society news. Geraldyn Dismond, whose gossip column ran in several African American newspapers (sometimes under the pseudonym Lady Nicotine), served as the *Tattler*'s managing editor from 1928 to 1931. Early in 1928, the *Tattler* put out a "Sports Special Issue," in which Dismond noted in her column, "I suppose I am expected to cooperate by writing on society sports" (Dismond 4). The rest of the column consisted of a list, pairing favorite Harlemites with their "favorite sports." For example, A. Philip Randolph's was "being fascinating," and James Weldon Johnson's "ditto." Charles S. Johnson's preference was "being mysterious," while Carl Van Vechten's was, predictably, "coming uptown." Dismond listed her own favorite sport as "dieting."

Still, some of the most vibrant voices in the Renaissance movement found the *Tattler*'s style worthy of merit. Theophilus Lewis, the drama critic for the *Messenger*, served as the editor of the *Tattler* in the late 1920s. In 1928, the paper ran a letter by Langston Hughes, in which the poet offered, "I might send you a story, since the Tattler is a 'Race Paper' (if it doesn't get too tight) and also designed for the proletariat (or used to be ere it became clever and slightly ritzy)." Hughes's jaunty tone fit right in with the rest of the editorial page, which was highlighted by an editorial belittling the Ku Klux Klan ("The Suckers Disband"). This mixture of political protest and stylized vernacular represents the Renaissance ethos embodied more by younger aesthetes such as Hughes than by the era's established intellectuals. Hughes concluded his letter approvingly, saying of Lewis, "You're an all right editor!"

The *Tattler*'s primary sports editor in the Renaissance years, Bennie Butler, exemplified the paper's talent, style, and bravado. In the mid–1920s, Butler served as the paper's editor-in-chief as well as its primary sports and theatre columnist. He had started his journalistic career in 1913, working alongside his later rival, Romeo Dougherty, for the newly launched *New York News*; the influential journalist and poet Fenton Johnson served as the paper's sports and theatre editor. In 1915, Butler became the sports and theatre editor of the *Amsterdam News*, causing the *Indianapolis Freeman* to note that the *Amsterdam* "knows how to pick up live wires" ("Short Flights" 2). After a brief career in vaudeville, Butler returned to newspaper work with the *Kansas City Call*; in 1920, *Billboard* magazine noted in its "News from Kansas City" that "Butler, a colored comedian of some importance, is here as sport writer and handles the amusement page of *The Call*" (Jackson, "News" 41; "Here and There" 64). Upon moving back to New York, Butler joined the Garvey movement and again worked with Dougherty on the *Negro Times*, Garvey's short-lived attempt to publish a daily paper in 1923. After that venture faltered, Butler found a confluence of

6. "A Course in the Curriculum of the Institution"

Garveyite leanings and his interest in popular culture at the *Tattler*. On one occasion, he took Garvey's successful weekly, *Negro World*, to task for not paying more attention to such matters. Praising the extent of the African American press coverage of the Wills-Firpo fight in 1924, Butler noted: "Yes, even the *Negro World*, which makes no pretense of featuring sports, had a Captain Saltus on the job" (Butler, "Sports and Theatrical" 6).

In time, Butler restricted his *Tattler* duties to coverage of the theatre and handed the sports editor's job to Moses, who seems to have been his hand-picked successor. In one column, Butler praised Moses as the "King of All Colored Writers" (Butler, "Sport Sparkles" 11). Such hyperbole appeared frequently in the unrestrained pages of the *Tattler*, as did the more commonplace tendency, practiced by many of the African American sportswriters of the era, to substantiate their praise with comparisons to their white counterparts. "I believe," Butler asserted, "that Alvin Jack has been quoted more times by the white sport writers of the local daily papers than all the others put together." When discussing himself, however, Butler dispensed with such comparative praise. Instead, he singled out the leading white sportswriter of the day and declared himself superior. "Some years ago," he wrote in his society column, "some of my friends started calling me the 'Black Grantland Rice.' I stopped that real quick and when they asked me why I objected, I told them I was better than Grantland Rice. Since then, nobody has called me anything other than Bennie Butler" ("This Harlem Urge" 7).

Butler fueled his columns with the same strident tone that characterized much of the paper's writing. In a review of the sports and entertainment events of 1927, headlined "A Most Disastrous Year," Butler lamented the deaths of Florence Mills and boxer Tiger Flowers before taking aim at the Negro Leagues. After declaring dourly that "Negro baseball is in a bad way and has been for several years," he further noted that "the Aframerican has little interest in the playing of colored teams." Butler suggested the lack of seriousness in the teams' play had deterred fan interest in Harlem. Opposing James Weldon Johnson, who found the Negro League clubs overly serious and imitative of white teams, Butler accused the teams of resorting to sideshows to attract audiences. Attempts at interracial appeal particularly disgusted the Garveyite in Butler, who believed most of the white fans who attended Lincoln Giants' games were drawn by "the buffoonery and amusing comedy actions and atmosphere that is to be found in such contests."

Only a lack of cooperation among African Americans disgusted Butler more than did such appeals to white patrons. While the Lincoln Giants left the Eastern Colored League to play as an independent club in 1927, Rube Foster's Negro National League had fallen into disarray. Foster, who had founded and ruled the league almost single-handedly, suffered a nervous breakdown in 1926, leaving open the power to book games and, perhaps, to collect the ten-percent fee that Foster had been charging. After Foster's death, infighting among the other owners—or, as Butler termed it, "petty jealousies, treachery and whatnot"—bogged down the league, which would fold in 1931. "As for the Negro National Baseball Debacle League," Butler concluded, "well the less said about this stupid, miserable effort of coniving [sic] fools, the better" ("1927" 11).

Though sometimes flippant, Butler's critiques evinced a fierce pride and an emphasis on the originality of his newspaper's style. In the followup column to "A Most Disastrous Year," headlined "Our Ambitious Program for 1928," Butler looked back on the "tremendous strides made by the *Interstate-Tattler* despite the many unfortunate events that hampered us during 1927" (possibly referring to the controversy following Florence Mills' funeral). Still, he promised more of the same, asserting: "What you read in the *Tattler* is our own version of what transpires. We are not a looking glass or a parrot" ("Our Ambitious Program" 12). In short, Butler's goal—a plainly stated one—was to raise the *Tattler* above the level of a gossip sheet and assume a more respected niche in the Harlem market. That niche needed to be something more than that of an independent, progressive voice, for the *Amsterdam News* had already laid claim to that; instead, Butler continually put forward the *Tattler*'s audacity and style. Always brazen and ambitious, he essentially declared the *Tattler* the paper most clearly aligned with the radical politics and aesthetics of the Renaissance.

While Butler ran the *Tattler* with an aggressive seriousness that he saw lacking in Harlem's ball clubs and sports sections both, his approach to journalistic standards left him open to charges of recklessness. On two separate occasions, the *Amsterdam News* sports editor, Dougherty, criticized Butler for printing erroneous information; each time, the *Tattler* dismissed the errors as inconsequential and insisted that the charges revealed the arrogance and insecurity of the community's largest newspaper. Ignoring the charges themselves, Butler responded with virulence and insults, referring to Dougherty as "Snoops" and the paper as "The Damnews."

Attacking Dougherty personally in the first incident, Butler called his error (misidentifying a boxer) a simple mistake and accused "Snoops" of arrogantly presenting himself as the "best sport and theatrical editor that ever pounded an Underwood" ("Butler's Challenge" 10). Then, converting the issue entirely to one of their respective talents, Butler—who made a point of comparing himself to Dougherty in print more often than did any of the Harlem sportswriters—challenged Dougherty to a competition. He suggested they each submit their twelve best issues to an impartial judge, "for decision as to which of us is the 'Goods.'" Butler suggested that Eugene Gordon judge the contest, even though Gordon had declared in *Opportunity* a few months earlier: "Readers care nothing for the personal dislikes, petty jealousies and silly prejudices of editorial writers. They regard, and rightly, the newspaper as a public institution and do not like to see it subverted to the use of selfish and vulgar personalities" ("Outstanding," 1925, 359). Two years later, Gordon complained in another assessment: "There is still too much vindictive editorial squabbling back and forth" ("Outstanding," 1927, 360). In any event, the contest seems not to have come off.

For his part, Butler stayed uninvolved in the second incident, as Wilfred R. Bain substituted and wrote the responsorial diatribes. According to Bain, Butler was "enjoying a little vacation"—he was working for Mayor Walker's 1929 re-election campaign. However, Bain, who had worked with Dougherty on the *New York News* in the early 1920s, continued in Butler's style, referring to Dougherty only as "the self-styled dean" of sports and theatre editors. Dougherty, he charged, simply resented the fact that he wasn't invited to a welcome-home party for Paul Robeson (Bain 9). The *Tattler* hierarchy had been invited, of course, and Bain proved as much by citing the location of the fete and naming several of the other guests.

More than his confrontational tone, Butler's support for separatism probably helped end his newspaper career in the Depression years; Vincent cites Butler as one of many columnists whose "Garveyite" viewpoints caused them to be run out of journalism by the early 1930s (*Voices* 37). In 1932, the *Pittsburgh Courier* profiled Butler in his "enforced retirement," sitting at home in his pajamas and talking about the past (Calvin 3). Like many Harlem newspaper writers, Butler found work later in the decade on the Federal Writers Project, working on a history of *The Negroes in New York*. Butler contributed essays on cricket and Harlem's athletic clubs to the project, along with a lengthy discussion of the celebrations that followed Joe Louis's victories (a topic that Richard Wright captured more succinctly in a brief piece that ran in *New Masses*). Butler also wrote a ruminative essay for the project, arguing that African American athletes and entertainers had done more to help the race than had intellectuals. The essay, "Negro Athletes," takes on the intelligentsia in Butler's characteristically confrontational manner, but it also belies a defeatist undertone. Butler, who had expressed disgust at the idea of pandering to white audiences in the 1920s, argued in the 1930s that the cross-cultural appeal of sports and entertainment promised to do the most for the race. Butler submitted the study to the FWP in January 1940, with his subject described as "Public re-action or the influences for 'good will' of Negro athletes, musicians and entertainers of prominence" (Butler, "Negro Athletes" 1).

"Negro Athletes" begins with a summary of the broad popularity enjoyed by African American boxers, especially Louis, and the 1936 Olympic track team. "That interest makes for studied interest and tolerance," Butler observes somewhat optimistically. The athletes "aroused the white man's curiosity to such a point that the white man wanted to find out—what made the Negro tick" (Butler, "Negro Athletes" 2). Anticipating the possibility that his position could be considered naïve, Butler argues that the interest and tolerance aroused by such performers comes about subtly, without the spectators even being aware of their onset. Here Butler confronts the intellectual position, put forth by Du Bois in the Renaissance, that art requires an element of propaganda to be effective. Instead, Butler recommends, the message should be delivered with stealth:

> It must be born[e] in mind that the Negro entertainer be he athlete, musician or stage artist carries an in-direct message of protest. He is not looked upon with hostility because he is a propagandist or, seeking to invade the so-called "white man's world" of higher learning such as art, science etc. And the sense in which I refer to art is that of sculpture, painter and kindred professions; not the actor, musician or singer. Therefore he is most freely accepted and in homes that hundreds of other Negroes—far more better trained—would not even be admitted to the back door ["Negro Athletes" 4].

Butler's theory abandons the separatism of Garvey (also endorsed, in different terms, by Du Bois in the 1930s) and embraces the integrationist pragmatism of James Weldon Johnson and Walter White. Butler's viewpoint in this regard is not unusual, as the militancy of the African American press generally faded in the otherwise more radical 1930s. As Theodore Vincent argues, the integrationist ethos of the New Deal era subsumed the community's more radical voices; Garvey's *Negro World*, for example, folded in 1933, despite having "endorsed Democrats consistently since 1928" (Vincent,

Voices 35). Butler, however, keeps his distance from both Du Bois and the NAACP by generally rejecting intellectualism, a viewpoint that would seem to keep him connected to Garvey.

Butler sees no difference between the intellectual aspects of the performing arts and the ones he dismisses; neither does he hesitate to group athletes with actors and musicians on one side, with painters, scientists, and "intellectuals" on the other. He concerns himself strictly with their effects. In Butler's view, white interest in African American culture "would not be what it is to-day had it been left to the Negro intelligentsia" (5). Intellectuals, he argues, do not understand the lives and tastes of the masses. "They are too far removed from the lay public," he argues, "and their respective fields do not have the spectacular, forceful appeal of the entertainer" (5). Although performers protest indirectly, the spectacle and force of their appeal carries supreme weight: not only do they affect their audiences subtly, but they also do so to enormous crowds. The entertainer, Butler points out, "gets in direct touch with the masses" (6). In this regard, his argument falls in line with the radical writing of the Thirties, when protests aimed at a multi-racial proletariat widely subsumed specific appeals to race.

Although Butler's analysis retains a measure of the oppositional viewpoint of the Garvey movement, the radical emphasis on self-sufficiency that marked his *Tattler* columns has subsided. He implies that some African American performers get under their white audience's skin, but he seems to have surrendered the fight for control of the game. "It did not and does not matter to whites," he observes, "that there were a score or more Negroes at one time or other in the House of Representatives.... But a champion! A Negro 'World's Heavyweight Champion' ye gods what are the Negroes doing to us? That's the question that apparently had to be answered" (5–6). Performers, more than intellectuals, seemed capable of raising questions. For Butler, who once had all the answers, dialogue promised more than the confrontational columns and separatist politics of the Garvey era had provided.

Above the Fray and into the Past: Alvin J. Moses and Sol White

Butler's successor as sports editor of the *Tattler*, Alvin J. Moses, represented the more folksy style of the Harlem press. Moses's columns were breezy, traditional and respectful, in the antiquated tone of the *Age* but without the moralistic tone. He seemed eager to show that he was well connected and friendly with everybody, white sportswriters included. In 1929, soon after Moses succeeded Butler, the *Tattler* noted that Moses had won a World Series contest in the white *Evening Journal*.

Moses, who had previously worked with Dougherty at the *New York News* and would later join the *Pittsburgh Courier*, could scarcely have been more different from Butler. While the *Tattler* grew even more political, running serious features such as a four-part update on Garvey's activities in 1932, the *News* increasingly offered more gossip and sensationalism. The relationship between the two publications seems to have been by design: In 1930, Butler indicated that the *News* was in the "same hands" as the *Tattler*, although they would not merge.[4] In 1921, when Dougherty was one of the paper's editors, the paper identified itself on the masthead as "A Medium That Reaches the Masses/Most Popular and Most Progressive," but in the late 1920s and early 1930s, the front pages featured huge headlines and "beauty photos."

Moses, seemingly alone among the Harlem sportswriters, considered Dougherty a friend more than a rival. After the *Tattler*'s second skirmish with Dougherty, Moses lobbed a few gentler gibes at the "dean" in his column, pointing out that it was he who had given Dougherty his alpha nickname in the first place. "Words fail us in our attempt to tell you how hard we'll strive to live up to all you had to say of us in your columns last week, old pal," Moses wrote. "It sort o' crept under the skin hard fashion—you understand."[5] In 1931, Moses reported that Dougherty had decided the two of them had only one peer at the top of their profession: Wilson, formerly with the *Pittsburgh Courier*, who was then the sports editor of the *Philadelphia Tribune* and soon to become the secretary and publicist for the Negro American League. "The sage of Jamaica, Long Island," Moses wrote, referring to Dougherty, "styled Rollo Wilson, the writer and himself as 'The Triumvirate' of the eastern sport world that is of interest to folk of African descent—chiefly, and quite a number of Nords. Its [sic] most refreshing in these days of 'baby killers,' racketeers, and gang-overlords to inhale a genuine bouquet of flowers like this one, from a contemporary we esteem" ("By Way of Report" 16). Moses showed more interest in elevation than confrontation, writing columns that praised and elegized figures in African American sports.

Moses called his column, variously, "Blazing the Trail," "Crashing the

6. "A Course in the Curriculum of the Institution"

Line," "Sportive Tidbits" or "The Sportive Horoscope." He specialized in lengthy profiles of figures he clearly considered historically significant, frequently drawing on subjects from the Negro Leagues. In the summer of 1929 alone, Moses profiled Homestead Grays owner Cumberland Posey and veteran ballplayers Oscar Charleston and Joe Williams. These features ran alongside his own columns, while his accounts of actual games, even when played at home, were scanty (by this time, most newspapers seemed to have grown suspicious of road-game accounts, which were provided by the clubs themselves). In his midyear analysis of the 1929 season, Moses noted that the Lincoln Giants were enjoying a surprisingly successful season—and then proceeded to concentrate solely on their manager, "the not-so-old John Henry Lloyd." Underscoring his affinity for the past and his desire to create legends in the African American game, Moses praised Lloyd's leadership: "He has taken a bunch of cast-offs and made pennant contenders out of them."[6] Even in this midseason report, however, Moses included no information on victories or defeats, much less any other evidence that the Lincolns were "pennant contenders." Over the course of the season, the *Tattler* printed the standings of the Negro American League about once per month.

At times, Moses meshed his encomiums to the legends of the game with attempts to transcribe colloquial speech, leading to strange results. In 1932, referring to Charleston's desire to continue playing while managing the Pittsburgh Crawfords, Moses declared: "If like Rogers Hornsby he feels like playing this season, how in H—, can you keep a guy who can hit .300 in any old kinda league.... OUTA THAT LINEUP ... you ... jes kant felLURES."[7] At other times, Moses simply fell into the habit of transposing every possible word with one from a thesaurus: thus he described Charleston, then a first baseman, as a "powerful guardian of the initial hassock."[8]

Moses's columns could also be inventive in other, more effective ways. He often made lists, as in "How'd You Like to See—," which included musings such as "Fats Jenkins playing left—or any old field for that matter, ... in the lineup of the New York Giants or Yankees?" ("How'd You Like" 8). Sometimes he printed dialogues of his own apparent creation, as in "Public Servants—Not Enemies." Moses did not identify who was Q and who was A:

Q: Say, what's a public servant anyway?
A: You ought to know that. Folk who eternally cooperate with movements that work for the good of the masses.

> Q: Would you call baseball players such?
> A: Boy ... and how ["Public Servants" 8].

Moses considered cooperation essential to the "public service" that sports provided. Unlike Butler, who, despite his own fractious nature, mocked the operators of African American sports organizations and expressed disgust at their bickering ways, Moses pleaded for togetherness.

By 1932, Moses seemed to consider the situation hopeless, offering a poem that bemoaned the catty competition between the owners of the Negro League clubs. Apparently berating himself for expecting fraternal bonds, he wrote of Gus Greenlee and Cumberland Posey, the owners of the rival Pittsburgh and Homestead teams:

> Gosh you're plenty dumb.
> Pittsburgh Crawfords Baseball Team
> Is headed by W.A. Greenlee,
> See what I mean?
> Spilled a lotta stuff about Posey,
> Wonder if it's okay?
> Well, I give up, I quit.
> They Won't Join East-West League,
> Can the Circuit stagger along
> Under the announcement—sure thing.
> Why can't both clubs patch it up,
> Colored folk scrap eternally
> While White Folk—"hold everything."[9]

Moses's use of vernacular and short, mostly end-stopped lines gives his poem an immediacy that undergirds the subject matter. The poem's hopelessness, however, reflects the stark mood of Harlem in the 1930s. Just a few years earlier, Moses had printed a starkly different kind of poem in the *News*. In "Garden Colloquy," he depicted a pastoral dialogue between a flower and the wind, consisting of formal rhymes and four tightly constructed quatrains.[10] The poem did not mention sports in any way, even though it appeared at the top of his sports column, "Blazing the Trail." Moses's unconventional, often innovative juxtaposition of traditional and popular styles may seem strange, especially in a newspaper's sports section, but it clearly demonstrates the aura and energy of the Harlem Renaissance.

Moses stood alone among the sports editors of the Renaissance press in his attempts to rise above competitive squabbling and redirect his papers' communal focus to racial advancement and equality. In the manner of

James Weldon Johnson, he tried to use his moderate views and disdain for personal attacks to effect reconciliation, both between the races and among warring camps within the race. Moses's peers took note. In a history of African American journalists for the Federal Writers Project, Ted Yates—a younger sports-and-theatre editor who worked for both the *Tattler* and the *Amsterdam News* in the 1930s—named Moses in a history of notable New York journalists (Yates, "Outstanding" 5).

Moses had at least one noteworthy compatriot in his attempts to rise above the infighting. Sol White, a former ballplayer and manager of African American teams, wrote columns on baseball for both the *Age* and the *Amsterdam News*. White's columns, like Moses's, stress the rich history of Negro League baseball. Their efforts, echoed in 1930 by James Weldon Johnson's historical emphasis in *Black Manhattan*, sketched a foundation for the explosion of scholarship concentrating on the Negro Leagues that would appear in the late-twentieth century. White, in particular, left behind one of the archives that became germinal to that scholarly enterprise.

White was a superb hitter and infielder around the turn of the century, playing primarily for the Philadelphia Giants. In 1907, he wrote *Sol White's Official Base Ball Guide*, a history of the early African American teams. White had attended Wilberforce University, where he "developed the innate interest in history that ultimately made him the Livy of African American baseball" (Malloy xlvii). By the time of Renaissance, he had served as a manager and secretary for several Negro League clubs, and his status as Negro League baseball's man of letters was widely known. In 1927, when White was beginning his career as a columnist, Floyd J. Calvin of the *Pittsburgh Courier* called him "a calm, quiet man ... who likes to go to the library and read good books when he is not at work."[11]

White's column in the *Amsterdam News* was called "At the Oval," a reference to the Catholic Protectory Oval, where the Lincoln Giants played their home games after the demolition of Olympic Field. He would wax poetic about the ballpark as a bucolic site where such societal concerns as racial strife were absent, where "creed, color and all the prejudice flesh is heir to is smothered in the regard for true sportsmanship."[12] In another column, White pursued the poetic aspects of the ballpark's name: "The word 'Protectory' is wide, deep and profound; but we like 'Oval.' To me, like the old game, it is poetically and romantically suggestive."[13] Despite such ruminations, however, White's snapshots of the past were hardly pastoral.

White emphasized the professionalism that Rube Foster had instilled in the players and coaches of early black teams, reminding players to act as role models for the African American community. As Chris Lamb has pointed out, "White wrote in black newspapers for decades about the need for ballplayers and fans to take the game seriously" (Lamb 68). In one column, he recalled the presence of African Americans on early professional teams before segregation was uniformly imposed in the 1880s and mocked the Negro intelligentsia by recounting his attendance, with a ball club, at a lecture by an unidentified African American scholar on the "Progress of the Negro." After the lecture, White concluded, "one of the boys said, 'He never said anything about the Big League; they've been Negroes in that too.'"[14] Although his tone echoed the rich tradition of baseball writing, White would sometimes conclude with a pragmatic piece of advice: "Rooting for the Lincoln Giants is an important course in the curriculum of the institution."[15]

White aimed unabashedly to promote Negro league baseball and, ultimately, to integrate the major leagues. After New York Yankees owner Jacob Ruppert rented out Yankee Stadium for a doubleheader played to benefit the Sleeping Car Porters' union, White addressed the union leaders in his column: "Any time any of your men run across Mr. Ruppert and his Yankees baseball team, treat 'em nice.... Mr. Ruppert knows how to get traveling service for his men and is also a sportsman."[16] Placing Negro League games in major-league ballparks became a popular project in the 1930s, primarily as a means of showcasing black talent to spur integration. By then the effects of the Depression had left most of the teams in the hands of white owners or gambling interests, and even they could not afford to own their own parks. This was a complete turnaround from the circumstances of the late 1910s, when the Negro Leagues were organized partly because independent black teams were owned almost exclusively by whites; the black press began to urge African American ownership so as to keep the profits within the community (e.g., Riess, *City* 118).

In such columns, White combined the unyielding push for integration that characterized the *Amsterdam* with the patient stance on racial accommodation that was the hallmark of the *Age* and its earlier patron, Booker T. Washington. While superficially obsequious, however, the substance of White's columns was savvy and practical. He argued that Negro League ballplayers, like artists, need patronage. "No man or group of men can be expected to expand their investments in the realm of athletics unless there is an appreciative response from the public by way of gate and turnstiles," he wrote. "A wonderful future would be the lot of a colored ballplayer could they get a patronage in ratio to their white brother of the craft."[17] White understood that the infusion of money he wished for was not entirely available in the community, and in other columns he fired salvos at the "business interests" that dominated Negro League baseball. White saw that the means to stability and success was money from the white sources, but he believed the responsibility for cultivating that patronage lay in the community.

White, like many of his fellow columnists in the Harlem press, openly urged fans to attend baseball games, calling on their civic pride as a reason to do so. "The Lincolns are going away," White wrote before a road trip in 1930. "They deserve an outing. They have been putting New York back on the map in a baseball way and they are going to use the Hilldales next Sunday."[18] This sort of civic appeal had an importance that went beyond support for a baseball team. In the eyes of sportsmen such as White, both baseball and the press represented the race. In the early years of the Depression, when the one was struggling, it was up to the other to raise it up. White found his ideals in poetry and nostalgia, but he based his recommendations in the bourgeois economic pragmatism of Booker T. Washington and the focus on integration promoted by the NAACP. White argued for cooperation with the existing sources of power; whether they were to reckon with him or to warmly accept him did not seem to matter.

However potent sports could be in commanding attention, White concluded that the ultimate responsibility for racial advancement lay with the press. "If baseball has veered toward the shoals of business inactiveness and sloth," White wrote, "let the press put it on the right course and bring it up to where it belongs—one of the greatest institutions of the race."[19] In particular, White believed in baseball's significance as a cultural institution, but such status needed to be actively imagined and created. It was up to the sportswriters and historians in the press to make it so.

7. "Race First" in the Sports Section
Romeo Dougherty and Harlem's Caribbean Circle

In 1925, Romeo Dougherty printed a column in the *Amsterdam News*, charging that Cumberland Posey was "up to his old tricks again." Posey, the manager of the Loendi basketball club of Pittsburgh, had demanded special terms and concessions if his team were to travel to New York City to play Harlem's top club, the Renaissance Five. As an experienced promoter of basketball games and other events in both sports and entertainment, Dougherty considered the terms unreasonable. Dismissing them and Posey, he speculated sarcastically: "Posey is either drunk from the gases of his native Pennsylvania or he has entered his dotage much earlier than is customary among men in the present century."[1] Dougherty suggested the owner of the "Rens," Bob Douglas, reject Posey's offer without any further consideration. "Our advice to Douglas," he wrote, "is to consign the undated and terribly constructed 'challenge' to the waste paper basket and continue on his successful way without a thought of challengers who have descended to the level of the parasites of the game."

Dougherty's ire had been provoked by more than Posey's tough negotiating terms. As the sports editor and lead columnist of Harlem's most prominent newspaper, Dougherty felt compelled to protect and nurture the local sports organizations, which he considered invaluable to African American cultural life. Posey's bargaining stance—one that would also help him build his baseball club, the Homestead Grays, into one of the most successful organizations in the Negro Leagues—struck Dougherty as selfish and unconcerned with the welfare of the community. Moreover, the disdain with which Dougherty regarded Posey was not new: In 1921, as Dougherty used his influence to help shape the growth of professional basketball, he printed a poem in *The New York News* that attacked Posey for refusing to play Harlem's powerful St. Christopher Machine at the St. Philip's Parish House Gym on 134th Street. "Mother, Dear, Why Do They Cry," his poem asked, as Dougherty accused the Loendi club of being "scared and forced to hide and stall" (Dougherty, "Things" 5). Dougherty's advice to Douglas extended beyond altruism, however. The men shared a deeper connection, as both were Caribbean-born, part of a circle of writers, entertainers, and activists that invigorated some of Harlem's most visible social and cultural organizations. Dougherty's public advisory encapsulates the uniquely influential role he played in the Harlem press in the 1920s: He argued, defended, nurtured, and provoked—all in an explicit attempt to advance the race.

Throughout the Renaissance years, Dougherty reigned supreme as the leading sportswriter in the Harlem press. For the better part of four decades, most as the sports and theatre editor of the *Amsterdam News*, his pages and columns helped define popular culture for his readers in Harlem. However, as historian Ted Vincent observes, "Considering his reputation in theatre and sports circles, it seems odd that journalist Romeo Lionel Dougherty is not better known today" (*Keep* 80). Vincent concentrates on Dougherty's influence as a music critic, but Dougherty wielded comparable influence in theatre, sports, and Harlem society. The *Messenger* magazine, identifying intellectuals, writers, and artists as members of the "Aframerican Academy," featured Dougherty prominently alongside Langston Hughes in its April 1927 segment ("Aframerican" 115). Earlier that year, the media critic Eugene Gordon had praised Dougherty's column, "The Sportive Spotlight," as one of the "first-class" features of the *Amsterdam News*. "That man Dougherty," Gordon noted, "is a true sport as well as a fine sports writer" ("Survey" 11). To be sure, Dougherty had his detractors, though many of them were his competition. Papers referred to him as the "Dean of Negro Sport Writers," or simply "the Dean." In his own columns, he called himself "your Dean," while his rivals, such as William E. Clarke of the *New York Age* and Bennie Butler of the *Interstate-Tattler*, derided him as "the self-styled Dean"; Dougherty rarely resisted the urge to trade insults with them in print. In 1922, *Billboard* magazine called Dougherty "the most widely known Negro writer on sports and playhouses," observing evenly: "He is much criticized but his copy is widely read" (Jackson, "James" 46).

In *Black Writers/Black Baseball* (2007), Jim Reisler reprinted six of Dougherty's columns in a chapter titled "Romeo Dougherty: Poet of Press

Row." Dougherty's pages featured poetry extensively—both his own and poems by others, such as the songwriter Andy Razaf—and were representative of the era. American newspapers, white and black, regularly published poetry in the first half of the twentieth century, and sportswriters in particular experimented with different forms of verse (Carroll, *Black Press* 24). However, as Brian Carroll has pointed out, historians have largely ignored the poetry written and published by African American sportswriters, "who continued with the form long after it was dropped by the mainstream press" (23). While Dougherty's use of poetry has recently attracted the attention of anthologists and critics such as Reisler and Carroll, he also experimented with fiction, contributing a serialized novella to the *Crusader* magazine in 1919. In *Punta, Revolutionist*, Dougherty depicted an uprising against white imperialism during the Spanish-American War. Although the work was uneven (and apparently unfinished), it represents the spirit of the Caribbean circle of writers with whom he collaborated at the *Crusader* and other radical periodicals in the tumultuous years of the early Renaissance.

Dougherty considered himself a writer in tune with the pulse of his times, and in a fleeting way, he often was: as African American newspapers sprang up during the years of the Great Migration, he helped found or popularize several; in the highly charged climate following World War I, he contributed to one of Harlem's most radical publications; at the height of Marcus Garvey's nationalist influence, he lent his efforts to Garvey's most ambitious journalistic project; and when the first professional African American basketball and baseball leagues in New York were formed, he was instrumental in their organization. He could argue for radicalism or pragmatism. He could be individualistic or moralistic. Always, however, he argued for the elevation of the race, a viewpoint that attracted him first to leftist causes and then to Garvey's movement.

Though not so virulent or radically separatist as Garvey—their association did not last long—Dougherty's idea of racial advancement often took its cues from similarly traditional sources. Like Claude McKay, Dougherty eventually disavowed dogmatic radicalism—either left-wing or nationalist—in favor of a more individualistic ethos; the "race first" politics of his early years, however, always stayed foremost in his work. Dougherty criticized those who lacked "the urge for the advancement of the race" and showed interest only in making money (213). He thought of baseball and basketball clubs as cultural institutions that would help build a community in Harlem, which its residents therefore had a duty to support. According to Vincent, Dougherty's writing "was distinctive in the way he tried to instill his theatre and sports pages with a broad vision of a better community" (Vincent, *Keep* 80).

After Dougherty's death in 1944, one of his successors at the *Amsterdam*, Dan Burley, reminded readers that for years Dougherty had "reigned unchallenged as the really big sports and theatre writer of his race" (Burley 8B). Already, Dougherty's name had become relatively obscure. The reasons may lie in his ever-shifting political positions, which found him inside Harlem's circle of Caribbean radicalism one year and aligned with the conservative crowd the next. More likely, though, Dougherty's willingness to promote sports and entertainment events—both as a newspaperman and as a paid agent—stained him in the eyes of radicals and ideologues. Still, he infused his pragmatism with an idealism of his own. In Dougherty's view, community institutions such as sports and entertainment required acknowledgment, cultivation, and protection. Only then could an authentic cultural Renaissance represent and include the entire community.

Looking Backward at the Caribbean Circle through C.L.R. James

The son of an American naval officer, Dougherty was born in 1885 in St. Thomas (then in the Danish Virgin Islands) but grew up in New Jersey. American involvement in the Caribbean remained a shifting, often controversial subject in Dougherty's career. The United States purchased its territories in the islands from Denmark during World War I, hoping to establish a naval presence in the Caribbean. *The Amsterdam* ran several stories in the 1920s examining the economic state of the Virgin Islands, which saw its lucrative rum trade banned after Prohibition went into effect throughout the U.S. territories in 1919. In 1922, Dougherty printed a series of front-page features built largely around a trip taken to the islands by his wife, who, according to his introductory note, "made our Sporting Editor what he is today."

While the sports section of the *Amsterdam* regularly printed cricket news from the islands under his purview, the Caribbean strain in Dougherty's writing emerges not so much in his cultural references as in the political underpinnings of his views. Like C.L.R. James a generation later, Dougherty considered sports a medium for racial expression; in time, he recognized in sportswriting an opportunity for political and cultural critique. Early on, Dougherty expanded his interests beyond sports and newspaper writing, joining Harlem's burgeoning literary circle of Caribbean migrants in the post-war years and contributing to both Communist and separatist publications.

The Caribbean-born population of New York City exploded in the years preceding and, to a slightly lesser extent, during the Harlem Renaissance. The number of foreign-born blacks living in the United States, about 20,000 in 1900, nearly doubled in each of the first two decades of the century; by 1930, slowed by immigration restrictions, it reached almost 100,000. The vast majority of these migrants—more than 75 percent—came from the islands of the Caribbean, and most of them landed in New York. At the height of the Renaissance in the 1920s, between a fifth and a quarter of Harlem was Caribbean-born (James, *Holding* 12, 355–358; Hill viii; Domingo 341–342).

The most famous of the Caribbeans in Harlem was undoubtedly Marcus Garvey, the Jamaica-born founder of the "Back to Africa" movement. Claude McKay, also from Jamaica, arrived in 1914 and contributed to radical magazines while becoming one of the major poets and novelists of the Renaissance. Caribbean migrants played major roles on the staffs of several newspapers and magazines, especially those with a radical bent. Hubert Harrison, of St. Croix in the Virgin Islands, began publishing *The Voice* in 1917. Soon after, Garvey launched the *Negro World*, which Harrison edited from 1920 to 1922. W.A. Domingo, of Jamaica, and Richard B. Moore, of Barbados, took a socialist, anti–Garvey stance in their *Emancipator*, mirroring the position of the *Messenger*, for which Domingo had worked. In 1918, Cyril Briggs, of Nevis in the Leeward Islands, founded the *Crusader*. Meanwhile, Caribbean migrants also contributed substantially to Harlem's literary and cultural life: Eric Walrond of British Guiana, the literary editor of the *Negro World*, also wrote for *Opportunity* and *New Masses* while distinguishing himself as a writer of short fiction; Arturo Schomburg of Puerto Rico, a collector and bibliophile, began the library of black culture that now bears his name; Casper Holstein of the Virgin Islands, the mobster who became Harlem's "numbers king," sponsored literary contests in *Opportunity* and wrote articles in that magazine and in the *Negro World*. Dougherty regularly referred to Holstein as "Our Casper"

7. "Race First" in the Sports Section

in stories about events in the Virgin Islands or Holstein's contributions to *Opportunity*.

In the years immediately following World War I, Caribbean migrants in Harlem formed and led radical movements ranging from black separatist groups to leftist political parties (James, *Holding* vi). Winston James, pointing out the "conspicuousness" of the islanders in such radical movements, argues that the Caribbean presence in Harlem not only produced some of the most prominent intellectuals of the Renaissance era, but did so out of proportion to the group's weight in the population (*Holding* 184). James attributes this level of involvement to the experiences of many of the migrants in the British West Indies, which left them more widely educated than their African American counterparts and less inclined towards American social and political traditions. The migrants' status as British citizens, James argues, gave them further confidence to oppose those traditions—a confidence primed by the anti-colonialist sentiments that sparked their migration in the first place.

If, as James argues, the number of Caribbean migrants involved in radical organizations and publications was disproportionately high, the emphasis that the migrants placed on sports seems equally remarkable. Richard B. Moore, the co-founder of the *Emancipator*, also co-founded the Ideal Tennis Club in 1911; the club built the first tennis courts in Harlem (Turner 24–25). Cyril Briggs, who succeeded Dougherty as the sporting and theatrical editor of the *Amsterdam News*, regularly included basketball coverage in his leftist monthly, the *Crusader*. This interest in sports, for which Moore and Briggs found time (and space in print) even as they carved themselves places as two of the most prominent radical writers and activists of the Renaissance, might have seemed ill-considered to many of the era's intellectuals. But it would not have seemed strange at all to their successor a generation later, C.L.R. James.

James, who played cricket in Trinidad as a young man and covered sports for newspapers in Manchester and Glasgow in the 1930s, arrived in New York in 1938, after (most observers agree) the Renaissance had ended. Fifteen years later, his activism in the Socialist Workers Party led to internment and expulsion from the country. In 1963, he published a memoir on cricket and culture, *Beyond a Boundary*, in which he traced his own realization that the sport was not a diversion from the more serious pursuits of his life, but rather the basis of them. James discusses sports not so much as an aspect of folk or popular culture—though he does that—but as a forum in which the racial restrictions and class codes of Western society are played out. James asserts:

> I believe and I hope to prove that cricket and football were the greatest cultural influences in nineteenth-century Britain, leaving far behind Tennyson's poems, Beardsley's drawings and concerts of the Philharmonic society. These filled space in print but not in minds. This is heresy but a heresy which for years was not so much a heresy to me as a nonentity. Cricket was entertainment. Its physical and moral value concerned me not at all. If I stuck rigidly to its code it was because I had learnt it that way [James, *Beyond* 70].

James speaks of the "code" of British colonialism. In *Beyond a Boundary*, James struggles to reconcile its tenets, which he intrinsically admires, with its effects, which he observed firsthand and endured. When James arrived in the United States, however, he had not yet recognized this paradox: he left the empire believing he had molted the restrictive skin of the code.

James's exposure to American sports cured him of all that. At baseball games, the unruly behavior of the fans, the players, and even the coaches shocked him; when instructing his friends in how to play cricket, he noticed the same "hue and cry" (51–52). But while he dismissed that dissonance as a simple difference in demeanor, the point-shaving scandal that struck college basketball in 1950 convinced James otherwise. "My usual restraint vanished and I expressed my horror to friends with an unaccustomed freedom that astonished them," he recalled. "That young men playing for school or university should behave in this way on such a scale was utterly shocking to me" (52–53). The source of James's shock was their lack of loyalty, of adherence to a code. The notion seemed naïve and antiquated to James's American friends, especially the "political people." As a result, James felt forced to examine his own loyalties—to school and team, more than country or king—and the confluence of Puritanism and Marxism that had created his world view.

The examination led James to a conclusion that many of the sportswriters of the Harlem Renaissance also expressed in more rudimentary terms. Their chronicles of athletic achievement and arguments for racial justice, sometimes ill-fitting and often paradoxical, reveal the same sort of awakening: much of what they knew about the world had come from sport itself. Although they inclined towards celebration, their knowledge of the games served them well when they shifted their focus. James, looking backward, reversed the playing field and found that his years of teaching had taught him little—his focus was myopic. The lessons he learned as a sportswriter, by contrast, carried greater significance despite their subtle, slow emergence:

> What stands out a mile is that I was publicly involved only in cricket and soccer. I played both of them, but the playing was only the frame. I was a sports journalist. The conflicts and rivalries which arose out of the conditions I have described gripped me. My Puritan soul burnt with indignation at injustice in the sphere of sport.... I was in the toils of greater forces than I knew. Cricket had plunged me into politics long before I was aware of it. When I did turn to politics I did not have too much to learn [71].

Romeo Dougherty described the political awakening he experienced in the postwar years in similar terms. Dougherty, then the sporting editor at the *New York News*, had been connected with radical causes and publications throughout the decade, but he always restricted his involvement to promotional work and writing narrowly about sports or entertainment. In the first issue of the *Crusader*, Cyril Briggs named Dougherty among the "patriotic Race men and women" listed in the magazine's "Roll of Honor." In the third number, Dougherty took a more assertive stance, contributing an elaborate, though somewhat tortured, statement of support. After confessing that he had hesitated to contribute his own voice to the venture, presuming the space would be reserved for "an academic treatise on the race question," Dougherty announced his debut as a serious writer. In the convoluted, rather pedantic style that would become his hallmark, Dougherty took his fellow newspapermen to task and distanced himself from their narrow focus:

> To many this article from the pen of the writer will come as a surprise, for it has been a custom among our people in the newspaper world to look with ill-concealed contempt upon the brother who dares to take upon himself the Herculean task of carrying the light of a new day among his much abused brethren through the medium of a magazine, but I feel that it is a duty I owe myself to say how very welcome The Crusader is in a field surfeited with mountebanks if I am to be taken seriously in my own little sphere ["A Contemporary's Appreciation" 24].

Dougherty infused his theme of seriousness with more than self-congratulations, however. Praising the *Crusader*'s message of racial pride and unity, he suggested that a lack of purpose was holding back not only newspapers but also the race. "If we would but take life a little bit more seriously and instill in our children love of race," he concluded, "the road toward unity in our midst would not be so hard" (24). This combination of factors—love of race and a serious engagement with life, even when covering sports and entertainment—encapsulates the aura of the Harlem's Caribbean-influenced, radical press in the early Renaissance.

The Crusader *and "The Fight to Keep Sport Clean"*

As a Virgin Islander, Dougherty must have noticed and been inspired by the Caribbean character of the radical publications that sprung up in Harlem immediately after World War I. Indeed, Winston James asserts that, after the Jamaican migrants, Virgin Islanders were the most radical of the Caribbean groups in Harlem (*Holding* 319 fn65). Dougherty's postwar period marks the most radical phase of a career that is hard to follow, much less to label, politically. After beginning his career as a reporter with the Brooklyn *Eye* in 1906, Dougherty joined the *Amsterdam News* soon after its founding in 1909. He left the *Amsterdam* to help Alderman George Harris launch another Harlem tabloid, the *New York News*, in 1913. A year later, Dougherty briefly left New York to handle the sports and theatre page of the Washington *Sun*. Dougherty's mentor at the *Sun* was T. Thomas Fortune, the pioneering African American journalist who had founded the *New York Age* in 1884 (as the *Freeman*) and had ghostwritten several books for Booker T. Washington; Fortune embarked on a late period of radicalism, editing papers for Garvey in the 1920s after returning to New York from Washington. When the *Sun* folded in 1915, Dougherty also returned to New York and worked for the *News* again until 1921. At this time, he became involved with Briggs's organization and contributed to the *Crusader*.

Despite these associations, Dougherty, like most sportswriters and the African American press in general, came to be seen as an apologist for the bourgeoisie and an opponent of radical causes. In a study of communism in the Harlem Renaissance, Mark Naison notes that Dougherty sponsored a "send-off" party in 1932 for a group of actors and writers (including Langston Hughes and Louise Thompson) who were going to the Soviet Union to work on a film project. Dismissing the party as essentially a "society event," Naison claims: "Some of the people sponsoring the party, such as sports and society columnist Romeo Dougherty ... had never previously associated with the left" (Naison 68). In fact, the *Crusader*, which Dougherty conspicuously supported and appeared in from its inception, stood out as one of the most radical of the leftist periodicals that swept Harlem after the war (Solomon 6-7).

Even the *Amsterdam*, while not strictly leftist, plunged into the progressive movement of the 1910s and occasionally waded into more radical waters. At the time of the *Amsterdam's* birth in 1909, the *Age* stood unchallenged as the dominant African American newspaper in New York. James Anderson founded the *Amsterdam* to counter the influence of Booker T. Washington, who secretly supported the *Age*. By 1918, the *Amsterdam* was considered a radical paper by the U.S. government: a post office report to the U.S. assistant district attorney called the *Amsterdam* the "most objectionable of all the Negro publications" (as qtd. in Hill xxiii). In 1919, the New York postmaster held up the March 12 edition of the paper because of an editorial that called the League of Nations a "League of Thieves"; at least twice before, postal authorities had delayed circulation of the paper (Hill xxii–xxiii).

Dougherty's successor at the *Amsterdam*, Cyril Briggs, wrote the editorial that caught the government's attention. Briggs, who had come to New York from the Caribbean at the age of 17 in 1905, began his journalism career in 1912 as a society reporter for the *Amsterdam*. When Dougherty left the next year for the *New York News*, Briggs took over his position as the paper's sports and theatre editor. Briggs eventually became the *Amsterdam's* city editor, and by 1917 he had become the paper's lead editorial writer. Seeking a broader, more militant outlet for his views, Briggs founded the *Crusader* in 1918 with the help of a donation from J. Anthony Crawford, a Caribbean importer. (Briggs later edited the communist *Harlem Liberator* and co-wrote *The Position of Negro Women* with Eugene Gordon in 1935.)

Briggs continued to work for the *Amsterdam* until June 1919. Scholars disagree on the circumstances that surrounded his departure: Most accounts say he resigned after the paper attempted to tone down his anti-war editorials, but Robert Hill suggests that Briggs created this version of the events years later, in a Federal Writers Project interview (Hill xvii). After examining the suppression of the *Amsterdam* by the post office and the paper's reaction, Hill concluded: "From the evidence presently available, there is no indication that the two earlier instances of censorship led to any muzzling of Briggs" (Hill xxiii). Theodore G. Vincent, on the other hand, notes that Briggs "founded his revolutionary *Crusader* monthly in 1918, after having been fired as editorial writer for the weekly *Amsterdam News* because of his antiwar editorials" (*Voices* 25). Hill notes that Theodore Draper cites "the same misleading account" in *American Communism and Soviet Russia* (Hill liv fn61).

However acrimonious Briggs's departure from the *Amsterdam* might have been, he enjoyed wide support from the paper's editors as he was launching his magazine. The *Amsterdam's* sales agents also distributed the *Crusader*, while Briggs thanked the paper's managing editor, Edward H. Warren, for his support by listing him—along with Dougherty and the Lafayette Theatre, then managed by former *Age* sports editor Lester Walton—in the magazine's "Roll of Honor." According to Briggs, Warren's "broadminded manly attitude made possible the wide advertisement of the *Crusader* and its purpose" (Briggs, "Roll" 23).

The magazine's purpose, initially, was to argue for equality for African Americans and all peoples of African descent. The *Crusader* aligned itself first with the Hamitic League of the World and later the African Blood Brotherhood, two secret organizations also supported by Crawford that argued for independence in African colonies and black separatism in the United States (Daniel 148). The African Blood Brotherhood, which advocated "armed defense of American black communities," claimed a membership of 50,000 in 1920 (Dodson 171). It was part of the same movement as Marcus Garvey's United Negro Improvement Association, though Briggs considered Garvey a rival and referred to him as "Judas" in his editorials; Briggs's anger, and a lawsuit, had been provoked when Garvey called him "white," though he was not the first to make light of Briggs' pale pigmentation: in the *New York News*, George Harris had called him an "angry blond Negro." The rivalry quickly consumed Briggs and his magazine: the final issues are dedicated almost entirely to criticism of Garvey and his organization, and publication ended soon after Garvey's arrest on charges of mail fraud in 1921 (Hill xliv). Briggs and W.A. Domingo conducted their own investigation of Garvey's legal activities and reported their findings to FBI agents (Hill xliv). In the December 1921 and January 1922 issues of the *Crusader*, Briggs claimed credit for exposing Garvey. Domingo, as director of publicity and propaganda for the ABB, called the *Crusader* "primarily an anti–Garvey publication" (Hill xlv).

The *Crusader* focused on cultural issues as well as political ones: Briggs wrote occasional theatre reviews and published features by Lester Walton and the vaudeville comedian Bert Williams (Daniel 150). Estimates of the *Crusader's* popularity vary widely: According to Vincent, its circulation reached 37,000 at its peak, while Daniel says the highest figure was 8,000 (Vincent 25; Daniel 151).

The *Crusader's* honor roll also included Robert L. Douglas, a friend

7. "Race First" in the Sports Section

of Dougherty's and the manager of the Spartan Braves amateur basketball club. "Smilin' Bob," who became better known in later years as the founder of Harlem's dominant professional team, the Renaissance Five, "took out the first subscription while yet The Crusader was but a literary expression" (Briggs, "Roll" 22). Douglas also worked on behalf of the magazine, helping organize the "Liberty Dances" held in its benefit and, according to the third issue, contributing to the attraction of "several hundred new subscribers" ("A Contemporary's Appreciation" 7). While their common Caribbean background—Douglas was a native of Nevis's neighboring island, St. Kitts—might have played a part in Briggs's support for Douglas's teams, the *Crusader* covered all of New York's basketball teams extensively. Briggs, like Dougherty, presciently pointed out basketball's significance in African American society.

For Briggs and Dougherty, basketball's status as a cultural institution in the Harlem community meant the sport needed to be kept free from the "taint of professionalism." Dougherty, in fact, had helped organize and promote the Metropolitan Basketball Association, formed in the late 1910s to coordinate games among the amateur African American clubs of Manhattan, Brooklyn, and Jersey City (Henderson 127). Along with Douglas's Spartan Athletic Club, the MBA originally included the Smart Set Athletic Club and the St. Christopher Athletic Club; these clubs are credited with initiating organized basketball in New York. Later, the league added the Alpha Physical Culture Club, the Jersey City Athletic Club, the Indian Athletic Club, the Laetitia Athletic Club, the St. Cyprian Athletic Club, the Salem Crescent Athletic Club, and the Williamsbridge Colored Men's Association (Henderson 127). Reflecting the influence of Caribbean migrants, many of the clubs also fielded teams in soccer and cricket.

Dougherty considered such promotional work part of his role as a community advocate. In the second decade of the century, as basketball became increasingly popular at the segregated African American colleges, Dougherty began arranging and promoting games between southern schools in the larger venues of New York City (Henderson 131–33; Boris 58). Dan Burley, the *Amsterdam*'s sports editor in the 1940s, observed after Dougherty's death: "In these clubs and organizations were the athletes the old-timers still rave about. Such history was at the fingertips of the grand old man of the press row who has just passed on. He considered it part of his Harlem and a constant chore to keep deserving athletes, then the future stars, in the limelight" (Burley 13b).

Throughout its first basketball season in 1918–1919, the *Crusader* covered the sport thoroughly and enthusiastically. Briggs, writing under the pseudonym "C. Valentine" (using his middle name), lauded the dominant St. Christopher club in March and named "Valentine's All-Negro All-Star Five" in April. Three members of Briggs's all-star team played for the St. Christopher "Machine," including "Headache Band" Capers, of whom Briggs observed: "[L]ike the Greeks at Thermopylae, Johnnie Capers is there with a spectacular shot at any time his team is in danger of defeat. It has never been known to fail in the memory of living fan" (Briggs, "Valentine's" 14). For the remainder of the season, the Crusader remained focused on the Machine. Briggs's praise gave way to protest the following season, however. Will Madden, the former "guiding hand" of the St. Christopher club, had formed a semi-professional team and signed several of his former players to exclusive contracts. Soon other teams formed, offering players cash incentives, and the clubs also began to trade players in the manner of professional baseball clubs (Henderson 130). The *Crusader* called on the clubs to maintain their amateurism as Briggs instituted a campaign he called "The Fight to Keep Sport Clean."

In the notes to his unfinished autobiography, Briggs described the campaign as "THE FIGHT FOR THE SOCIAL AND ATHLETIC CLUBS IN HARLEM" (as qtd. by Hill, xviii; emphasis in original). Robert Hill notes that Briggs embarked on a personal campaign to convince Hampton Institute to cancel a series of games it had scheduled with Madden's club, the Incorporators. Although the effort failed, Briggs enlisted the cooperation of Paul Robeson, who was then a law student at Columbia. (Robeson, who had starred in basketball as well as football at Rutgers, played briefly for the St. Christopher club in New York.) Hill suggests that the meeting was Robeson's first with a member of the Communist Party (xviii–xix). Briggs also visited schools with James H. Ravenell, a former track star who had written an essay in the *Crusader* of May 1919 recounting his experience as an officer in France during World War I.

Dougherty became Briggs's chief lieutenant in "The Fight to Keep Sport Clean." In a highly dramatic exposé, appearing in the *Crusader* of January 1921, Dougherty revealed the details of one of the key battles in the fight. Using language heavily redolent of the Great War and the peace negotiations that followed it, he cited the sacrifices of the amateur clubs, particularly the "Triple Alliance" of Alpha, Spartan, and St. Christopher (Dougherty, "Behind the Scenes" 13). Despite their efforts, the "germ" of "under cover professionalism" had infiltrated the sport: Players were secretly taking money for jumping from one club to another, and certain clubs had reportedly offered bonuses to players if they defeated St. Christopher. The officers of the St. Christopher club, "realizing the mire into which they were being drawn, came together hoping to devise some plan whereby an attempt could be made to stamp out this evil and its baneful influence for all time" (14). Acting unilaterally, St. Christopher dismissed all players "carrying the taint of professionalism" from its team. Soon afterwards, in a conference that convened at St. Philip's Church, the delegates of the local clubs drafted what Dougherty called "Treaty of the Parish House," prohibiting acts of "under cover professionalism."

The location of the conference was significant. St. Philip's Episcopal Church, originally located on 25th Street in Chelsea before moving to Harlem soon after the turn of the century, remains one of the largest African American congregations in the United States. In 1901, W.E.B. Du Bois, who became a parishioner, called St. Philip's the primary meeting place of established, well-to-do African American families in New York City ("The Black North" 151–2). The church and rectory, designed by African American architects George W. Foster, Jr., and Vertner W. Tandy in 1911, still stand; the original Parish House, to which Dougherty refers, was replaced by a new multi-purpose facility in 1970.

The language Dougherty used in his exposé might have been exaggerated, but it was fraught with seriousness and purpose. He claimed basketball, played by social clubs and church teams, had an ability to attract and inspire people that few institutions could match. More important, the absence of financial gain proved the amateur clubs were dedicated to the community. The importance of basketball could be shown by comparing it to baseball, which had been organized into the first formal Negro National League only a year before. For all the significance of that venture, it seems not to have impressed Dougherty or Briggs (who never ran a story on the Negro Leagues in the *Crusader*) because it carried the "taint of professionalism" from the start. Local basketball, by contrast, had grown to prominence with an amateur spirit, and Dougherty considered the fight to be one between good and evil, with no neutral ground:

> Those of you in the class of the "Stay-at-Home" who read with slight interest the accounts of basketball, our chief pastime during the fall and winter months, will never appreciate the threatened danger to our institutions that in years past unselfishly fostered this game which has been the means of bringing together a

large number of our people under the best auspices. Here in Greater New York and New Jersey basketball has meant more to us than baseball, for the latter sport among colored people has been so closely allied to the saloon and underground dives the majority of sport writers passed it up in behalf of the game which is fostered by religious and other institutions working for the uplift of our people [13].

While Dougherty's rhetoric seems histrionic, it differs little from that of some Renaissance intellectuals, including W.E.B. Du Bois, who disapproved of the supposed excesses and irreverence of the "New Negro" movement.

Dougherty considered himself a defender of community-minded organizations in general, and of Harlem athletic clubs in particular. Bob Douglas, for one, seems to have agreed with Dougherty's self-assessment. Douglas took a deferent attitude towards Dougherty, occasionally asking him for advice in letters signed "Yours in Sport," which Dougherty printed in the *Amsterdam*. In the waning days of the "Fight to Keep Sport Clean," while still managing the amateur Spartan club team, Douglas asked for Dougherty's approval in scheduling games against clubs that used professional players (Douglas 4). The Spartan club, in attempting to stay "clean," had had trouble filling out its schedule, and Douglas suspected he was alone in abiding by the rules of the amateur ideals of the Metropolitan Basketball Association.

Dougherty, returning to the jargon of World War I, pointed out that Douglas and his partner at the Spartan Club, Cecil Carter—whom Dougherty referred to as "Lloyd George"—had not yet severed "diplomatic relations" with the other clubs (Dougherty, "Spartans" 4). After a "careful inquiry in the matter," Dougherty gave the actions of the Spartan club his imprimatur. But the idealism of his *Crusader* expose seemed to be gone. Conceding "it is a grandstand play to hastily come out and suggest things radical the moment something goes wrong," Dougherty noted that the Spartan club had dropped its arguments against the St. Christopher club's use of professional players in hopes of simply scheduling games between the two. In the end, he gave Douglas the green light to drop his adherence to amateur contests and play professional teams.

The next winter, Douglas organized the Renaissance Five. The club became the most popular team in Harlem in the 1920s and surpassed the Original Celtics as the dominant team of the era (George 34–40). Dougherty's influence in that arena has been recognized by historians: He was featured prominently in the "Black Fives" exhibition on the history of African American basketball at the New-York Historical Society in 2014.

When Dougherty died in relative obscurity in 1944, Douglas—who would serve as a pallbearer—reminded the public of Dougherty's prominence, stopping a Rens game in progress for one minute as a band played "Taps" (Snelson 16A).

From Leftism to Nationalism: The Radical Ideology of *Punta, Revolutionist*

Dougherty's involvement with Briggs and the *Crusader* marked the beginning of a period in which Dougherty experimented with radical ideas. Dougherty's interest in leftism did not last long: as Briggs moved the *Crusader* closer to cooperation with the Communist Party, Dougherty fell away from the group. Rather than reverting to the ostensibly apolitical world of the sports pages, however, he plunged into rockier waters by joining the black nationalist movement led by Briggs's adversary, Marcus Garvey. The controversial move underscores one of the principles that runs throughout Dougherty's work: he consistently focused on racial rather than class consciousness. Even in his basketball coverage for the *Crusader*, before Briggs made antagonism of Garvey his primary goal, Dougherty made his priorities clear.

Dougherty demonstrated his inclination towards Garvey's "race first" ethos in his other major contribution to the *Crusader*, a serial novella that appeared in seven installments in 1919. *Punta, Revolutionist*, billed in advertisements as a "thrilling adventure," explores the idea of a racial revolt that would unify all people of color under one flag. W. F. Santiago-Valles cites Dougherty's novel as an example of the literary radicalism practiced by the community of Caribbean migrants who were then "at the center of radical activity in Harlem" (Santiago-Valles 5). Dougherty never published the novella's conclusion, probably after a falling out with Briggs over the direction of the magazine. Possibly, Dougherty never finished it; perhaps his romantic, aristocratic hero brought the political differences between him and Briggs into irresolvable conflict. Whatever the revolutionary Briggs thought of the novella's endorsement of aristocratic ideals, however, its call to arms most likely appealed to him: When the last chapter appeared in October 1919, Punta and his cohorts were in seclusion with German chemists, building a bomb that would initiate a war for black freedom. Dougherty's melding of literary experimentation and historical perspective is unique among Renaissance writers, especially in this circle of radical journalists, and it demands a detailed close reading.²

Set in the Caribbean during the Spanish-American War, the story is revolutionary in terms of race but not class. Dougherty's protagonist, the improbably named "Puntacious Hernandez," represents the aristocrats who seek to overthrow white control of the islands while maintaining the genteel propriety of plantation society. Significantly, Punta's leadership stems from his natural athletic abilities, enhanced by his upbringing: he is a horseman *non pariel*. Indeed, Dougherty takes the novella's operating metaphor from the world of sport at its most aristocratic: Punta must ride in a high-stakes horse race to demonstrate his natural talent and defeat a symbolic foe.

Much as he did in his coverage of "The Fight to Keep Sport Clean," in his novel Dougherty uses the terminology and themes of World War I. The Germans in his story, seemingly incongruous in the setting of the Spanish-American War, know their country "is preparing to strike a blow at a certain nation within the next fifteen or twenty years that will throw the world into the most terrible war in history" (*Punta VI* 14). Indeed, Germany did join the scramble for Spain's former possessions after the war, sending ships to the Philippines and eventually acquiring several Pacific islands. Punta prophetically announces that he can see ahead to that war, when nations ("with the possible exception of France") will again ask black soldiers to fight alongside whites despite denying them equality otherwise; at that time, those countries will be unprepared to fight on another front, as Punta leads an uprising of "the brave sons and descendants from Africa's sunny clime." Dougherty might also have been playing on political hysteria here: During World War I, for example, the New York *Herald-Tribune* suggested that Germans tried to encourage disloyalty among African Americans (Kornweibel 4–5).

Although the story eventually devolves into science fiction, for the most part Dougherty strives for Romantic grandiosity. In the first installment, Dougherty's protagonist, Harry Longsdale, describes himself by recounting his own reading tastes. After noting that wild-west adventure tales dominated his interest as a boy, he assures the reader he has never given in completely to them: "Although I had earlier in life read books that usually give youngsters a desire to hike for the west and hunt Indians, I never lost my balance" (*Punta I* 9). In spite of this balance, his mature tastes lean decidedly towards the Romantic: His favorite writers range from British melodramatics (Marie Corelli, Charles Garvice, Mrs. Southworth) to French naturalists (Alphonse Daudet, Eugene Sue).[3] Harry's list culminates with Alexandre Dumas, whose aristocratic, mixed-race background (his father was a general in Napoleon's army, his mother a Haitian slave), helped make him a celebrated figure in the Renaissance era, as demonstrated by Gwendolyn Bennett's poem, "Lines Written at the Grave of Alexandre Dumas." In fact, Dumas's biography embodies many of the features of Dougherty's novella.

Dougherty's story also blends aspects of *Bildungsroman*. In the first installment, he quickly leads the reader through Harry's youth and eventual employment as a reporter for the fictional *New York Thunderer*. Light-skinned and passing for white, Harry finds that his earnestness and ambition meet with quick approval in the era of the emergent New Journalism: "Color your story, boy, color your story was all that I could hear and believe me, I painted everyone of mine with a rainbow finish" (10). The setting of Dougherty's story—the Spanish-American War—represents a flashpoint in the rivalry between Joseph Pulitzer and William Randolph Hearst, as many critics considered the Spanish-American War the result of Hearst's "yellow journalism," an extreme version of Pulitzer's sensationalistic New Journalism (e.g., Bessie 40–41). Despite Harry's apparent cynicism, however, Dougherty depicts him as occasionally naïve. After submitting a particularly colorful and overblown story ("a rip-roaring corker"), he earns a promotion, and the paper sends him to the Caribbean as a war correspondent. Harry basks in the glamour of this assignment, even though he knows he will be stationed in Santo Amalia (a fictional, Spanish version of the capital of St. Thomas, Charlotte Amalie), sending home embellishments of telegraph reports from the war in Cuba. "I did not take the trouble to explain to my friends that I would only be engaged in the harmless 'indoor sport' of stretching stories from the direct cables," he admits. "And how I did 'stretch' those stories!" (10).

Safely ensconced five hundred miles from the front, Harry spends his days as most fictional correspondents do: at the race track, in restaurants and bars, in luxurious hotels. His first impressions of the teenaged, "almost imperial highness" Punta seem an extension of the opulent colonial setting: "Tall for his age, with features of a boy much younger, almost girlish in their aristocratic refinement, hair and eyes jet black, body lithe and supple and an easy stride which showed the athlete in every move" (*Punta II* 10). While Punta's refinements impress Harry, his natural talents prove more prodigious and central to the story. Harry investigates Punta's background, and nearly everything he learns revolves around athleticism:

> Son of Elacios Hernandez, biggest retail merchant in the capital. Born rich. Plenty money. Great horse back rider. Unequalled when it comes to sailing a boat. Swimmer of no mean ability. Holds a racquet with the best of men. Even rides his own horses at El Fonda race track when he doubts the ability of his jockeys. And say, when it comes to rising in the stirrups and stretching his mount for a win right under the wire, the best in the land are forced to take a back seat [*Punta I* 8].

The foreshadowed centerpiece of Dougherty's story appears in the third installment, when a horse race serves as a symbolic contest between opposing political and racial forces. Punta's "jet black horse," Del Fuego, runs against a field of competitors from the Caribbean as well as, "for the first time," an American thoroughbred. The American horse, ridden by a renowned white Southern jockey, inspires record wagering and jingoistic revelry among the Americans in attendance. When the local fans respond by showing similar support for Punta and his entry, the racial chasm becomes clear and poisonous:

> One uncouth son of Georgia or Alabama, who up to this time had attracted the attention of the people in the stand where he sat by his boisterous conduct[,] wanted to know who was "the high muchamuck nigger" and but for the hateful look which darted from the eyes of a score of natives around and the suggestive manner in which their hands sought their back pockets, he might have forgotten that he was from a certain part of the United States where the popular sport is taking the lives of unoffensive Negroes [*Punta III* 15].

For Harry—a Southerner himself—the scene offers an opportunity to analyze the aggressive behavior of the local residents. His description of the victims of lynching as "unoffensive" demonstrates a common theme in the African American press of the era and in Dougherty's work in particular. Just as he promoted traditional mores of public decorum, he and other traditionalists argued that African Americans must always be on their best behavior, so as to debunk any attempts by whites to defend racial oppression as "discipline." By implication, however, Dougherty here also endorses a militant response to racist behavior.

As the horses leave the paddock and appear on the track, Dougherty highlights Del Fuego's symbolic characteristics. He is not only black and powerful, but also difficult to control; none of his handlers knows which direction he will lurch. The fearful laborers, cast here as the henchmen of colonialism, try haplessly to fulfill their assigned tasks: "This animal was plunging, rearing, jumping, in fact, he was doing everything in his power to get away from the undersized natives who tried valiantly to quiet him" (16). In short, none of the locals wants any part of his uprising, though it leaves them all entranced. After Del Fuego throws his jockey (a "little English boy"), Punta comes out of the crowd to calm the horse "before he again started his tactics of plunging and rearing" (27).

The American contingent, made up mostly of military men, anticipates Del Fuego's withdrawal, giving their entry victory without serious opposition. The possibility of winning so easily throws the Americans into a frenzy that the island's upright policemen subdue: "But for the timely arrival of 'rurales,' a body of mounted men, a few heads might have been cracked and a stiletto or two might have flashed, but these hardy sun-tanned sons of the island on their even hardier steeds swept back the sailors and marines and kept them from precipitating a clash" (28). The *rurales*, far from representing overreaching authority, exemplify the islanders' self-determination and dignity, especially in contrast to the dishonorable lust for easy victory exhibited by the American thugs.

Of course, Del Fuego does not withdraw; Punta climbs aboard and the metaphorical race is on. Riding "without whip or spur," Punta effortlessly guides his black horse past the pack. Echoing Dougherty's scene-setting descriptions of the Caribbean islands, and overcoming Del Fuego's innate wildness, Punta "breezed by" the other horses, as calm as "a gentle zephyr." By contrast, the American soldiers "now acted like wild men" (29). Dougherty swiftly reduces the race to a contest between Punta and the American rider, whose willingness to use his whip symbolizes his desperation. After Punta waves to the crowd, Del Fuego accelerates and wins the race by a length, the "speed and stamina" of the "black animal" barely tested.

After the race, the islanders rush the track in celebration and a riot ensues as the American servicemen attack. Punta immediately diffuses the uprising in a scene that combines the best elements of Caribbean society, brought together by a surpassing athletic performance:

> Having Del Fuego under perfect control although he was inclined to plunge, he headed a party of 'rurales' and pleaded with the people to come to their senses. The presence of the horse that won the race had a splendid effect upon the natives, especially as the sailors and marines were now on the run with the riff raff after them [29].

Punta himself dispenses with the last rambunctious soldier, using his whip for the first time and giving the American officer a "cut across the shoulder."

The ever-neutral, almost neutered grooms rescue the American as Punta laughs "heartily" (15).

Dougherty's depiction of Punta as an aristocratic leader expands in the fourth chapter. Dismounting his horse "with the easy manner of the well bred" and vaulting "gracefully" into the box, Punta invites Harry to his country estate. Along the way, as Harry observes the Caribbean juxtaposition of colonial mansions and squatter's huts, Punta points out the significance of the uprising at the race track:

> Quite an unusual sight, is it not, my dear Longsdale? If I am not mistaken, affairs of this kind where whites and Negroes come together in your country the Negroes always get the worst of it. We have had so much of this thing in the islands the natives are getting tired of it you can rest assured that when your marines and sailors "start something" these children of the sea will be ready for them [15].

The declaration sparks in Harry a rumination on race relations in the United States and his own Americanness. Harry, still passing as white, wonders if the equality enjoyed by Punta on the island would also apply to him, an African American. Harry becomes momentarily distraught, remembering his "lot in life—a lot which condemned me to be what I am not" (16). Just as quickly, though, he calms down, much as the raging black horse had relaxed under the influence of Punta. Harry thinks of the American flag and imagines African Americans saluting it in parades but doing so silently, in a manner that would "remind the white man that something was lacking and that something the wild enthusiasm which we too readily display." The image alludes to the Silent Protest Parade in New York in 1917, when fifteen thousand African Americans protested lynching by marching down Fifth Avenue to the sound of muffled drums. "Such an attitude," Harry continues, "would make the people who keep us down and refuse to allow us to enjoy God's right to a full measure of this earth can give toss restlessly at night. Their conscience would reproach them and in fear when they realize that we are at last THINKING DEEPLY, they would give us what is justly ours" (16; emphasis in original).

Again, Dougherty tempers his radicalism with a deeper belief in the intrinsic fairness of American society. In this sense, he reveals his difference from the radicals of the *Crusader*, seeming closer in temperament to Harlem's "old crowd," as Domingo termed the establishment intellectuals in the *Messenger*. Domingo delineated a split between the New Negro movement and "old crowd Negroes," specifically rejecting what he called the old crowd's "doctrine of non-resistance" (Huggins 53). For many younger radicals, however, the "old crowd" also included W.E.B. Du Bois because, like Dougherty, he retained a devotion to bourgeois values, even when his views on race relations tended towards separatism.

Like James Weldon Johnson and others in the "old crowd," Dougherty resisted as the many in the new crowd explored the possibilities of Marxism. In particular, he withdrew as Briggs and Domingo led the African Blood Brotherhood into close association with and eventual absorption into the Workers Party (James, *Holding* 178). The ABB "shared goals" with the Garvey movement, according to Winston James, as late as April 1921 (James, *Holding* 160). At the UNIA convention in August of that year, Briggs broke ranks as his views grew increasingly left-leaning; Garvey already had fired Domingo from his position on the *Negro World* because of his Marxist views (171, 270). In Winston James's view, this transition from black nationalism to orthodox socialism "was the continuum that the New Negro ideology of the era also traversed" (*Holding* 157). Not everyone, of course, belonged to one camp or the other. Hubert Harrison, for example, remained faithful to both causes: ultimately, he refused to put socialism above "the call of his race," though he considered separatism a last resort (*Holding* 126–28).

Dougherty apparently felt no such dilemma. For radicals who adhered to the "race first" philosophy but would rather not have turned left, there was one place to go. In 1922, Dougherty began writing for the *Negro Times*, Marcus Garvey's attempt to publish a daily newspaper (Jackson, "Romeo" 49). The ambitious enterprise lasted for less than two months, comprising twenty-six issues in September and October, amid the pervasive distraction of Garvey's indictment and impending trial for mail fraud (the trial began May 18, 1923, and ended with Garvey's conviction on June 15; he was sentenced to five years in prison on June 21, began serving the sentence in 1925, and was deported after President Coolidge commuted his sentence in 1927). Dougherty's participation in the project indicates his relative importance at the time, as Garvey aimed to hire prominent names for the project. Dougherty, for example, was described in the *Who's Who of Colored Americans* (probably by himself, as the publication gathered its information by questionnaire) for years after his split with Garvey as the "Sports authority on the staff of the *Negro Times*" (*Who's Who* 58). According to the editor of the *Who's Who*, Joseph J. Boris, "persons whose careers were deemed of sufficient importance to warrant inclusion were invited to submit the required facts" (*Who's Who* 5). Among the African American sportswriters of the era, only Dougherty was mentioned regularly, starting in 1927. W. Rollo Wilson of the *Pittsburgh Courier* was also listed in the 1930s.

Most of the prominent figures in Renaissance journalism and politics took sides in the Garvey debate, though their positions were not always fixed. Dougherty's mentor from the Washington *Sun*, T. Thomas Fortune, completed an about-face from his tenure as Booker T. Washington's ghostwriter, signing on as Garvey's editor; after the demise of the *Times*, he would take over Garvey's weekly, the *Negro World*. John E. Bruce, the syndicated *New York Age* columnist better known as "Bruce Grit," served as associate editor (Garvey, v.4, 891 fn4). Garvey's notoriety drew several contributors, such as sociologist Carter G. Woodson, who were not necessarily part of the movement but seemed to want to oppose and attach themselves to him at the same time. The *New York News*, for example, published Garvey's memoirs in 1926; supposedly, they were ghostwritten by a witness for the prosecution (Martin 332). *News* editor George Harris, meanwhile, circulated a petition on Garvey's behalf during the trial, even though he had signed a letter to Attorney General Henry Daugherty in 1923, urging surveillance of Garvey (Martin 327). The letter was also signed by Robert Abbott, the editor of the Chicago *Defender*; Julia Coleman, a cosmetics manufacturer who had owned the Washington *Sun* and hired T. Thomas Fortune as the paper's editor; Chandler Owen, the co-editor of the *Messenger* and a subject of governmental surveillance during World War I; Harry H. Pace, an Urban League officer, former partner of W.C. Handy in the Pace and Handy Music Company and founder of the Black Swan record label; John E. Nail, a Harlem real estate magnate and father-in-law to James Weldon Johnson; and two NAACP officers, Robert W. Bagnall and William Pickens.

Garvey's world roiled with such curlicues of association and denial. Edgar Grey, another Caribbean migrant who had served as Hubert Harrison's "faithful lieutenant" in the Liberty League and executive secretary of the Universal Negro Improvement Association, became a key figure in Garvey's mail-fraud trial (James, *Holding* 162). Grey had also directed the Black Star Line, the shipping company that became the centerpiece of Garvey's legal troubles. After Garvey expelled Grey from the UNIA, Grey testified against him; Garvey later claimed his attorney's mishandling of Grey's unexpected appearance in court had led to his conviction. Specifically, Garvey argued that his attorney's failure to cross-examine Grey forced him to dismiss his counsel and act on his own behalf for the remainder of the trial. In his closing statement on June 15, 1923, Garvey gave his impression of Grey: "Who is Edgar Gray [sic]? You saw him on the stand—a reckless, irresponsible man, full of talk, representing nothing, a great politician who has no office, a great know-all who has nothing in all his years, who is still a messenger at probably a meager eighteen dollars a week" (Garvey, vol. 5, 333). In a rhetorical conclusion, Garvey asked the jury: "Would the great God condemn a Christian soul on the testimony of the devil?" (333). Later, as Garvey sat in jail, Grey joined the *Amsterdam*, where he covered tennis for Dougherty.

Dougherty's association with Garvey made him a target for criticism among the Harlem sportswriters. Almost immediately after leaving the *Negro Times*, he disavowed any allegiance to Garvey and separatism. He bristled, for example, when William Clarke referred to Garvey in the *Age* as Dougherty's "friend." Dougherty shot back, insisting that as far as he was concerned, Garvey's paper "is the same as if it never existed," and charged that Garvey had once used the *Age*'s printing press for more than a month.[4] In other words, both Dougherty and the *Age* had dallied with Garvey, but for financial rather than political reasons. "If because I edited his *Times* for a time makes me a friend then he must be a boon companion of the *New York Age*," Dougherty continued. "When payday came we both stalked the African Provisional President in search of our coin of the realm."

Dougherty's brief affiliation with Garvey perfectly characterizes his activities in the early Renaissance years, when a storm of radical ideas and causes engulfed the Harlem literary and journalistic worlds. It may be that individual ambition, more than radical idealism, provoked Dougherty's "adventurous association" with Garvey's movement and the African Blood Brotherhood of Briggs and Domingo (Vincent, *Keep* 80). Much as his association with the *Crusader* had inspired him to attempt a novel, the height of Dougherty's journalistic ambition coincided with his most radical venture.

8. The Dean's Demise

The Sudden Fall and Long Disappearance of Romeo Dougherty

In the days after the folding of the *Negro Times*, Marcus Garvey's short-lived attempt to produce a daily newspaper, Romeo Dougherty considered starting his own, all-sports newspaper (Jackson: 1922, 49). Clearly, Garvey's audacity and enterprise appealed to Dougherty, even if the warfare between radical leftists and black separatists had failed to convert him to either side. After his return to the *Amsterdam News* in 1922, Dougherty ascended to the position of "Dean" of the sports-and-theatre writers in the Harlem press, an influential role that he held for more than a decade. In the turbulence of the 1930s, however, the inconsistency of his political viewpoints undermined his authority as the newspaper's voice in a labor battle, and he disappeared from the scene suddenly and completely. In his absence, Dougherty seemed to plunge as deeply into obscurity as he had thrown himself into every controversy he had covered, from the founding of the Eastern Colored League to the development of professional basketball. Despite the shifting nature of Dougherty's affiliations, perhaps to his ultimate detriment, he never hesitated to endorse a viewpoint passionately or to commit himself to a cause that he believed would benefit the community.

African American newspapers regularly offered space in stories and columns to the promoters of sporting events and the owners of teams, particularly those of Negro League baseball clubs in the early twentieth century. While the relationship benefitted the press as black baseball became more organized and popular, many newspapers later acted as publicity organs and advocates to help teams stay afloat (Carroll, *Black Press* 15–16). As an experienced promoter of both athletes and entertainers, Dougherty embraced this role with relish, although he tended to promote himself at the same time. As a result, Dougherty's positions frequently appeared inconsistent and self-serving, sometimes shallow and contradictory. However, Dougherty remained consistent in one regard: He always aligned himself with a particular organization or cause by arguing for its importance to the African American community. Indeed, he may well have fallen into relative obscurity after the Renaissance because he built his fame and influence as a promoter of events more than as a critic.

While covering theatre for the *New York News* in the 1910s, for example, Dougherty helped book films in Harlem theatres as an agent for the Lincoln Motion Picture Company (Bowser and Spence 74). Dougherty publicized and endorsed as much as he reported and critiqued, seeing no conflict between his objectivity as a newspaperman and his efforts to promote his subjects. This contradiction was not so unusual in this era, when sportswriters—black and white—commonly played a part in the stories they covered. For example, Arch Ward, the lead sports columnist at the time for the *Chicago Tribune*, became best known for originating the major-league All-Star Game in 1933. In the African American press, Lester Walton also received commissions for bookings while covering film and theatre for the *Age*; Tony Langston and D. Ireland Thomas did the same in Chicago while working for the *Defender* (Bowser and Spence 73). Certainly, the conflict of interest could sometimes be egregious: In one column, Walton emphasized the size of the crowds at a Lafayette Theatre screening of the documentary *From Harlem to the Rhine*, a film he also distributed (Bowser and Spence 236 fn65).

Nonetheless, Dougherty prided himself on his independence and objectivity. In 1921, J. A. Jackson, the editor of *Billboard*'s section of African American entertainment news, noted that Dougherty was "regarded as an authority by his people."[1] A year later, Dougherty's return to the *Amsterdam* made headline news in *Billboard*. Jackson called Dougherty "probably the best-known of the colored sporting and theatrical writers of the metropolis," marveling at his "immense personal following of readers and advertisers" (Jackson 49). Dougherty, however, critiqued the "symposium of praise" that Jackson contributed weekly to *Billboard*, which he dismissed as "the Ofay theatrical weekly." Only recently, in Dougherty's opinion, had Jackson begun "telling the truth" and ceased putting forward only the most favorable news possible about African Americans. Dougherty compared Jackson's "conversion" to one he had recently detected in no less a critic than W.E.B. Du Bois. Meanwhile, Dougherty boasted, he himself had been practicing such truth-telling for years.[2]

As an example, Dougherty pointed to his own criticism of Jess McMahon, the white owner of the Commonwealth Casino. Unlike other Harlem club owners, Dougherty claimed, McMahon refused to blame negative publicity in the newspapers when business lagged. Instead, McMahon dealt with the press pragmatically, as Dougherty—the seasoned promoter himself—contended promoters should. McMahon, he wrote, "being versed in what he is doing, gives us the glad hand at all times and not once has he by word or action ever suggested that everything must be praise from our hands where the Commonwealth is concerned."[3] Dougherty saw sports and theatre as cultural institutions in Harlem, but he took a less idealistic view when it came to business and promotion. He expected only fair play—whether pragmatic or idealistic—from Harlem's entrepreneurs.

At about the same time, Dougherty took the owners of the local Negro League ball clubs to task for not properly promoting their teams, especially in the "sundown papers."[4] The Eastern Colored League's revenues had decreased in 1924 after a successful debut the year before, and the upcoming season would accelerate its swift demise. That winter, Dougherty pointed out that William Clarke, his counterpart with the *New York Age*, was moonlighting as the publicist for the Lincoln Giants. Rather than accuse Clarke of a conflict of interest, however, he merely chastised him for not doing a more thorough job. "We believe it to be the duty of a press agent," Dougherty wrote, "to hand around the news instead of keeping it under cover."[5]

In the winter of 1922–23, Dougherty presided over the controversy that led to the formation of the Eastern Colored League, the first Negro League to include teams from New York City. At the time, Rube Foster's Negro National League, operating in the Midwest, had effectively frozen out the biggest teams on the eastern seaboard: Foster had labeled four clubs "outlaws" and prohibited teams in his league from playing even exhibition games against them (Ribowsky 103). Two of the clubs, the Bacharach Giants of Atlantic City and the Hilldale Daisies of Philadelphia, agreed to "associate memberships" in Foster's league. This agreement allowed the Bacharachs and the Hilldales to play NNL clubs, but the hefty membership fee of $1,000 (twice the amount paid by the actual members of the league) and the cost of traveling to the Midwest (they could play only each other among the major clubs in the East) proved financially crippling (Ribowsky 113). The Bacharachs folded in 1922; after the season, the Hilldales' owner, Ed Bolden, organized a rival league.

8. The Dean's Demise

Bolden and Foster, who had become bitter enemies as the owners of independent teams in the late-1910s, began criticizing each other in the press. Foster used African American papers—first the *Indianapolis Freeman* and later the *Chicago Defender*—as sounding boards, while Bolden enjoyed free rein in the *Philadelphia Tribune*. This practice was not rare: Much as the *New York Age* attached itself to the Bacharach Giants in 1920, sports editors in the African American press often allowed their sections to become promotional sites—even mouthpieces—for the owners of ball clubs. Many editors, well aware that the clubs could afford little advertising, considered such promotional work part of their civic duty. Dougherty, however, considered himself above any one team and promoted what he considered a greater good: the betterment of the game itself. As a result, both Foster and Bolden appealed to him and he assumed the role of moderator, printing diatribes from each about the other under headlines such as "Colored Baseball Men in Sensational War of Words."[6] In Dougherty's view, the interest the feud might generate merited its detailed publication.

Foster, fearing the formation of an eastern league would provoke a new bidding war for players, announced in the *Defender* that he was going to New York, where he would be willing to debate Bolden and the Lincoln Giants owner, Nat Strong, "before newspapermen in that city" (Cottrell 165). In February, Bolden accepted the challenge in a column printed in the Baltimore edition of the *Afro-American* (Lester 146). The contest never came off, though Foster did travel to New York. In February, Dougherty printed a letter from Foster accusing Bolden of reneging on an offer to debate. "Running away with such a bluff," Foster charged, "is one of Bolden's great efforts to save people from allowing me to show the facts and the kind of man he really is and how little he means to help advance the Negro in his profession."[7] Foster challenged Bolden to send "proof to any newspaper" that the Hilldales and the Bacharachs had been mistreated. Appealing directly to Dougherty, he added: "Make him prove this for the sake of fairness to me."

Dougherty stayed uncharacteristically silent on this matter. He supported the formation of an eastern league but must have been chagrined by Foster's denigration of Bolden's racial fealty. Indeed, although Bolden largely modeled his league on Foster's, it differed in one distinct way: four of the six owners were white. In the *Kansas City Call*, Foster charged that referring to Bolden's organization as a black league would be like calling "a street car a steamship" (qtd. in Ribowsky 121). He attacked Bolden's alliance with Strong in particular, branding the new league "Nat Strong's Booking Agency" and reminding Harlem readers of Strong's domineering ownership of several New York City teams in the 1910s (Cottrell 164). As historian Larry Lester notes, Foster feared that Strong "would economically exploit black baseball and eventually control all of black baseball in the eastern states" (Lester 151). While Bolden had conspired with Strong to take advantage of the booking agent's established operation in New York, the primary beneficiary was Bolden himself. Only the Hilldales kept all the gate receipts from their home games—an arrangement that Foster also had in his own league.

Dougherty stayed above the fray through the winter. Instead, he offered periodic updates on the progress of the league's formation and made it clear that African American fans supported the effort. "Organized baseball in the East is arousing much interest," he wrote on January 24. He left no doubt about the source of his information, however, as most of his news focused on Bolden club in Philadelphia rather than any of the three teams based in New York. The veneer of neutrality fell away in March, as Dougherty printed a gushing profile of Bolden. Calling him "a human dynamo," Dougherty cited Bolden's nineteen years as a clerk in Philadelphia's central post office ("an efficiency record for case examinations and floorwork unsurpassed and seldom equaled") and praised his acumen in running the self-incorporated Hilldale club: "This man's unselfishness put quite a few stockholders on salary, and has developed a race corporation that not only leads in Pennsylvania, but is held up as a beacon light to other organizations all over the country."[8] Most of all, Dougherty stressed Bolden's importance as an inarguably successful African American businessman. Two weeks after allowing Rube Foster's direct appeals and charges against Bolden to go unanswered, Dougherty had allowed his promotional inclinations—if not his tendency for hyperbolic praise—run wild. His enthusiasm for the Eastern Colored League, and his desire to see it succeed, apparently got the best of his reportorial judgment.

Trying to maintain a position of some objectivity, Dougherty noted that it was "the consensus of opinion that no other manager of color could have called such a powerful aggregation together and whipped them into a concrete organization, holding the guiding hand through constitutional tilts, and emerging as head with everybody satisfied" (4). It seems unlikely that Dougherty would have forgotten that just three years earlier, Foster had organized the first Negro League, or that the exchange of accusations in the *Amsterdam* the month before would have been enough to diminish Foster in Dougherty's mind. More likely, Bolden's effort struck him as more immediate, precarious, and in need of promotional support. Although white interests owned the majority of the teams in Bolden's league, his status as chairman of the enterprise was paramount; indeed, the fact that Bolden had authority over four white businessmen, including the notorious Nat Strong, underscores Dougherty's description of the members as "such a powerful aggregation." The rarity of such an arrangement at the time only made it more imperative that the league not fail.

For his part, Bolden claimed the league demonstrated the benefits of integrated efforts. He argued that business efforts brought real gratification only when "the color line fades and cooperation instituted. ... Segregation in any form, including self-imposed, is not the solution" (qtd. in Ribowsky 107). Whatever Bolden's motives were, he maintained a constant, ruthless adherence to the bottom line. His rivalry with Foster did great damage to the Negro National League, while his partners in the Eastern Colored League grew restless after a profitable first year. In 1928, they voted Bolden out as president and he withdrew his club from the league. In 1929, he joined a new organization, the American Negro League, which quickly folded; the next year, he declined to renew the lease on the Hilldales' ballpark and barnstormed for games. Bolden sold the club in 1931 and it folded in 1932. In 1934, he resurfaced as a part-owner of the Philadelphia Stars and served for many years as that team's public face, a figurehead that recalled a more glorious past. Meanwhile, Dougherty's unmitigated support of Bolden's highly visible entrepreneurship moved him farther away from the leftist politics of Briggs and the *Crusader*. Similarly, his endorsement of Bolden's "race neutral" stance, in the midst of Bolden's war with Rube Foster's "race first" approach, marked Dougherty's complete split with Garveyism.

Throughout the Renaissance years, Dougherty's positions grew increasingly pragmatic. On several occasions, he praised boxing promoters, such as Jess McMahon, for staging interracial bouts.[9] In one blatantly promotional article, previewing an upcoming fight card at the McMahon brothers' Commonwealth Casino, Dougherty's elaborate sub-heading read: "Jess McMahon Continues to Offer the Best Cards While Other Managers Are Floundering Around and Asking What It's All About When They See the Big Crowds."[10] The "best cards," of course, not only included African American boxers but pitted many of them against white fighters—a consistently good draw that many promoters found too hot to touch. One such promoter was Tex Rickard, who refused to allow his best-known fighter, Jack Dempsey, to face his primary challenger, the African American Harry Wills. Rickard built and ran the present incarnation of Madison Square Garden, which Dougherty called "the graveyard of the hopes and aspirations of the colored fighters." Dougherty suggested that when African American boxers had competed at the Garden, the fights more often than not were fixed.[11] Like James Weldon Johnson, Dougherty believed the public's desire to see interracial competition, for reasons admirable or otherwise, would force promoters to arrange such bouts, and that such contests would inevitably lead to greater opportunities.

Jess McMahon and his brother Rod had originally owned the Lincoln Giants, founding the team in 1911. They built the Lincolns' home park, Olympic Field, in the heart of Harlem at Fifth Avenue and 136th Street, and the Lincolns quickly became the community's favored team. Although the McMahons sold the club in 1916, they maintained control of the players they had under contract and briefly fielded a rival team, the Lincoln Stars. The brothers also ran the Commonwealth Casino at 135th and Madison, featuring basketball and boxing as well as musical entertainment. In the early 1920s, before the Renaissance Casino played home to the dominant Renaissance Five, sportswriters considered the Commonwealth the primary basketball venue in Harlem, and the McMahons' Commonwealth Five its primary professional team.

Dougherty's protectiveness of the Commonwealths drew him into another controversy in which he defended the McMahons, this time attacking a "race first" entrepreneur on grounds of selfishness and a lack of community-mindedness. Cumberland Posey, the owner and manager of the Homestead Grays, one of Negro League baseball's legendary teams, repeatedly found himself at war with Dougherty, especially when the two wielded unparalleled influence as pioneers in the development of professional basketball as an urban fixture. According to Nelson George, "Posey's involvement in several Black entertainment entities is an excellent preview of the way different aspects of Black show business and basketball would be linked in years to come. Cumberland Posey ... was one of the first to recognize this connection" (George 19).

Well before he built the Homestead Grays into a force in Negro League baseball, Posey achieved a measure of fame in Pittsburgh as a basketball player and manager, running the Loendi Big Five. He had been born into such prominence: his father was the first African American riverboat engineer on the Ohio, one of the wealthiest black men in Pittsburgh, and a member of the exclusive Loendi Club. After starring briefly in basketball at Penn State, where he was kicked off the team for academic reasons in 1909, "Cum" Posey returned home and played center field for Homestead's factory baseball team. He also organized a semi-professional basketball club, the Monticello Rifles, which competed with college teams in Pittsburgh and traveled to New York to play the top amateur clubs there (Ruck 126). In 1913, Posey put together a more ambitious operation, sponsored by the relatively well-heeled Loendi Club, combining former collegiate players with athletes from the Homestead mills (Ruck 127). By the early 1920s, when professional basketball began to displace the amateur game, Loendi reigned as one of the dominant teams in the East.

Posey had no interest in playing the Commonwealth Five, however, apparently because of the team's close connections to Dougherty. For several weeks in the winter of 1922–23, Dougherty criticized Posey in his column—which also ran in the Pittsburgh *Courier*—for not bringing his team to New York. Dougherty attacked Posey's insistence on setting the terms of any meeting between Loendi and the Commonwealths, calling such demands unprofessional. Dougherty particularly objected to Posey's requirement that the winner take all of the revenue from any contest.[12] Posey had spelled out fourteen conditions in a letter to the McMahons, which Dougherty printed in the *Amsterdam*. Although the brothers had been sports promoters in Harlem for more than a decade, Posey suggested their naiveté as basketball managers had caused them to trust Dougherty in spite of his proclivity for airing out such disputes in print: "While it is hard to excuse your association, of course in a public way, with Romeo Dougherty, whom the Loendi Club has learned through various experiences, financially and otherwise, to studiously avoid, we again attribute this to your first year in basketball."[13]

Dougherty responded by casting himself in the role of the public watchdog. "Say," he asked, "who wouldn't avoid a man who is constantly on guard to tell the public of the doings of those who would bring disgrace to a game which we all enjoyed for many years? Is it not a fact that a criminal at all times tries to avoid the police?"[14] Dougherty's extreme language attests to the gravity he saw in the situation: African American basketball, having followed baseball into professionalism, risked falling into the hands of profiteers. Jess McMahon was assuredly no saint: he offended his more upstanding players with his hard drinking and conspicuous spending, but he paid his players well (Ribowsky 82). Dougherty argued that McMahon's commitment to Harlem sports clubs and integrated boxing cards added substantially to the cultural life of the community, regardless of how much he profited from those investments.

Dougherty extended his arguments beyond hyperbolic charges and self-serving seriousness. He mocked Posey's list of requirements by comparing him to Woodrow Wilson (by then especially unpopular among African Americans): "Posey's 'Fourteen Points' reminds us of another bunch of points that received the same consideration at the hands of the European papers that Posey's received at the hands of the colored papers here in New York."[15] After Posey emended his demands and agreed to play two games with the Commonwealths, Dougherty sarcastically condemned him for deploying "ways that are dark and tricks that are futile," paraphrasing Bret Harte's poem "Plain Language from Truthful James." Harte's popular satirical poem, more widely known as "The Heathen Chinee," depicts a naive protagonist and his friend, duped in a game of euchre by a Chinese immigrant. Although the immigrant claims not to understand the game, he wins, and in the subsequent scuffle it is revealed that he has hidden 24 packs of cards up his sleeves. The poem is hardly subtle: the immigrant's name is "Ah Sin," and the speaker's friend observes that "We have been beaten by Chinese cheap labor" before instigating the brawl. Still, the simplicity of Truthful James (he admits as he recalls Ah Sin's name, "And I shall not deny/In regard to the same/What that name might imply"), along with the poem's jaunty rhythm, hint at an irony that undercuts the racism of the message: James concludes that "the heathen Chinee is peculiar," a hesitant assertion that he feels compelled to defend. The lines paraphrased by Dougherty read:

> Which I wish to remark—
>   And my language is plain—
> That for ways that are dark
>   And for tricks that are vain,
> The heathen Chinee is peculiar:
>   Which the same I would rise to explain [Harte 131].

Adopting the "plain talk" and truthfulness, though not quite the pathos, of Harte's protagonist, Dougherty re-asserted his responsibility as a relentless muckraker: "He has ducked and prolonged a conference at the Commonwealth, hoping we'd go to press without knowing whether he had stopped singing the blues. No use, brother."[16]

8. The Dean's Demise

While Dougherty continued to endorse the McMahons and their boxing cards throughout the decade, his animosity towards Posey faded a bit over the years. In Rob Ruck's authoritative history of African American sports in Pittsburgh, *Sandlot Seasons*, he quotes a much later column of Dougherty's as evidence that "the dean of black American sportswriters ... never tired of writing of Posey's era and exploits" (Ruck 127). Even in the passage Ruck cites, however, Dougherty mentions Posey's great basketball clubs and several players (including Posey's brother, Seward), but not Cum Posey himself. The column ran in the *Pittsburgh Courier* in 1943, late in Dougherty's life, after an acrimonious split with the *Amsterdam*. By then, Dougherty had grown nostalgic and resigned to the conclusion that profiteering and professionalism had a stranglehold on sports and entertainment.

Dougherty aimed in all his endeavors to exhort African Americans to support and produce their own entertainment. Undoubtedly, he could be self-serving and self-righteous in those exhortations. Still, while few intellectuals of the era recognized sports as a cultural institution, some of the leading critics of the Renaissance shared Dougherty's views regarding the popular theatre. Dougherty had a noteworthy ally in the drama critic Theophilus Lewis, who wrote a monthly column in the *Messenger*. Lewis not only shared Dougherty's viewpoint but also endorsed and recommended him to his readers, from whom he commanded considerable respect. According to Theodore Kornweibel, the younger artists and writers of the Renaissance considered Lewis "the only drama critic they could take seriously" (Kornweibel 109).

Lewis called Dougherty the best theatre critic in the African American press and claimed credit for nicknaming him the "Dean" (Lewis, "New" 10). Lewis had taken only Dougherty's writing into account when originally anointing him, however: In his column of January 1927, he noted that he had recently become aware of Dougherty's promotional efforts as well. Calling him a "journalistic wet nurse to almost a tenth of the colored theatrical profession," Lewis noted that Dougherty also served as a "friend, helper and adviser of scores of colored actors and athletes." This discovery carried great weight for Lewis, who had been calling for a national black theatre. Until more African American playwrights and capital in the community emerged, Lewis believed popular performers would have to be the lifeblood of such a movement (Kornweibel 109–110).

Despite their common social interests, Lewis insisted he admired

Dougherty's aesthetics most of all. "The distinguishing marks of Mr. Dougherty's writing," he declared, "are his sincerity and simplicity of expression" (Lewis, "New" 10). Given the meandering nature of most of Dougherty's prose, Lewis must have been referring to simplicity of content rather than style. In Lewis's emphasis on Dougherty's sincerity, his opposition to cynicism and support for certain causes, a social critique becomes clear. Aesthetics are important, but the promotion of a socially engaged artistic expression trumps all. In the end, these attributes place Dougherty in opposition to "the decadent intellectuals of Greenwich Village."

Dougherty's position, described and endorsed by Lewis, smacks of bourgeois rectitude and self-satisfaction, but his sense of purpose—in the context of the times—cannot be easily dismissed. Consistently, whether writing on the theatre or sports, Dougherty emphasized the advancement of the race. And the publications that printed his exhortations burnished his creditability, if only by association: the *Crusader* and the early *Amsterdam*, like the *Messenger*, were hardly middlebrow magazines, and Dougherty's flirtation with Garveyism attests to his disinterest in mainstream, white acceptance. The community and the race always took precedence in Dougherty's work; as Lewis observed, "his interest seldom wanders south of 125th Street" (Lewis, "New" 10). Far from being provincial, however, Dougherty's single-minded vision impressed Lewis as an act of resistance. Such a spirit of self-determination, Lewis argued, transformed Dougherty's apparently moralistic approach to racial "uplift" into a kind of black aesthetic:

> [Dougherty] knows, too, that the Negro Theatre cannot be stimulated from the outside and that the most white people can do is not put any barriers in its way. The barriers which have already been erected he is unremittingly laboring to break down. This, I say not as a moralist, but as a man who loves beauty, is a more wholesome esthetic creed than has ever been expressed by all the intellectuals put together [Lewis, "New" 10].

In Lewis's view, Dougherty's promotion of the popular arts helped define and advocate specifically African American institutions. Dougherty never elucidated this theory to the same extent, though he considered his work serious business. Dougherty, in his self-styled role (Lewis defended him by observing that "all leaders are self-appointed"), not only shone a light on products of popular culture; he also tried to imbue African American performers, like sportswriters, with a seriousness he believed they lacked.

In "The Negro and the Theatre," Dougherty laid out his own theory on race and popular entertainment. Again, he expressed scorn for African Americans who failed to support entertainment produced by and in the community, especially attacking investors who profited from such ventures but ignored their social responsibilities. In most instances of investment in the theatre, Dougherty argued, "it has been with the same tendency of simply making money without the urge for the advancement of the race along this line of necessary human endeavor" ("The Negro," 213). While his thesis regarding the "necessity" of the theatre in society could be simplistic and proscriptive, calling for "comedy of a clean and wholesome nature," Dougherty emphasized wider opportunities for performers above all else. The moral importance of drama, Dougherty argued, lay in its ability to depict opportunities and "lend inspiration to the efforts of our people in all walks of life," but he considered the cultural significance of the entertainment industry to be broader than that. The relationship between performers and the people was intrinsic to the community, and therefore needed to be consciously cultivated. "In Negro communities," he concluded, "the little Theatre is a necessity" (216).

Dougherty encouraged greater appreciation of the theatre not only to edify the audience, but also to expand the race's roster of performers and artists. As Ted Vincent points out, Dougherty intertwined his advocacies of the "serious" and "popular" theatres:

> He championed Black dramatic productions, first because he felt African America deserved drama, and second, because he felt it essential to the reputation of the blues and the comedy-based musical revues that light entertainment be reinforced by evidence of ability in serious art forms such as drama and concert music [Vincent, *Keep* 82].

Noting the lack of African American producers (and financial capital) in the Depression years, Dougherty decried the failure of black businessmen to build upon the visibility of African American stage performers in the heyday of the Renaissance. Dougherty's analysis here was decidedly pessimistic, however, especially when contrasted with the impassioned attack on professionalism in sports he had published in the *Crusader* fifteen years earlier. Recognizing the attempts of the African American-owned Quality Amusement Corporation to stage dramatic shows, Dougherty remarked bluntly that "it did not take long for them to be washed up upon the sands of disaster" (214). He sadly referred to himself as "one who in early life believed and hoped that at this time a larger number of Negro performers would be enjoying a more secure place" (213).

Dougherty published "The Negro and the Theatre" in 1936, soon after his attempts to promote both activism and business had proved untenable. When the New York newspaper guild attempted to unionize the *Amsterdam* in 1935, Dougherty, by then the paper's general manager, stood firmly with management. The newspaper, he argued with some validity, had done more for the community than had labor unions. In the midst of the Depression, the Harlem community turned against the *Amsterdam* and Dougherty in favor of the union and its president, Heywood Broun, a longtime supporter of African American causes—including Negro League baseball. After a three-month standoff, the paper was sold and Dougherty was dismissed. The paper's staff walked out for three months after its publisher, Sadie Warren Davis, refused to deal with the union. The *Amsterdam* suffered significantly during the walkout, and Davis sold the paper to two Harlem doctors, C.B. Powell and P.M.H. Savory, in January 1936. The Powell-Savory Corporation came to terms with the union and quickly promoted the *Amsterdam* as a labor-friendly paper. In a front-page sign-off, Dougherty thanked the 5,000 readers who had "rejoined The Amsterdam News family of readers" after the paper rescinded a strike-induced, five-cent price increase. Personalizing the situation, Dougherty continued: "No man enjoys the loss of friends it has taken years to draw to him. Never does a man rise so high nor become so mighty that he cannot be stung to his heart by the lowliest of his friends who turn from him" (Dougherty, "Appreciation" 1).

This outcome stood in stark contrast to the triumphant position Dougherty had claimed a decade earlier. In 1926, he inserted himself into a labor dispute involving the motion picture operators at the Harlem theatres and took credit for forcing the union to integrate. That strike threatened to shut down the Harlem theatres, which had grown reliant on motion pictures to subsidize their dwindling number of dramatic productions. Along with Dougherty, the cultural critic Harold Cruse later observed, "several spokesmen from other levels of Harlem life joined in what was to become one of the most significant controversies ever to arise in this community" (Cruse 74). Assessing the conflict a generation later, Cruse argued that the strike "glaringly revealed the inexperience, the incompetence, the backwardness—but at the same time the eagerness and the militancy—of the young Harlem Communist leftwing" (75). Complicating matters further, Cruse has been accused of having an anti–Caribbean bias: For example, he counters his critique of the Caribbean radicals with praise for Edgar Grey, who reported on the strike for the *Amsterdam*; Grey, however, was also of Caribbean origin and had formerly been an assistant to Harrison (James, *Holding* 162). As a result, Winston James argues, Cruse "inevitably gets tangled up into some very uncomfortable knots" (*Holding* 268). In 1972, C.L.R. James more harshly accused Cruse of bigotry: "My objection to Cruse's book is that he doesn't like West Indians, he doesn't like Jews, he doesn't like too many people" (qtd. in James, *Holding* 291).

By the time of the strike, Dougherty had largely detached himself from Harlem's radical left, and in fact his position was a slippery one: Not only did he cover the theatres being struck, but he had also worked with one of the theatres as a booking agent for the Lincoln Motion Picture Company (Bowser and Spence 74). The Lincoln criticized Dougherty's connections in its newspaper advertisements, though he claimed objectivity when the theatre's management avoided the strike by agreeing to a contract with its projectionists (Dougherty, "Will the Operators" 10). The Lafayette Theatre—Harlem's largest venue—became the focal point of the dispute, which ended with the union integrating but failing to gain most of its demands. In the course of the strike, Dougherty essentially worked for all the interested parties, arguing that his primary obligation was "to take the side of the matter that would help our boys."[17] Dougherty took the same position in the two labor disputes that his fellow Virgin Islander, Hubert Harrison, had taken in his tenure as the editor of Garvey's *Negro World*. In choosing to stay with Garvey's nationalist movement rather than follow Cyril Briggs, W.A. Domingo, and other socialists into the Communist Party, Harrison famously pointed out that his primary devotion, as opposed to Abraham Lincoln's, was to saving his race and not the union. (After breaking his own ties with Garvey, Harrison continued to focus on racial equality as well as economic revolution, founding the International Colored Unity League in 1924.)

In 1944, Dougherty died at his home on Long Island at the age of fifty-nine, largely forgotten. Still, his obituary in the *Amsterdam* ran on the front page, as it did in the *Age*. The *Amsterdam* recalled Dougherty's popularity, power, and intellectual prowess (his private library was said to have held more than 2,500 volumes); the sub-heading declared: "Poet and Philosopher, Once Amsterdam News Writer Was Well Known." A story in his former paper the following week summarized Dougherty's declining fame and influence:

> The once famous journalist of Harlem whose prolific pen was a mighty power in wielding his ideals in the principles of Democracy for his race was an important factor during his time. But in latter years since his termination with the Amsterdam News, Mr. Dougherty unfortunately was unable to find himself, and obviously lived in a life of obscurity, and his pen was dormant [Snelson 16A].

That Dougherty's heavy-handed role in a labor dispute precipitated his descent into obscurity would have come as a surprise to those who read his columns when he was connected with radical positions and publications a generation earlier. In the course of his career, Dougherty argued intermittently for labor and management, integration and separatism. Perhaps these apparent contradictions reflect a less sophisticated political outlook than those of radicals such as Harrison. But in his steadfast attention to race and unwavering defense of the transformative power of popular culture—especially sports—Dougherty left a distinctive and indelible mark as the primary voice in the sports pages of the Renaissance press.

Epilogue
Arna Bontemps, Sterling Brown and the End of an Era

While the economic onslaught of the Great Depression undoubtedly hastened the demise of the Harlem Renaissance, critics disagree on the exact end date. In his introduction to recent critical anthology, Jeffrey O.G. Ogbar declares that the Renaissance began amid the race riots of 1919 and "the Great Depression and the Harlem riot of 1935 brought an end to it" (Ogbar 2). Ogbar's demarcation echoes that of David Levering Lewis, who identifies "three stages" of the Renaissance, with the riot of 1935 delivering the final blow (Lewis, *Portable* xv). That date differs slightly from the one Lewis uses in *When Harlem Was in Vogue*, where he describes the movement's "sputtering end in 1934, with the Great Depression deaths of two principals": Wallace Thurman and the writer/physician Rudolph Fisher (Lewis, *When Harlem* xxviii). In the seminal *Norton Anthology of African American Literature*, Henry Louis Gates, Jr., and his co-editors define the end date of Renaissance as 1940, though they concede that by the publication of Zora Neale Hurston's *Their Eyes Were Watching God* in 1937, "the movement was absolutely finished" (Gates et al., *Norton* 936).

In *Figures in Black*, however, Gates asserts that the publication of Sterling Brown's *Southern Road* in 1932 ended the movement, "for that slim book undermined all of the New Negro's assumption about the nature of the black tradition and its relation to individual talent" (Gates, *Figures* 227). In Gates's view, Brown's collection of poems marked a departure from the sensibility that had made Harlem the putative center of African American culture and also from the idea that the black poet needed to choose between vernacular, folk forms and the Anglo-American tradition. Gates argues that Brown "transcended" the vernacular tradition, while Langston Hughes, for example, "seemed content to transcribe the popular structures he received" (*Figures* 228). Gates declares: "[Brown's] language, densely symbolic, ironical, and naturally indirect, draws upon the idioms, figures, and tones of both the sacred and the profane vernacular traditions, mediating between these in a manner unmatched before or since" (227–28).

Brown, who argued for the inclusion of athletics among the arts, pointed out their comparable importance in the fight for integration. Moreover, Brown's interest in folk culture and regional traditions caused him to reject the name "Harlem Renaissance" altogether. "The New Negro," Brown observed, "has temporal roots in the past and spatial roots elsewhere in America, and the term has validity, it seems to me, only when considered to be a continuing tradition" (as qtd. by Singh, *Novels* 3). While terms such as the "New Negro" and the "Negro Renaissance"—first used in the late-nineteenth century—gained wide use during and after the Great Migration of the 1910s, the appellation "Harlem Renaissance" was apparently coined by the New York *Herald Tribune* in 1925 (Lewis, *When Harlem* 116).

Arna Bontemps, like Brown, has been credited with having an indirect hand in bringing the era to a close. Bontemps recalled that as early as 1931, when he was honored with a reception in Harlem after publishing his first novel, he "couldn't help thinking of legendary people of antiquity pleasuring themselves and celebrating as their cities were about to be destroyed" ("Awakening" 26). Brown seconded this notion in the anthology *The Negro Caravan* (1941), describing Bontemps's role in the Renaissance: "[H]e contributed to it the book that marked the end of that period: *God Sends Sunday*" (254).

The Renaissance itself seemed almost illusory and unreal to Bontemps. "Within a year I was far away," he wrote of that 1931 reception in Harlem. "The golden days were gone" ("Awakening" 26). His belief in the social significance of sports persisted throughout his life, however, finding form in a book for children, *Famous Negro Athletes* (1963). The publisher, Dodd, Mead and Company, first proposed the *Famous Negro Athletes* project to Langston Hughes, who had written three previous volumes in the "Famous Negroes" series. Hughes wrote to Bontemps: "Allen Klots phoned today to discuss a possible Famous Negro Athletes for their young folks Famous series. The subject is not down my alley, but I told him of your long interest in sports from the jockeys at the turn of the century through the boxers of the twenties up to current baseball" (*Arna Bontemps-Langston Hughes Letters* 384). Bontemps and Hughes also collaborated on an anthology, *The Poetry of the Negro, 1746–1949*, which included two poems by the former track star Henry Binga Dismond. As a medical student at the University of Chicago, Dismond had matched the American record in the quarter-mile and made the U.S. Olympic team; he later became a physician at Harlem Hospital.

Brown and Bontemps share more than an overlapping history as young writers whose early works are considered final gestures of a waning artistic era. Although both saw the Harlem Renaissance, in Bontemps's words, "from a grandstand seat" (*Negro Caravan* 254), they also took the lead in expanding the scope of African American literature to include a wider range of subject matter, including sports and the sometimes unsavory world in which they exist. While Brown sketched portraits of unstudied—and often unsavory—characters in his poem cycle *Southern Road*, Bontemps's debut, *God Sends Sunday*, broke ground by depicting the world of sports and sportsmen, following the rise and fall of a jockey. Brown praised Bontemps's novel as "an accurate picture of sporting life" (Fleming 85).

In *God Sends Sunday*, Bontemps followed the lead of Claude McKay, painting a picture of a world that some critics found garish and primitive. Du Bois, the leading voice among the novels' detractors, called the book "a profound disappointment" (Review 304). Decrying the author's lack of gentility in much the same way he had criticized McKay's *Home to Harlem*, Du Bois said of Bontemps's work: "There is a certain pathetic touch to the painting of his poor little jockey hero, but nearly all else is sordid crime, drinking, gambling, whore-mongering, and murder.... In the 'Blues' alone Bontemps sees beauty" (304). Few critics agreed with Du Bois, however. Bontemps's novel received generally laudatory reviews and the Writer's Guild feted the author with the "glittering reception in Harlem" that he later described in his memoir (Bontemps, "Awakening" 26). The *New York Times* praised the novel, while Gwendolyn B. Bennett, writing in the *New York Herald-Tribune*, commended Bontemps's devotion to art rather than to "propaganda" (as qtd. by Fleming 80).

Unquestionably, Bontemps saturates the life led by the novel's protagonist, Little Augie, with decadence and punctuates it with brutality: Augie drinks to dissipation and flaunts his success by wearing expensive clothes; in turn, these displays help him attract "fast" women, with whom he shares intimacy only through physical violence. Unlike McKay, however, Bontemps "shows little interest in using primitivism to define ethnic identity" (Singh, *Novels* 56). Instead, according to Amritjit Singh, the novel represents Bontemps's "simple identification with black folk"—a rendering of traditional morals and manners as he saw them in the rural South, devoid of either explicit or implied comment. Bontemps later recalled that his father, who had moved his family from Louisiana to southern California when Bontemps was three years old, disapproved of the book on the same terms as Du Bois, "and I, in my exhilaration, was convinced that neither quite understood" (Bontemps, "Awakening" 26).

Much of *God Sends Sunday* revolves around Augie's early successes and later failures as a jockey, which he believes are determined by chance rather than by competition. Although Augie possesses the right size and skill to become a top rider, he considers folkloric omens the source of his fortune. Augie was born with a caul, signaling his inherent good luck; as a consequence, the narrator tells us, Augie "believed in conjure and 'signs'" (*GSS* 10). Several critics have traced the connections between the folk traditions in the novel and those Bontemps describes in another autobiographical essay, "Why I Returned." In the essay, Bontemps recalls his Uncle Buddy, who was his model for Lil Augie. Bontemps's uncle "likely enlightened the young Bontemps about the sporting life," according to Lisa Abney, who explains Bontemps's references to games and beliefs specific to the Louisiana "sporting subculture" (Abney 89 and *passim*). Abney notes that the novel "documents the many recreational and occupational cultural traditions of this group" (93 fn4). In this regard, Augie seems hardly unusual in his world, a folk culture that Bontemps depicts as neither magical nor uncivilized.

The milieu of the novel is that of "sports," with all the term's connotations. Bontemps, like McKay and other Renaissance writers, uses "sports" in reference to both athletes and gamblers. Augie, for example, "decided to identify himself exclusively with a fancier crowd—macks, pimps, gamblers, prize-fighters, and other jockeys like himself" (*GSS* 26). "Sport," in this context, could also refer to a dandy, though in a hyper-masculine rather than an effeminate way. In the Renaissance era (and in African American culture for several decades preceding), the word more generally connoted gambling, prostitution, and, by extension, jazz: Louis Armstrong called bordellos "sportin' houses," according to Jack Schiffman in *Harlem Heyday* (49); Jelly Roll Morton's jazz was called "sporting house music." In his autobiographical essay, Bontemps specifically recalled hearing Morton, by then widely famous and playing in public dancehalls, in Los Angeles in the early 1920s ("Awakening" 7–8).

In both the rural fairs and the city streets, "rounders and sports" populate the novel (*GSS* 27). These characters live on the edge—often between life and death—just as they are on those margins of society in spite of occasional wealth and fame. Augie remains on the margins even when he moves from the rural South to cities where he races and, eventually, to the outskirts of Los Angeles, where he takes refuge with his sister. Even in St. Louis, the city with "the glowing reputation of capital of the Negro sporting wheel," Augie's awareness of the capriciousness of success tempers his contentment (*GSS* 52). He yearns to get back on the road, though no one destination—not even Harlem—specifically attracts him:

> He looked forward to the many races he would ride on Churchill Downs, to those in Mobile and New Orleans, and to the vague uncertain ones in New York and Maryland. But it was not so much the actual racing he craved as the unbroken companionship of the horses. Life as he had experienced it in St. Louis was much too complicated for his taste. It was like trying to puzzle out a combination lock [*GSS* 92].

Horse racing, even at the most prestigious tracks, offers Augie sanctuary from the strangeness of the city. Breaking ranks with many Renaissance writers (and American culture at large), Bontemps chooses not to depict urban modernity as "faster" than the slow, languorous South: Augie, after all, prefers the fast pace of nightlife and the track. Similarly, Bontemps resists the simple dichotomy of civilization and nature, with the latter embodied by horses. Augie seeks "unbroken companionship"—a society in which traditions remain uncomplicated—just as he prefers his superstitions unquestioned and his farewells unsaid.

While Bontemps rejects certain Renaissance notions about the city and the South, his hero's quest and artistry render *God Sends Sunday* a distinctly modernist work. Certain aspects of Augie's quest, particularly his desire for "self-respect and, in turn, wholeness," can be placed in a long tradition of African American literature (Abney 88). Augie's fascination with speed, however, complicates the novel's approach to modernity. At the end of the book, Augie leaves his sister's house, hopping a freight train bound for Tijuana, where he has heard that horse racing and liquor were to be found (197). Although aging and alcoholic, with his fine clothes tattered and his beloved Prince Albert coat left behind, he feels vital again: "A strangely familiar feeling of exhilaration came to Augie, an illusion that came with speed" (199). Despite the illusory, even pathetic nature of this final venture, the "thrill" of the race revives Augie's will to suspend disbelief.

Epilogue

A year after the publication of *God Sends Sunday,* Brown published his poem cycle *Southern Road*. Brown, who called Bontemps's novel "a well-done portrait of a winning character," expanded the range of subjects in African American literature further by including similar slices of life among his own "portraitures" (Brown, *Negro in American Fiction* 155). Working in the wider wake of James Weldon Johnson's exploration of African American cultural history in *Black Manhattan*, Brown drew attention to subcultures in both rural folk and urban Bohemian settings in his sketches of unstudied "sporting life."

One of Brown's "sports," the title character of "Sporting Beasley," bears resemblance to Bontemps's Augie—right down to his Prince Albert coat. Like Augie, Beasley stirs sympathy despite his ridiculous self-grandeur:

> Good glory, give a look at Sporting Beasley
> Strutting, oh my Lord.
>   Tophat cocked one side his bulldog head,
>   Striped four-in-hand, and in his buttonhole
>   A red carnation; Prince Albert coat
>   Form fitting, corset like; vest snugly filled,
>   Gray morning trousers, spotless and full-flowing,
>   White spats and a cane.
> Step it, Mr. Beasley, oh step it till the sun goes down.
> [Brown, "Sporting" 1224]

While Beasley's outfit brands him both out of touch and out of date, he also represents the "resilience, strength, and perseverance that sustained previous generations" (Sanders 77). The speaker, aware of the anachronism, not only urges Beasley (respectfully calling him "Mister") to continue strutting "until the sun goes down," but he also ends the poem by asking God to let Beasley wear his spats and cane in heaven ("Sporting" 1225). Mark A. Sanders reads the poem as a confirmation of the sporting man's agency:

> His clothes, emblems of pride and resilience, provide him with his only avenue toward self-affirmation. In a cultural tradition that insists on his absence, his spats and cane confirm presence. In the tradition of cultural heroes, though Beasley represents one of the smaller personal gains, he reveals simply a modicum of agency with a hope for restitution in the next life [Sanders 77].

Beasley's status as a "cultural hero," however minor, encapsulates the significance of *Southern Road* to the culminating years of the Renaissance. Brown emphasizes the agency and humanity of Bohemians and other outcasts in his poems. In later years, he would do the same for sports and athletes, defending their distinctive cultural contributions rather than their shallow status as celebrities.

Brown demonstrated an interest in sports throughout his life. In the early 1920s, he played tennis as an undergraduate at Williams College, where he "learned to drive" (serve and volley) at college after playing "the scrambling game" on the playgrounds in Washington, D.C. (Brown, "A Son's Return" 10). Brown's doubles partner was the sociologist Allison Davis (he played first singles as well). In the early 1940s, he proposed an ambitious history of "The Negro in American Culture" as part of the Carnegie-Myrdal research project that resulted in *An American Dilemma* (1944). Brown devoted the first section of his study to sports, outlining seven specific chapters, devoted respectively to pugilism, baseball, football, track, basketball, tennis, and "others."[1] Brown completed only three chapters (pugilism, baseball, and, perhaps following his own personal preference, tennis) before apparently turning to more pressing subjects. None of his sports research found its way into the final study.

In 1951, Brown responded by arguing for the inclusion of sports in such studies. In "Athletics and the Arts," he examined the progress of integration in American society and suggested sports deserved equal status with the arts. Assessing the progress and effects of integration in sports, jazz, concert music, dance, art, drama, motion pictures, and literature, he asserted: "All of these stories are of significance to the student of American culture" (Brown, "Athletics" 99). Defining the goals of integration, Brown called for equal opportunity to be judged on one's abilities:

> The integration of the Negro athlete or artist means his acceptance as an individual to be judged on his own merits, with no favor granted, and no fault found, because of race. It means that, whether second-baseman or pugilist, jazz trumpeter or concert singer, poet or painter, the Negro will be judged evenly, neither over-rigorously nor over-gently, according to the standards of his calling [99].

Although Brown's emphasis on merits is at the heart of the complaints by some contemporary critics that popular culture rewards African Americans more for natural talents than intellectual achievement, the arc of his essay aims to bridge the gap between sports and literature. "This subject is a Goliath," Brown admits, "and I am not sure that my slingshot can bring it down" (99). Rather than concentrate on sheer feats of physical prowess, Brown analyzes the social effects of integration in sports. He concludes that the political ideals of citizenship may be highlighted by the achievements of athletes and artists but that they are unlikely to achieve "full integration in American culture" until the social ideal becomes a reality (135).

Brown's essay, appearing four years after Jackie Robinson broke baseball's color line, concentrates heavily on baseball. Despite his obvious enthusiasm about Robinson's achievement, Brown resists the notion that integration in sports would "lead the way" to social equality or even that baseball could be considered a "mirror," reflecting the changing structure of society. Brown understood that social change would be more complex and difficult than that. However, just as he argued for a broader, continuing conception of the New Negro Renaissance than one restricted to Harlem and the 1920s, Brown called for the inclusion of sports in a broad-based idea of culture that would, in turn, include all the complexities and elements of African American life.

This integration of athletics and the arts—celebrated by Bontemps and summoned by Brown—was acknowledged in the later years of the Renaissance by figures such as Langston Hughes and James Weldon Johnson, but it had been already been explored in the sporting pages of the Harlem press. Even as Bontemps and Brown helped to deliver the final blows to the movement, they recognized and nurtured what the sportswriters of the Renaissance organically knew: that writing and sports, like literature and popular culture, were intrinsically linked rather than diametrically opposed. The cultural contradictions that would need to be negotiated in later years were forged by writers who drew abounding energy and saw little distinction between high and low. As Renaissance Men, they represented Harlem's full range of culture on its most unlikely canvas: the newspaper's sports page.

Chapter Notes

Introduction

1. The poem was reprinted later that year in Frederick G. Detweiler's *The Negro Press in the United States* as part of a series of passages that demonstrated the sports coverage in the black press (Detweiler 234).
2. *New York News*, 14 April 1921 (as qtd. by Singer, 67–68).
3. Chicago *Defender* 21 March 1921: 1.
4. Lewis says further of *The Crisis*: "In an era of rampant illiteracy, when hard labor left Afro-Americans little time or inclination for reading Harvard-accented editorials, the magazine found its way into kerosene-lit sharecroppers' cabins and cramped factory workers' tenements" (*When Harlem* 7).
5. In the biographical notes to *American Negro Poetry* (New York: Hill and Wang, 1963), Arna Bontemps writes that Allen was "discovered" by Wright, who helped him publish his poems in France (187). Robert Hayden quotes much of the same information provided by Bontemps in his own biography of Allen in *Kaleidoscope: Poems by American Negro Poets* (New York: Harcourt, Brace, and World: 1967).

Chapter 1

1. See Du Bois and Guy B. Johnson, *Encyclopedia of the Negro: Preparatory Volume with Reference Lists and Reports,* 2nd ed. (New York: 1946). The *Encyclopedia* project, conceived by Du Bois in 1901, was to be funded by the Phelps-Stokes Fund but was doomed by disagreements over the makeup of its editorial board. The funding eventually went to the Carnegie-Myrdal study that resulted in *An American Dilemma* in 1944 (Gates, "W.E.B. Du Bois" 204; Lewis, *W.E.B. Du Bois*, II, 427–53).

Chapter 2

1. In a speech at Williams in 1973, Brown recalled: "Allison Davis and I were the Commons Club's doubles team, and we were pretty good" (Brown, "A Son's Return," 10).
2. The 119-page memorandum is part of the Carnegie/Myrdal Collection, Schomburg Center for Research in Black Culture. In *American Dilemma*, the conclusions of Frazier's study are summarized in four pages (982–986). Frazier condensed the findings of his research even more briefly, in one page, in his textbook *The Negro in the United States* (1949).
3. Statistics reflect the salaries of teachers in public schools in southern states (including Maryland and Missouri) and the District of Columbia. According to Tuskegee's *Negro Year Book* (1931–32), statistics from the era are not available for northern states because they did not officially maintain separate schools and salaries (203).
4. Lester's *Rube Foster in His Time* (Jefferson, NC: McFarland, 2012) is an authoritative biography that uses a "hybrid" method of embedding Foster's writings (along with other documents and records) into the text.

Chapter 3

1. For further discussion on Johnson and interracial audiences at sporting events, see below.

2. In *Death in the Afternoon*, Hemingway specifically compares a matador to the former major-league pitcher Nick Altrock, who had become famous as a clown in ballparks and on the vaudeville stage: "Martin Aguero ... was a boy from Bilbao who did not look like a bullfighter at all but more like a husky, well-built, professional ballplayer, a third baseman or shortstop. He had a full-lipped face, German-American looking in the sense that Nick Altrock's was..." (Hemingway 258). Although the reference is brief, Hemingway repeats it later (Hemingway 276). Miriam B. Mandel considers the connection between Aguero and Altrock to be significant, as it alludes to Hemingway's interest in clowns throughout the book and also in several of his novels. In addition to his descriptions of the clowns, or mojigangas, who perform central roles in bullfights in the manner of American rodeo clowns, Hemingway also devotes much of the book to a discussion of bullfighting as comedy and tragedy. Ultimately, he asserts, these aspects make bullfighting more a theatrical performance than a sport: "The bullfight is not a sport in the Anglo-Saxon sense of the word, that is, it is not an equal contest or an attempt at an equal contest between a bull and a man. Rather it is a tragedy; the death of the bull, which is played, more or less well, by the bull and the man involved and in which there is danger for the man but certain death for the animal" (Hemingway 16). Mandel also points out that Hemingway describes the bullfighter Luis Freg by noting that Freg had been "a full matador in Mexico since Johnson fought Jeffries at Reno, Nevada, in 1910" (Hemingway 263). This "seemingly irrelevant" comparison carries weight because Freg's popularity was, like Johnson's, racially controversial, "both in Mexico (because Freg was an Indian) and in Spain (because Freg was Mexican)" (Mandel 154).

3. Novak, examining sports within the context of American philosophical and religious traditions, defines baseball as the fulfillment of a white myth, while assigning basketball the same role for African Americans and football for European immigrants. He traces baseball's WASP character through such familiar metaphors as its preponderance of numbers and rules, which expand into capitalist ethics (bookkeeping) and Christian symbology ("a gentle Trinitarian mysticism"), as well as its rural, pastoral qualities. Ultimately, it is the individualist nature of baseball that Novak describes as white, Anglo-Saxon, and Protestant—in contrast to what he calls the corporate character of football and the communality of basketball (58–60). But while Novak points out that "anthropological details" suggest that non-white, non-Protestant cultures—he analyzes the French at length—are not disposed towards baseball, he accounts for the game's popularity in Latin America and the Pacific Rim by noting that "*anyone* can learn to operate within the Anglo-Saxon mythic world" (60–61; emphasis in original). The game's appeal, for Novak, lies in its formality, and he compares it to bullfighting in this regard. "Those who appreciate the rules and formality of the bull ring and the toreadors," he notes, "can see how Latins would like the order and the nerve called upon in baseball, and similarly with the Japanese" (61).

Chapter 4

1. Schuyler, incidentally, was a finalist for that year's Harmon Award for Literature, for which Johnson was a judge. *Chicago Defender* sportswriter Frank A. Young was also a candidate, though his sportswriting was not mentioned in his dossier (James Weldon Johnson Papers; subsequent references to the collection will be cited as JWJP).

2. *New York Age*, 21 June 1930, 6.

3. This correspondence is in Box 7 of the James Weldon Johnson papers at Yale University.

4. *New York Age*, 31 July 1920, 4. Johnson's "Views and Reviews" column in the *Age* ran weekly on page four, with that title as its headline. All references hereafter will indicate only the date of publication.

5. To avoid confusion with Jack Johnson, I will refer to "Weldon Johnson" here.

6. *New York Age*, 18 April 1915.

7. *New York Age*, 12 July 1919.
8. *New York Age*, 24 June 1915.
9. *New York Age*, 24 June 1915.
10. *New York Age*, 11 March 1922.
11. *New York Age*, 31 July 1920.
12. New York Age, 17 February 1923.
13. *New York Age*, 30 November 1930.
14. *New York Age*, 24 July 1920.
15. *New York Age*, 7 August 1920.
16. *New York Age,* 12 October 1920.
17. *New York Age,* 22 November 1919.
18. Among the AfricanAmerican intellectuals, Du Bois and Claude McKay were the most outspoken critics of *Negro Americans, What Now?* (Levy 340–46). Du Bois, like Johnson, had recently resigned from the NAACP, though under more contentious circumstances. McKay was generally critical of the organization, whose officials he described as "the more conservative Negro leaders" (*A Long Way* 109). Still, McKay admired Johnson and considered him a man of "real sophistication," even though the two "differed profoundly" on some issues (Cooper, *Claude McKay* 337). Although Johnson "felt that McKay had unfairly disparaged the black middle class," he was a lifelong supporter and had been one of the few established African American intellectuals to defend *Home to Harlem* (Cooper, *Passion* 32–33).

Chapter 6

1. *Amsterdam News*, 30 October 1929, 12. (Newspaper articles that appeared under the same standing title will be cited hereafter by date and page number only.)
2. *New York Age*, 15 November 1930, 6.
3. *Interstate-Tattler*, 9 December 1927, 3.
4. *Baltimore Afro-American*, 8 February 1930.
5. *Interstate-Tattler*, 15 November 1929, 12.
6. *Interstate-Tattler*, 28 June 1929, 13.
7. *Interstate-Tattler*, 18 February 1932.
8. *Interstate-Tattler*, 16 January 1931, 8.
9. *Interstate-Tattler*, 24 March 1932, 16.
10. *Interstate-Tattler*, 12 March 1927, 11.
11. *Pittsburgh Courier*, 12 March 1927.
12. *Amsterdam News*, 23 April 1930.
13. *Amsterdam News*, 16 April 1930, 17.
14. *New York Age*, 27 December 1930, 6.
15. *Amsterdam News*, 23 April 1930.
16. *Amsterdam News*, 9 July 1930, 19.
17. *Amsterdam News*, 11 June 1930, 17.
18. *Amsterdam News*, 9 July 1930, 19.
19. *Amsterdam News*, 18 December 1929.

Chapter 7

1. *Amsterdam News*, 18 March 1925, 5.
2. The seven chapters of *Punta, Revolutionist* ran in the *Crusader* from January through April, in July, and in September and October. References here will indicate the chapter and page number.
3. C.L.R. James confirms the popularity of these writers in the Caribbean at the time. In *Beyond a Boundary*, he also mentions Garvice, who wrote children's books, and "a woman called Mrs. E.D.E.N. Southworth" among the writers read by his mother (James, *Beyond* 26). Her "taste in novels was indiscriminate," a predilection she passed along to the young James.
4. *Amsterdam News*, 23 February 1923, 5.

Chapter 8

1. *Billboard*, 6 August 1921, 64.
2. *Amsterdam News*, 20 May 1925, 6.
3. *Amsterdam News*, 20 May 1925, 6.
4. *Amsterdam News*, 11 March 1925, 5.
5. *Amsterdam News*, 4 February 1925, 5.
6. *Amsterdam News*, 17 January 1923.
7. *Amsterdam News*, 21 February 1923, 5.
8. *Amsterdam News*, 7 March 1923, 4.
9. *Amsterdam News*, 10 January 1923, 4.
10. *Amsterdam News*, 4 February 1925, 5.
11. *Amsterdam News*, 18 March 1925, 5. On the Wills-Dempsey controversy, see also Chapter 4.
12. *Amsterdam News*, 7 March 1923, 4.
13. *Amsterdam News*, 14 February 1923, 4.
14. *Amsterdam News*, 14 February 1923, 4
15. *Amsterdam News*, 21 February 1923, 4.
16. *Amsterdam News*, 7 March 1923, 4.
17. *Amsterdam News*, 8 September 1926, 10.

Epilogue

1. Brown's drafts are held in the Carnegie/Myrdal Collection at the Schomburg Center for Research in Black Culture, New York Public Library.

Bibliography

Archives, Exhibitions, & Special Collections

Andy Razaf Papers. Schomburg Center for Research in Black Culture, New York Public Library.
"Black Fives" (exhibition). New-York Historical Society Museum and Library. 14 March–20 July 2014. http://www.blackfives.org/exhibition/
Carnegie/Myrdal Collection. Schomburg Center for Research in Black Culture, New York Public Library.
Federal Writers Project Research File. Schomburg Center for Research in Black Culture, New York Public Library.
Rube Foster Player File. Giamatti Library and Research Center, Cooperstown, N.Y.
James Weldon Johnson Papers. James Weldon Johnson Collection, Beinecke Rare Book and Manuscript Library, Yale University.

Periodicals

Amsterdam News (New York)
Billboard (New York)
Chicago Defender
Crisis (New York)
Crusader (New York)
Interstate-Tattler (New York)
Messenger (New York)
Negro World (New York)
New York Age
New York News
New York Times
Opportunity (New York)
Phylon (Atlanta)
Pittsburgh Courier

Books and Articles

"The Aframerican Academy." *Messenger* 9:4 (April 1927) 115.
"Aframerica Snapshots." Messenger 9:5 (May 1927) 152.
"Afternoon Teas Now the Rage in Harlem." *New York Age*. 16 April 1914: 1.
Abney, Lisa. "Dualism and the Quest for Wholeness in Arna Bontemps's *God Sends Sunday*." *Upon Further Review: Sports in American Literature*. Eds., Michael Cocchiarale and Scott D. Emmert. Westport, CT: Praeger Publishers, 2004. 87–95.
Anderson, Jervis. *This Was Harlem: A Cultural Portrait, 1900–1950*. New York: Farrar, Straus, Giroux, 1982.
Arna Bontemps-Langston Hughes Letters, 1925–1967. Ed. Charles Nichols. New York: Dodd, Mead & Company, 1980.
Associated Negro Press. "'Pop' Lloyd, Baseball Player, Spurns Limelight." *Amsterdam News*. 6 November 1929: 12.

Bibliography

"Athletics and the Church." Editorial. *New York Age*. 8 October 1914: 4.
Bain, Wilfred R. "Don't Mention it, Mr. Dougherty." *Interstate-Tattler*. 15 November 1929: 9.
Baker, Houston A., Jr. *Turning South Again: Re-Thinking Modernism/Re-Reading Booker T*. Durham, NC: Duke University Press, 2001.
Baldwin, James. Preface. *The Negro in New York: An Informal Social History*. Roi Ottley and William J. Weatherby, eds. New York: New York Public Library, Oceana Pub., 1967.
Berlack-Boozer, Thelma. "Amsterdam News: Harlem's Largest Weekly." *The Crisis* 45:4 (April 1938), 105–6.
Berliner, Brett A. *Ambivalent Desire: The Exotic Black Other in Jazz-Age France*. Amherst: University of Massachusetts Press, 2002.
Bessie, Simon Michael. *Jazz Journalism: The Story of the Tabloid Newspapers*. New York: E.P. Dutton, 1938.
Bontemps, Arna, ed. *American Negro Poetry*. New York: Hill and Wang, 1963.
_____. "The Awakening: A Memoir." *The Harlem Renaissance Remembered*. Ed. Arna Bontemps. New York: Dodd, Mead & Company, 1972. 1–26.
_____. *God Sends Sunday*. New York: Harcourt, Brace and Company, 1931.
Bowser, Pearl, and Louise Spence. *Writing Himself into History: Oscar Micheaux, His Silent Films, and His Audiences*. New Brunswick, NJ: Rutgers University Press, 2000.
Brooks, Van Wyck. *America's Coming-of-Age*. New York: B.W. Huebsch, 1915.
Briggs, Cyril V. "Roll of Honor." *Crusader* 1:1 (September 1918), 22–23.
_____. [as C. Valentine]. "Valentine's All-Negro All-Star Five." *Crusader* 1:8 (April 1919) 14.
Brown, Sterling A. "Athletics and the Arts" (1951). *A Son's Return: Selected Essays of Sterling A. Brown*. Mark A. Sanders, ed. Boston: Northeastern University Press, 1996. 99–137.
_____. "A Son's Return: 'Oh, Didn't He Ramble'" (1973). *A Son's Return: Selected Essays of Sterling A. Brown*. Mark A. Sanders, ed. Boston: Northeastern University Press, 1996. 1–21.
_____. "Sporting Beasley." *The Norton Anthology of African American Literature*., Henry Louis Gates, Jr. et al., eds. New York: W.W. Norton & Company, 1997. 1225–1226.
Brown, Sterling A., Arthur P. Davis, and Ulysses Lee. *The Negro Caravan: Writings by American Negroes*. New York: Citadel Press, 1941.
Bruni, Frank. "Baseball and Black History." *The New York Times*, 14 June 2015: Sunday Review 1, 3.
Burley, Dan. "Grand Old Man of Press Row Passes On." *Amsterdam News*. 16 December 1944: 13B.
Butler, Bennie. "1927 A Most Disastrous Year." *Interstate-Tattler*. 6 January 1928: 11.
_____. "Butler's Challenge." *Interstate-Tattler*. 2 July 1926: 10.
_____. "Negro Athletes" (unpublished), 1940. Federal Writers Project research file. Schomburg Center for Research in Black Culture, New York Public Library.
_____. "Our Ambitious Program for 1928." *Interstate-Tattler*. 13 January 1928: 12.
_____. "Sport Sparkles." *Interstate-Tattler*. 9 December 1927: 11.
_____. "Sports and Theatrical News," *Interstate-Tattler*. 28 September 1924: 6.
_____. "This Harlem Urge." *Interstate-Tattler*. 25 February 1932: 7.
Calhoun, Donald W. *Sport, Culture, and Personality*. 2nd ed. Champaign, Ill.: Human Kinetics Publishers, 1987.
Calvin, Floyd. "Bennie Butler, Former 'Tattler' Editor Now in Enforced Retirement, Talks of Past." *Pittsburgh Courier*. 24 December 1932: Sec. 2, 3.
Campbell, Mary, et al. *Harlem Renaissance: Art of Black America*. New York: Harry Abrams, 1987.
Carroll, Brian. *The Black Press and Black Baseball: A Devil's Bargain*. New York: Routledge, 2015.
_____. *When to Stop the Cheering? The Black Press, the Black Community, and the Integration of Professional Baseball*. New York: Routledge, 2007.
Clark, Dick, and Larry Lester, eds. *The Negro Leagues Book*. Cleveland: Society for American Baseball Research, 1994.
Clarke, William E. Letter. *Amsterdam News*. 28 February 1923: 5.
Cooper, Wayne F. *Claude McKay: Rebel Sojourner in the Harlem Renaissance*. Baton Rouge: Louisiana State University Press, 1987.
_____. Foreword. *Home to Harlem*. By Claude McKay. Boston: Northeastern University Press, 1987. ix–xxvi.

Bibliography

_____, ed. *The Passion of Claude McKay: Selected Poetry and Prose, 1912-1948.* New York: Schocken Books, 1973.
Cottrell, Robert Charles. *The Best Pitcher in Baseball: The Life of Rube Foster, Negro League Giant.* New York: New York University Press, 2001.
Cruse, Harold. *The Crisis of the Negro Intellectual.* New York: William Morrow, 1967.
Daniel, Walter C. *Black Journals of the United States.* Westport, CT: Greenwood Press, 1982.
Davis, Allison. "The Second Generation." *The Crisis* 35 (March 1928): 87.
Detweiler, Frederick. *The Negro Press in the United States.* Chicago: University of Chicago Press, 1922.
Dismond, Geraldyn. "Social Snapshots." *Interstate-Tattler.* 27 January 1928: 4.
Donnelly, Peter. "Subcultures in Sport: Resilience and Transformation." *Sport in Social Development: Traditions, Transitions, and Transformations.* Ed. Alan G. Ingham and John W. Loy. Champaign, IL: Human Kinetics Publishers, 1993. 120-39.
[Dougherty, Romeo]. "Black Sox Heads North; Play All the Way Up." *Amsterdam News.* 4 June 1930. 17.
Dougherty, Romeo L. "About Things Theatrical." *Amsterdam News.* 20 May 1925: 6.
_____. "Appreciation." *Amsterdam News.* 9 November 1935: 1.
_____. "Behind the Scenes in Basketball." *Crusader* 3:5 (January 1921) 13-14.
_____. "Bolden Made Chairman of Eastern Colored Baseball League." *Amsterdam News.* 7 March 1923: 4.
_____. "A Contemporary's Appreciation." *Crusader* 1:3 (November 1918) 24-25.
_____. "Eastern Ass'n of Colored Clubs Hold Big Pow-wow." *Amsterdam News.* 24 January 1923: 5.
_____. "Lincoln Theatre Manager Signs Contract Giving Operators Chance." *Amsterdam News.* 8 September 1926: 10.
_____. "More Fistic Fireworks Promised at the Commonwealth This Coming Saturday." *Amsterdam News.* 4 February 1925: 5.
_____. "The Negro and the Theatre." Faye P. Everett, et al. *The Colored Situation: A Book of Vocational and Civic Guidance for the Negro Youth.* Boston: Meador, 1936. 213-16.
_____. "Personal But Not Private." *Amsterdam News.* 28 February 1923: 5.
_____. "Punta, Revolutionist." *Crusader* 1:5-8, 1:11, 2:1-2 (1919).
_____. "Spartans Did Not Withdraw From M.B.A." *Amsterdam News.* 20 December 1922: 4.
_____. "Things in General—Basketball in Particular." *New York News.* 24 February 1921: 5.
_____. "Thousands See Howard-Lincoln Football Game." *Amsterdam News.* 6 Dec. 1922: 1.
Douglas, Robert L. Letter. *Amsterdam News.* 6 December 1922: 4.
Du Bois, W.E.B. "The Black North in 1901." *W.E.B. Du Bois on Sociology and the Black Community.* Dan S. Green and Edwin D. Driver, eds. Chicago: University of Chicago Press, 1978.
_____. *The College-Bred Negro American.* Atlanta: Atlanta University Press, 1910.
_____. *The Correspondence of W.E.B. Du Bois.* Vols 1 & 2. Ed. Herbert Aptheker. Amherst: University of Massachusetts Press, 1973-1978.
_____. "Criteria of Negro Art" (1926). *Writings.* Ed. Nathan Huggins. New York: Library of America, 1986.
_____. *Darkwater: Voices from Within the Veil.* New York: Harcourt, Brace, 1920.
_____. *Dusk of Dawn: An Essay Toward an Autobiography of a Race Concept* (1940). New York: Schocken Books, 1968.
_____. "Fisk." *The Crisis* 29 (April 1925): 247-251.
_____. *Newspaper Columns.* Vol. 1. Ed. Herbert Aptheker. White Plains, NY: Kraus-Thomson Organization, Ltd., 1986.
_____. "The Prize Fighter." *The Crisis* 8 (August 1914): 181.
_____. "The Problem of Amusement" (1897). *W.E.B. Du Bois on Sociology and the Black Community.* Dan S. Green and Edwin D. Driver, eds. Chicago: University of Chicago Press, 1978. 226-237.
_____. "Race Relations in the United States: 1917-1947" (1948). *Writings by W.E.B. Du Bois in Periodicals Edited by Others.* Vol. 4. Edited by Herbert Aptheker. Millwood, NY: Kraus-Thomson Org., Ltd., 1982. 66-76.
_____. Rev. of *God Sends Sunday*, by Arna Bontemps. *The Crisis* 38:9 (September 1931) 304.
_____. "This Law-Abiding Land." *The Crisis* 26: 151-152.

Bibliography

Du Bois, W.E.B., and Guy B. Johnson. *Encyclopedia of the Negro: Preparatory Volume with Reference Lists and Reports,* 2nd ed. New York: N.p., 1946.
Early, Gerald. "Baseball and African American Life." *Baseball: An Illustrated History.* Geoffrey C. Ward, ed. New York: Knopf, 2000. 412–417.
Edwards, G. Franklin. Introduction. *E. Franklin Frazier on Race Relations.* Chicago: University of Chicago Press, 1968.
Ehrmann, Jacques. "Homo ludens revisited." Trans. Cathy & Phil Lewis. *Yale French Studies* 41 (1968): 31–57.
Ellison, Ralph. *Shadow and Act.* New York: Random House, 1964.
Everett, Anna. *Returning the Gaze: A Genealogy of Black Film Criticism, 1909–1949.* Durham, NC: Duke University Press, 2001.
Ferris, William H. "Impressions and Reflections of Lincoln-Howard Game, Coliseum Reception and Howard University Affairs." *Negro World* 16 Dec. 1922.
Fleming, Robert E. *James Weldon Johnson and Arna Wendell Bontemps: A Reference Guide.* Boston: G.K. Hall, 1978.
Foster, Andrew (Rube). Letter. *Amsterdam News.* 21 February 1923: 6.
_____. Letter to W.T. Smith. 15 November 1922. Giamatti Library, Cooperstown, NY.
Frazier, E. Franklin. *Black Bourgeoisie: The Rise of a New Middle Class in the United States.* New York: Collier, 1962.
_____. *The Negro in the United States.* New York: Macmillan, 1949.
_____. "Recreation and Amusement among American Negroes." Carnegie/Myrdal Collection. Schomburg Center for Research in Black Culture, New York Public Library.
Gates, Henry Louis, Jr. *Figures in Black: Words, Signs, and the "Racial" Self.* New York: Oxford University Press, 1987.
_____. "W.E.B. Du Bois and the Encyclopedia Africana, 1909–63." *The Annals of the American Academy of Political and Social Sciences* 568 (March 2000): 203–219.
_____, et al., eds. *The Norton Anthology of African American Literature.* New York: W.W. Norton & Company, 1997.
Garvey, Marcus. *The Marcus Garvey and Universal Negro Improvement Association Papers.* 9 vol. Edited by Robert A. Hill. Berkeley: University of California Press, 1983–1995.
George, Nelson. *Elevating the Game: Black Men and Basketball.* New York: HarperCollins, 1992.
Gordon, Eugene. "The Contest Spotlight." *Opportunity* 5 (July 1927): 204–5.
_____. "The Negro Press." *American Mercury* 8 (June 1926): 207–15.
_____. "A Survey of the Negro Press." *Opportunity* 5 (January 1927): 7–11.
_____. "Outstanding Negro Newspapers." *Opportunity* 2 (December 1924): 365–7.
_____. "Outstanding Negro Newspapers: Reiteration and Detail." *Opportunity* 3 (February 1925): 51–4.
_____. "Outstanding Negro Newspapers of 1925." *Opportunity* 3 (December 1925): 358–61.
_____. "Outstanding Negro Newspapers, 1927." *Opportunity* 5 (December 1927): 358–63.
Gross, B. "Character of the Amsterdam News and the New York Age." 1939. Federal Writers Project file, Schomburg Center for Research in Black Culture, New York.
Harlan, Louis. *Booker T. Washington: The Making of a Black Leader, 1856–1901.* New York: Oxford University Press, 1972.
Harte, Bret. *The Poetical Works.* Boston: Houghton, Mifflin, 1883.
Hawkins, James E. *History of the Southern Intercollegiate Athletic Conference, 1913–1990.* Butler, GA: Benns Printing Co., 1994.
Hemingway, Ernest. *Death in the Afternoon.* New York: Scribner, 1932.
Henderson, Edwin B. *The Negro in Sports.* Washington, DC: Associated Publishers, Inc., 1939.
Hill, Robert A. Introduction. *The Crusader.* 3 vol. New York: Garland, 1987.
Hoberman, John. *Darwin's Athletes: How Sport Has Damaged Black America and Preserved the Myth of Race.* Boston: Houghton Mifflin, 1997.
Holmes, Dwight Oliver Wendell. *The Evolution of the Negro College.* New York: Columbia University, 1934.
Holway, John. *Voices from the Great Black Baseball Leagues.* Rev. ed. New York: Da Capo Press, 1992.
Hooks, Ted. "Bacharach Giants Lose on Opening Day." *New York Age.* 8 May 1920: 7.
_____. "Bacharachs Put Whitewash on Lincolns in First Game." *New York Age.* 17 July 1920: 1, 7.

―――. "Cyclone Williams vs. Cannonball Dick." *New York Age*. 15 May 1920: 7.
―――. "For Championship of the East." *New York Age*. 17 July 1920: 7.
―――. "Why Do Big Leagues Bar the Negro Baseball Player?" *New York Age*. 9 October 1920: 6.
Huggins, Nathan Irvin. *Harlem Renaissance*. New York: Oxford University Press, 1971.
Hughes, Langston. *The Big Sea: An Autobiography*. 1940. New York: Hill and Wang, 1993.
―――. Letter. *Interstate-Tattler*. 9 March 1928: 4.
―――. Letter to Arna Bontemps. 23 June 1959. *Arna Bontemps-Langston Hughes Letters*. Ed. Charles Nichols. New York: Dodd, Mead & Company, 1980. 384
Hughes, Langston, and Arna Bontemps, eds. *The Poetry of the Negro, 1746-1949*. New York: Doubleday & Company, 1949.
Huizinga, Johan. *Homo Ludens: A Study of the Play Element in Culture* (1938). Boston: Beacon Press, 1951.
Hurston, Zora Neale. "Characteristics of Negro Expression." *Negro: An Anthology*. Ed. Nancy Cunard. 1934. Ed., abr., introduction, Hugh Ford. New York: Frederick Ungar Publishing Co., 1996. 24-31.
Ingham, Alan G., and Stephen Hardy. "Sport Studies through the Lens of Raymond Williams." *Sport in Social Development: Traditions, Transitions, and Transformations*. Ed. Alan G. Ingham and John W. Loy. Champaign, IL: Human Kinetics Publishers, 1993. 1-14.
Jackson, James A. "Here and There among the Folks." *Billboard*. 6 August 1921: 62, 64.
―――. "James A. Jackson's Page." *Billboard*. 9 September 1922: 46.
―――. "News from Kansas City." *Billboard*. 20 November 1920: 41.
―――. "Romeo Back to the Amsterdam." *Billboard*. 25 November 1922: 49.
James, Bill. *The New Bill James Historical Baseball Abstract*. New York: The Free Press, 2001.
James, C.L.R. *Beyond a Boundary*. 1963. New York: Pantheon, 1983.
James, Winston. *Holding Aloft the Banner of Ethiopia: Caribbean Radicalism in Early Twentieth-Century America*. New York: Verso, 1998.
Jarvie, Grant, and Joseph Maguire. *Sports and Leisure in Social Thought*. New York: Routledge, 1994.
Johnson, Charles S. *The Negro College Graduate*. Chapel Hill: University of North Carolina Press, 1938.
Johnson, James Weldon. "Abolition in Football." *New York Age*. 22 November 1919: 4.
―――. *Along This Way*. New York: Viking, 1933.
―――. *The Autobiography of an Ex-Colored Man*. 1912. New York: Penguin, 1990.
―――. "The Big Fight." *New York Age*. 12 July 1919: 4.
―――. *Black Manhattan* (1930). New York: Da Capo Press, 1991.
―――. "The Color Line in Athletics and Sports." *New York Age*. 24 July 1920: 4.
―――. *Complete Poems*. Edited by Sondra Kathryn Wilson. New York: Penguin, 2000.
―――. "Dempsey and Wills." *New York Age*. 11 March 1922: 4.
―――. "The Egoism of the White Race." *New York Age*. 12 October 1918: 4.
―――. "Eulogy for Jack Johnson." *New York Age*. 18 April 1915: 4.
―――. "The Georgia Peach." *New York Age*. 6 July 1916: 4.
―――. "Gorillas." *New York Age*. 7 August 1920: 4.
―――. "Harlem: The Culture Capital." *The New Negro* (1925). Ed. Alain Locke. Intro. Arnold Rampersad. New York: Atheneum, 1992.
―――. "Jess Willard on Race Prejudice." *New York Age*. 24 June 1915: 4.
―――. "Muldoon and the Color Line." *New York Age*. 17 February 1923: 4.
―――. *Negro Americans, What Now?* New York: Viking, 1934.
―――. "Up to Mr. Dempsey." *New York Age*. 31 July 1920: 4.
―――. ed., preface. *The Book of American Negro Poetry* (1922). Rev. ed. (1931). New York: Harcourt Brace Jovanovich, 1969.
Kelley, Brent. *Voices from the Negro Leagues: Conversations with 52 Baseball Standouts of the Period 1924-1960*. Jefferson, NC: McFarland, 1998.
Kellner, Bruce, ed. *The Harlem Renaissance: An Historical Dictionary for the Era*. Westport, CT.: Greenwood Press, 1984.
Kornweibel, Theodore. *No Crystal Stair: Black Life and the Messenger, 1917-1928*. Westport, CT: Greenwood Press, 1975.

Lamb, Chris. *Conspiracy of Silence: Sportswriters and the Long Campaign to Desegregate Baseball*. Lincoln: University of Nebraska Press, 2012.
Lanctot, Neil. *Negro League Baseball: The Rise and Ruin of a Black Institution*. Philadelphia: University of Pennsylvania Press, 2004.
Leiter, Andrew B. *In the Shadow of the Black Beast: African American Masculinity in the Harlem and Southern Renaissances*. Baton Rouge: Louisiana State University Press, 2010.
"Lester A. Walton, Ex-Envoy, Is Dead." *New York Times*. 19 October 1965: 43.
Lester, Larry. *Rube Foster in His Time: On the Field and in the Papers with Black Baseball's Greatest Visionary*. Jefferson, NC: McFarland, 2012.
Levy, Eugene D. *James Weldon Johnson: Black Leader, Black Voice*. Chicago: University of Chicago Press, 1973.
Lewis, David Levering, ed. *The Portable Harlem Renaissance Reader*. New York: Penguin, 1994.
_____. *W.E.B. Du Bois: Biography of a Race, 1868–1919*. New York: Henry Holt, 1993.
_____. *W.E.B. Du Bois: The Fight for Equality and the American Century, 1919–1963*. New York: Henry Holt, 2000.
_____. *When Harlem Was in Vogue*. 2nd ed. New York: Penguin, 1997.
Lewis, Theophilus. "New Year Greeting to the Dean." *Messenger* 9:1 (January 1927), 10.
Light, Jonathan Fraser. *The Cultural Dictionary of Baseball*. Jefferson, NC: McFarland, 1997.
Locke, Alain. *The New Negro*. 1925. Ed. Alain Locke, intro. Arnold Rampersad. New York: Atheneum, 1992.
MacClancy, Jeremy, ed. *Sport, Identity, and Ethnicity*. Oxford: Berg, 1996.
Malamud, Bernard. *The Natural*. 1952. New York: Avon, 1993.
Malloy, Jerry. Introduction. *Sol White's History of Colored Base Ball, with Other Documents on the Early Black Game, 1886–1936*. Lincoln: University of Nebraska Press, 1995.
Mandel, Miriam B. *Hemingway's* Death in the Afternoon: *The Complete Annotations*. Lanham, MD: Scarecrow, 2002.
Martin, Tony. *Race First: The Ideological and Organizational Struggles of Marcus Garvey and the Universal Negro Improvement Association*. Westport, CT: Greenwood Press, 1976.
Maxwell, William J. *New Negro, Old Left: African American Writing and Communism between the Wars*. New York: Columbia University Press, 1999.
McKay, Claude. *Banjo: A Story without a Plot*. New York: Harper & Brothers, 1929.
_____. *Harlem: Negro Metropolis*. New York: E.P. Dutton & Co., 1940.
_____. *Home to Harlem*. 1928. Boston: Northeastern University Press, 1987.
_____. *A Long Way from Home*. New York: Lee Furman, Inc., 1937.
_____. *The Negroes in America*. 1923. Ed., Alan McLeod. Trans. P. Okhrimenko; trans. (from Russian) Robert J. Winter. Port Washington, NY: Kennikat Press, 1979.
McKible, Adam. "Our (?) Country: Mapping 'These "Colored" United States' in *The Messenger*." *The Black Press: New Literary and Historical Essays*. Edited by Todd Vogel. New Brunswick, NJ: Rutgers University Press, 2001. 123–39.
McPherson, Barry D., James E. Curtis, and John W. Loy. *The Social Significance of Sport: An Introduction to the Sociology of Sport*. Champaign, IL: Human Kinetics Publishers, 1989.
Meisenhelder, Susan L. *Hitting a Straight Lick with a Crooked Stick: Race and Gender in the Work of Zora Neale Hurston*. Tuscaloosa: University of Alabama Press, 1999.
Mishkin, Tracy. *The Harlem and Irish Renaissances: Language, Identity, and Representation*. Gainesville: University of Florida Press, 1998.
Morgan, Tom. "Jazz Roots: The Frogs." Jazz Roots, 1996. www.jass.com/frogs.
Moses, Alvin W., Jr. "By Way of Report." *Interstate-Tattler*. 24 December 1931: 16.
_____. "Garden Colloquy." *Interstate-Tattler*. 12 March 1927: 11.
_____. "How'd You Like to See." *Interstate-Tattler*. 13 February 1931: 8.
_____. "Public Servants—Not Enemies." *Interstate-Tattler*. 2 July 1931: 8.
Mote, James. *Everything Baseball*. New York: Prentice Hall, 1989.
Myrdal, Gunnar. *An American Dilemma: The Negro Problem and Modern Democracy* (1944). New York: Harper & Row, 1962.
Naison, Mark. *Communists in Harlem during the Depression*. Urbana: University of Illinois Press, 1983.
The Negro in New York: An Informal Social History. Edited by Roi Ottley and William J. Weatherby. Pref. James Baldwin. New York: New York Public Library, Oceana Pub., 1967.

Negro Year Book, 1931–1932. Edited by Monroe N. Work. Tuskegee: Negro Year Book Publishing Co., 1931.
Novak, Michael. *The Joy of Sports: End Zones, Bases, Baskets, Balls, and the Consecration of the American Spirit.* New York: Basic Books, 1976.
Ogbar, Jeffrey O. G., ed. *The Harlem Renaissance Revisited: Politics, Arts, and Letters.* Baltimore: The Johns Hopkins University Press, 2010.
Oleck, Joan. "Allison Davis: 1902–1983." *Contemporary Black Biography* 12: 38–41.
Osofsky, Gilbert. *Harlem: The Making of a Ghetto.* New York: Harper & Row, 1966.
Ottley, Roi. *New World A-Coming: Inside Black America.* Boston: Houghton Mifflin, 1943.
Patton, Venetria K., and Maureen Honey, eds. *Double-Take: A Revisionist Harlem Renaissance Anthology.* New Brunswick, NJ: Rutgers University Press, 2001.
Peterson, Robert. *Cages to Jump Shots: Pro Basketball's Early Years.* New York: Oxford University Press, 1990.
_____. *Only the Ball Was White.* New York: Oxford University Press, 1970.
Pochmara, Anna. *The Making of the New Negro: Black Authorship, Masculinity, and Sexuality in the Harlem Renaissance.* Amsterdam: Amsterdam University Press, 2011.
Posey, Cum. Letter to J. McMahon. *Amsterdam News.* 14 February 1923: 4.
Powell, Richard J., et al. *To Conserve a Legacy: American Art from Historically Black Colleges and Universities.* Cambridge, MA: MIT Press, 1999.
Pride, Armistead S., and Clint C. Wilson II. *A History of the Black Press.* Washington, DC: Howard University Press, 1997.
Rampersad, Arnold. *The Art and Imagination of W.E.B. Du Bois.* Cambridge: Harvard University Press, 1976.
_____. Introduction. *The Big Sea: An Autobiography.* By Langston Hughes. New York: Hill and Wang, 1993.
_____. *The Life of Langston Hughes.* Vol. 1. New York: Oxford University Press, 1986.
_____. "W.E.B. Du Bois, Race, and the Making of American Studies." Afterword. *W.E.B. Du Bois on Race and Culture.* Ed. Bernard W. Bell, Emily Grosholz, and James B. Stewart. New York: Routledge, 1996.
Reisler, Jim. *Black Writers/Black Baseball.* Rev. ed. Jefferson, NC: McFarland, 2007.
Rhoden, William C. "Matchup Isn't Simply Talent vs. Team." *New York Times.* 5 April 2005: C23, C27.
_____. "Talent Doesn't Equal Trouble as a Teammate." *New York Times.* 28 March 2005: C3.
Rice, Albert. "Albert Rice." *Caroling Dusk: An Anthology of Verse by Negro Poets.* Ed. Countee Cullen. New York: Harper & Brothers, 1927. 176–77.
Ribowsky, Mark. *A Complete History of the Negro Leagues, 1884 to 1955.* Secaucus, NJ: Carol Publishing Group, 1995.
Richardson, Joe M. *A History of Fisk University, 1865–1946.* University, AL: University of Alabama Press, 1980.
Riess, Steven A. *City Games: The Evolution of American Urban Society and the Rise of Sports.* Urbana: University of Illinois Press, 1989.
_____. *Sport in Industrial America, 1850–1920.* Wheeling, IL: Harlan Davidson: 1995.
Riley, James A. *The Biographical Encyclopedia of the Negro Baseball Leagues.* New York: Carroll & Graf, 1994.
"R. L. Dougherty, Veteran Sports Editor, Is Dead." *Amsterdam News* 16 December 1944: 1.
Roberts, James B., and Alexander Skutt. *The Boxing Register: International Boxing Hall of Fame Record Book.* 2nd ed. Ithaca, NY: McBooks Press, 1999.
Robeson, Paul, with Lloyd Brown. *Here I Stand.* New York: Othello Associates, 1958.
Rogosin, Donn. *Invisible Men: Life in Baseball's Negro Leagues.* New York: Atheneum, 1985.
Ruck, Rob. *Sandlot Seasons: Sport in Black Pittsburgh.* Urbana: University of Illinois Press, 1987.
Russ, Robert A. "'There's No Place Like Home': The Carnival of Black Life in Claude McKay's *Home to Harlem.*" *The Harlem Renaissance Re-Examined.* Ed. Victor Kramer. New York: AMS Press, 1987. 355–73.
Sammons, Jeffrey T. *Beyond the Ring: The Role of Boxing in American Society.* Urbana: University of Illinois Press, 1988.
Sanders, Mark A. *Afro-Modernist Aesthetics and the Poetry of Sterling A. Brown.* Athens: University of Georgia Press, 1999.

Bibliography

Santiago-Valles, W.F. "The Caribbean Intellectual Tradition that Produced James and Rodney." *Caribbean Voice*. New York: Gale Group, 2002. http://www.caribvoice.org/Caribbean Documents/intellectual.html

Schiffman, Jack. *Harlem Heyday: A Pictorial History of Modern Black Show Business and the Apollo Theatre*. Buffalo: Prometheus Books, 1984.

Schuyler, George. "Shafts and Darts." *Pittsburgh Courier*. 19 July 1930: 4.

Scruggs, Charles. *The Sage in Harlem: H.L. Mencken and the Black Writers of the 1920s*. Baltimore: The Johns Hopkins University Press, 1984.

"Short Flights." *Indianapolis Freeman*. 6 November 1915: 2.

Singer, Barry. *Black and Blue: The Life and Lyrics of Andy Razaf*. New York: Schirmer Books, 1992.

Singh, Amritjit. Foreword. *Infants of the Spring*. By Wallace Thurman. Boston: Northeastern University Press, 1992. vii-xxix.

_____. *The Novels of the Harlem Renaissance: Twelve Black Writers, 1923–1933*. University Park: Pennsylvania State University Press, 1976.

Snelson, Floyd G. "Boys of Yesteryear Pallbearers at Funeral for Romeo Dougherty." *Amsterdam News*. 23 December 1944: 16A.

Solomon, Mark. *The Cry Was Unity: Communists and African Americans, 1919–1936*. Jackson: University Press of Mississippi, 1998.

Stansell, Christine. *American Moderns: Bohemian New York and the Creation of a New Century*. New York: Metropolitan, 2000.

Stewart, Jeffrey C., ed. *Paul Robeson: Artist and Citizen*. New Brunswick, NJ: Rutgers University Press, 1998.

Thurman, Wallace. *Infants of the Spring*. 1932. Boston: Northeastern University Press, 1992.

_____. "Negro Life in New York's Harlem: A Lively Picture of a Popular and Interesting Section." *The American Parade*. Ed. E. Haldeman-Julius. Girard, KS: Haldeman-Julius Co., 1928.

Turner, Joyce Moore. Introduction. *Richard B. Moore, Caribbean Militant in Harlem*. Ed., W. Burghardt Turner and Joyce Moore Turner. Bloomington: Indiana University Press, 1988.

Veblen, Thorstein. *The Theory of the Leisure Class* (1899). New York: Penguin, 1994.

Vincent, Ted. *Keep Cool: The Black Activists Who Built the Jazz Age*. London: Pluto Press, 1995.

_____, ed. *Voices of a Black Nation: Political Journalism in the Harlem Renaissance*. San Francisco: Ramparts Press, 1973.

Walden, Daniel. "'The Canker Galls...,' or, the Short Promising Life of Wallace Thurman." *The Harlem Renaissance Re-Examined*. Ed. Victor Kramer. New York: AMS Press, 1987. 201–12.

Walton, Lester. "An Unwritten Law." *New York Age*. 17 June 1915: 6.

Ward, Geoffrey C. *Baseball: An Illustrated History*. New York: Knopf, 1994.

Washburn, Patrick S. *The African American Newspaper: Voice of Freedom*. Evanston, IL: Northwestern University Press, 2006.

Washington, Booker T. *Up from Slavery* (1900). Edited and with an introduction by W. Fitzhugh Brundage. New York: Bedford /St. Martin's, 2003.

Watson, Steven. *The Harlem Renaissance: Hub of African American Culture, 1920–1930*. New York: Pantheon, 1995.

"We 'Rile' the Crackered Department of Justice." *Crusader* 2:9 (May 1920), 5.

Webber, H.B., and Oliver Brown. "Play Ball!" *The Crisis* 45 (May 1938): 135, 137, 146.

Weber, Max. *The Protestant Ethic and the Spirit of Capitalism*. 1904–1905. Trans. Talcott Parsons. Intro. Randall Collins. Los Angeles: Roxbury Publishing Co., 1996.

West, Cornel. "Black Strivings in a Twilight Civilization" (1996). *The Cornel West Reader*. New York: Basic Civitas Books, 1999. 87–118.

_____. "Race and Modernity" (1982). *The Cornel West Reader*. New York: Basic Civitas Books, 1999. 55–86.

White, Walter F. *A Man Called White: The Autobiography of Walter F. White*. New York: Viking, 1948.

Who's Who in the American Negro Press. Ed. Roy L. Hill. Dallas: Royal Publishing Co., 1960.

Who's Who in Colored America. Vol. 1. Ed. Joseph Boris. New York: WWCA Corp., 1927.

Wilkins, Roy. "The Negro Press." *Opportunity* 6 (December 1928): 362–63ff.

_____, with Tom Mathews. *Standing Fast: The Autobiography of Roy Wilkins*. New York: Viking, 1982.

Bibliography

Williams, Raymond. *Marxism and Literature*. New York: Oxford University Press, 1977.
Wilson, August. *Fences*. New York: Penguin, 1986.
Wilson, Sondra Kathryn, ed. Introduction to *Complete Poems*, by James Wheldon Johnson. New York: Penguin, 2000. xv-xxi.
Wolseley, Roland E. *The Black Press, U.S.A.* Ames: The Iowa State University Press, 1971.
Wolters, Raymond. *The New Negro on Campus: Black College Rebellions of the 1920s*. Princeton, NJ: Princeton University Press, 1975.
Woodward, Stanley. *Sports Page*. New York: Simon & Schuster, 1949.
Yates, Ted. "Outstanding New York Newspapermen." Federal Writers Project file, Schomburg Center for Research in Black Culture, New York.
Young, P. Bernard, Jr. "News Content of Negro Newspapers." *Opportunity* 7 (December 1929): 370-72ff.

Index

Abbey Theatre (Dublin) 59
Abbott, Robert 162
Abney, Lisa 182
Aesop 120
"Aframerican" 102, 111–113, 129, 141
Africa 111, 144, 150, 156; *see also* French West Africa
African American press 4, 5, 7, 10, 14–15, 17, 22, 41, 42, 57, 59, 72, 81, 86, 99, 101–117, 118–119, 124–126, 129, 132, 133, 136, 138–129, 141, 148, 158, 164–166, 167, 173, 178, 186; see also journalism
African Blood Brotherhood 150, 161, 163
Afro-American (newspaper) *see* Baltimore *Afro-American*
Aguero, Martin 188*ch3n*2
Alabama 158
Algren, Nelson 16
All-Star Game (major league baseball) 165
Allen, Samuel 11
Along This Way (Johnson) 13–14, 72, 80, 88–89
Alpha Physical Culture Club 151, 152
Altrock, Nick 188*ch3n*2
amateur athletics *see* professionalism
American Mercury 102, 109, 110, 111
American Negro League 122, 169
American Studies 31
America's Coming-of-Age (Brooks) 8
Amsterdam News see New York *Amsterdam News*
Anderson, James 149
Anderson, Jervis 76
Anderson, Sherwood 63–64
Anderson Monarchs 10–11
Anson, Adrian "Cap" 54
Aristophanes 120
Armstrong, Louis 59, 182
Armstrong, Samuel 32, 33
"Athletics and the Arts" (Brown) 185–186
Atlanta 29
Atlanta University 29, 30
Atlantic City 83, 122, 166
Austin (Texas) 49
Austria 25

The Autobiography of an Ex-Colored Man (Johnson) 14, 64–65, 83–85

Bacharach, Harry 122
Bacharach Giants 82, 86, 121–125, 166, 167
Bagnall, Robert W. 162
Bain, Wilfred R. 131
Baltimore *Afro-American* 104, 108, 110, 111, 167
Baltimore Orioles 7
Baker, Houston A. 32–33, 53
Baldwin, James 84
Bandura, Steve 11
Banjo 67
Baraka, Imamu Amiri 13
Barbados 144
Barcelona 73
baseball 6–7, 15–17, 67, 72, 76–77, 84, 89–90, 106, 114, 120, 124, 146, 154, 165, 180, 185–186; see also Negro League baseball
basketball 7, 15, 21, 48, 57, 61–62, 65, 103, 140, 142, 145, 146, 151–155, 164, 170–171, 173, 185, 188*ch3n*3
Bateson, Gregory 32
Bavaria 25, 63; *see also* Germany
Bayreuth (Germany) 27
Beardsley, Aubrey 146
Beckwith, Johnny 86
Bennett, Gwendolyn B. 157, 181
Berlin 24, 25, 26, 27
Berliner, Brett A. 71
Bessie, Simon Michael 105
Bethune-Cookman University 47
Beyond a Boundary (James) 145–147
The Bible 9
The Big Sea (Hughes) 58–60, 62, 74, 84
Bilbao (Spain) 188*ch3n*2
Billboard 128, 141, 165
billiards 29
Black Arts Movement 11, 12–13
"Black Bohemia" 14, 57–58, 60, 77, 79, 82–87, 89, 97, 106–107
Black Bourgeoisie 45–46, 113
"Black Fives" 154
Black Manhattan (Johnson) 13, 60, 76–77,

Index

79, 80–83, 85–88, 89, 96, 137, 184; *see also* Bohemianism
Black nationalism 24–25, 103, 111, 144, 155, 161; *see also* Garvey, Marcus; separatism
Black Star Line 162
Black Swan (record label) 162
Blake, William 52, 54
Boas, Franz 29
boat racing 23
Bohemianism 14, 48, 57–63, 67–68, 73–79, 106, 107, 117, 184; *see also* "Black Bohemia"
Bolden, Ed 166–169
Bontemps, Arna 16, 43, 180–184, 186; *God Sends Sunday* 180, 181–184
The Book of American Negro Poetry (Johnson) 13, 52
Boris, Joseph J. 161
Boston 120
Boston Celtics 61, 154
Boston Guardian 126
Boston Post 109
bourgeoisie 34, 41–50, 55, 57, 58–60, 68, 70–77, 79, 107–108, 112–114, 116, 139, 148, 161, 174
boxing 5, 9, 11, 13, 16–17, 23–24, 57, 60–62, 66–75, 80–81, 83–84, 88, 91–94, 96, 120, 129, 131, 132, 133, 169, 171–173, 180, 182, 185
Briggs, Cyril (C. Valentine) 109, 144–145, 147–153, 155, 161, 163, 169, 177
British Guinea 144
British West Indies 145; *see also* Caribbean Islands
Briton, George 127
Brooklyn Dodgers 17, 24, 55–56, 106
Brooklyn *Eye* 148
Brooklyn Royal Giants 82, 86, 120, 125
Brooklyn Visitations 61
Brooks, Gwendolyn 11
Brooks, Van Wyck 8–9; *America's Coming-of-Age* 8
Brotherhood of Sleeping Car Porters 103, 138; *see also Messenger*
Broun, Heywood 106, 176
Brown, Sterling A. 42, 179–181, 184–186; "Athletics and the Arts" 185–186; *Southern Road* 179, 184
Bruce, John E. ("Bruce Grit") 162
Burley, Dan 143, 151
Burns, Ken 11–12
Butler, Bennie 126–133, 134, 136, 141

California 182
California Eagle (Los Angeles) 126
Calvin, Floyd 109, 137
Camp, Walter 36
Campanella, Roy 55
Cannady, Walter 126

Capers, Johnnie "Headache Band" 152
capitalism 8, 58, 65, 71, 73, 76, 79
Caribbean Islands 5, 72, 78, 113, 140–149, 151, 155–160, 162; *see also* Barbados; British Guiana; British West Indies; Charlotte Amalie; Cuba; Haiti; Havana; Jamaica; Leeward Islands; Puerto Rico; St. Croix, Trinidad; St. Kitts and Nevis; Virgin Islands
Carnegie-Myrdal study 45, 185, 187*ch*1*n*1
Carroll, Brian 10, 85–86, 105, 142
Carson City (Nevada) 91
Carter, Cecil 154
Catholic Protectory Oval 122, 124, 137
Charleston, Oscar 135
Charlotte Amalie (Virgin Islands) 157
Charpentier, Georges 70, 71
Chicago 16, 43, 61, 82, 113
Chicago American Giants 49, 50, 120
Chicago Defender 7, 48, 49, 87, 104, 108, 110, 111, 113, 117, 125, 162, 165, 167
Chicago School of Sociology 42
Chicago Tribune 165
Chicago Whip 117
Chicago White Sox 6, 124
Churchill Downs 183
Civil War 35
Clark University 47
Clarke, William 125–126, 141, 163, 166
Cleaver, Eldridge 13
Cleveland (Ohio) 3, 58
Cobb, Ty 120
Coffeyville Junior College 48
Cole, Bob 120
Coleman, Julia 162
"College Athlete" (Davis) 42–43
Collegiate Athletic Conference 39
Columbia University 14, 152
Comintern (Communist International) 69–70, 71
Comiskey, Charles 6
Committee of Fourteen 121
Commonwealth Casino 166, 169
Commonwealth Five 171, 172
communism 17, 69, 109, 112, 144, 148, 149, 176; *see also* Communist Party
Communist Party 73, 152, 155, 177; *see also* communism
Congress (U.S.) 6, 127; *see also* U.S. government; Justice Department; House of Representatives
Connor, John W. 122–123
Conroy, Jack 16
Continental League 3, 6–7
Coolidge, Calvin 161
Cooper, Wayne 69
Corbett, James J. 91

Index

Corelli, Marie 157
Cotton Club 7
Crawford, J. Anthony 149–150
cricket 67, 68, 131, 143, 145–147, 151
The Crisis 9, 16–17, 22, 23, 37, 39, 42, 55–56, 103
"Criteria for Negro Art" (Du Bois) 30, 39
Crusader 5–6, 7, 103, 113, 142, 144–145, 147–155, 160, 163, 169, 174, 175
Cruse, Harold 96, 176
Cuba 91–92, 158; *see also* Havana
Cuban Giants 82, 85, 88
Cullen, Countee 40, 52–53, 55, 75
Cuning, Waring 109

Daily Worker 17, 109
Daniel, Walter C. 109, 150
Darkwater: Voices from Within the Veil (Du Bois) 30
Daudet, Alphonse 157
Daugherty, Henry 162
Davis, Allison 42–43, 45, 185; "College Athlete" 42–43
Davis, Gordon 42
Davis, Mo'ne 11
Davis, Sadie Warren 176
Death in the Afternoon (Hemingway) 73–75, 76
Democratic Party 132
Dempsey, Jack 24, 72, 91–94, 170
Denmark 143
Depression *see* Great Depression
Dewey, John 7
Diagne, Blaise 70–71
Dill, Augustus Granville 29
Dismond, Geraldyn 109, 127–128
Dismond, Henry Binga 180
District of Columbia *see* Washington, D.C.
Dixon, George 57
Dodd, Mead and Company 180
Domingo, W.A. 144, 150, 160–161, 163, 177
Donnelly, Peter 83
Dougherty, Romeo L. 3, 4, 5, 6, 14, 102, 109, 118–119, 128, 130–131, 134, 140–145, 147–163, 164–178; "The Negro and the Theatre" 174–176; *Punta, Revolutionist* 142, 155–160
Douglas, Aaron 63
Douglas, Robert L. 140–141, 150–151, 154–155
Douglass, Frederick 83
Draper, Theodore 149
Du Bois, W.E.B. 4, 8, 21–40, 41, 42–43, 46, 47, 48, 49, 55, 56, 70, 77, 83, 95 103, 108, 109, 113, 115, 116, 118–119, 126, 132–133, 153, 154, 161, 165, 181–182, 188*ch*4*n*18; "Criteria for Negro Art" 30, 39; *Darkwater: Voices from Within the Veil* 30; "Fisk" 36, 37–38; "The Problem of Amusement" 28–29, 30, 31, 33; *see also* Du Bois–Washington debate
Du Bois, Yolande 37, 40
Du Bois–Washington debate 22, 28–34, 43, 55, 103, 118–119, 126
Dumas, Alexandre 157
Dunbar, Paul Laurence 53, 57
Duval Giants 122
Dyer Anti-Lynching Bill 127

Early, Gerald 11–12, 13
East-West League 136
Eastern Colored League 14, 21, 41, 82, 86, 122, 130, 164, 166, 168–169
Eastman, Max 69
Ebbets Field 124
education 5, 12, 21–22, 25–36, 40–44, 46–51, 55, 56, 92, 103, 118, 120, 146; *see also* historically black colleges and universities
Ehrmann, Jacques 33
Ellington, Duke 7
Ellison, Ralph 3, 15–16, 59; *Shadow and Act* 15–16
The Emancipator 144, 145
Emerson, Ralph Waldo 51
England 25–26, 84; *see also* Great Britain
Europe 7, 14, 23, 25, 26, 27, 63, 70, 75, 172, 188*ch*3*n*3; *see also* Denmark; England; France; Germany; Great Britain; Russia; Spain; U.S.S.R.
Europe, James Reese 120
Everett, Anna 116
Exclusive Club (New York) 121

Farrell, James T. 16
Faulkner, William 10, 16
Fauset, Jessie 41
Federal Bureau of Investigation 150
Federal Writers Project 16, 114–115, 126, 131–132, 137, 149
Ferris, William H. 101–102
Firkins, Marty 87
Firpo, Luis 129
Fisher, Rudolph 179
"Fisk" (Du Bois) 36, 37–38
Fisk News 28
Fisk University 14, 22, 28, 34–40, 44
Fitzsimmons, Bob 91
Florida 88, 91
Flowers, Tiger 129
football 5, 11, 14, 15, 21, 23, 24, 32, 36, 39, 41, 48, 95, 96, 101–102, 115, 118, 120, 146, 152, 185, 188*ch*3*n*3
Fortune, T. Thomas 127, 148, 162

203

Index

Foster, George W., Jr. 153
Foster, Rube 12, 21, 41, 47, 48–51, 55, 82, 130, 138, 166–168
Foster, William H. (Juli Jones) 87–88
Foster Photo Play Company 87
France 70–71, 84, 152
Franklin, Benjamin 31
Frazier, E. Franklin 41–42, 45–46, 113; *Black Bourgeoisie* 45–46, 113
Freg, Luis 188*ch*3*n*2
French West Africa 70–71
Frick, Ford 106
Frogs (musical group) 119–120
Fulton, Frank 92

gambling 29, 37, 46, 58, 60, 78–79, 83, 84–85, 125, 138, 144, 181–182; *see also* "sporting" world
Gans, Joe 57
Garvey, Marcus 4, 101, 103, 111–113, 118, 126–129, 131, 132, 133, 134, 142, 144, 148, 150, 155, 161, 162, 164, 169, 174, 177
Garvice, Charles 157
Gates, Henry Louis, Jr. 52–53, 55, 64, 179–180
George, Nelson 170
Georgia 158
Germany 25, 26–28, 84, 155–156
Gibson, Josh 56
Glasgow 145
God Sends Sunday (Bontemps) 180, 181–184
Goffman, Erving 32–33
Gold, Mike 69
Gordon, Eugene 102, 108–112, 114–116, 119, 126, 131, 141, 149
Grant, Eddie 125
Gray, Thomas 52
Great Britain 66–68, 146; *see also* England
Great Depression 17, 21, 45, 47, 55, 97, 105, 109, 113, 115, 126, 131, 138, 139, 175, 179
Great Migration 5, 45, 48, 104, 142, 180
Greenlee, Gus 136
Greenwich Village 60, 84, 174
Grey, Edgar 162, 177

Haiti 157
Haldeman-Julius Quarterly 75
Hall of Fame *see* National Baseball Hall of Fame
Hamitic League of the World 150
Hampton Institute 28, 29–30, 31, 32, 36, 48
Handy, W.C. 162
Hardy, Arthur 50
Harlan, Louis 36
Harlem Black Sox 47
Harlem Globetrotters 61

Harlem Hospital 181
Harlem Liberator 149
Harlem Stars 86
Harmon Award 188*ch*3*n*2
Harris, George 148, 150, 162
Harrison, Hubert 144, 161, 162, 177, 178
Harte, Bret 172
Harvard University 16, 25, 42, 101
Havana 91
Hayden, Robert 187*n*5
Hearst, William Randolph 94, 105, 157
Hemingway, Ernest 9, 73–77; *Death in the Afternoon* 73–75, 76; *The Sun Also Rises* 77
Henderson, Edwin B. 16
Here I Stand (Robeson) 15
Hill, Robert 149, 152
Hilldale Daisies 123, 139, 166–169
Hines, Ike 81
historically black colleges and universities 14, 21, 34, 36, 47–49; *see also* education
Hitler, Adolf 27
Hoberman, John 12
hockey 93
Holloway, Jonathan Scott 46
Holstein, Casper 144–145
Holway, John 50–51
Home to Harlem (McKay) 59, 67, 77–79, 181
Homer (poet) 23
Homestead Grays 44, 126, 134, 136, 140, 170
Hooks, Ted 122–125
Hoover, J. Edgar 5
Hornsby, Rogers 135
horse racing 57, 83, 85, 88, 91, 95, 157–160, 181–183
House of Representatives 133
Houston (Texas) 48
Howard University 48, 101–102, 115
Hudson River 91
Huggins, Nathan 38, 63
Hughes, Langston 10, 43, 57, 58–60, 62, 63, 74–75, 84, 97, 128, 141, 148, 179, 186; *The Big Sea* 58–60, 62, 74, 84
Huizinga, Johan 33
Hume, David 53
Hurston, Zora Neale 64, 179

Ideal Tennis Club 145
"If We Must Die" (McKay) 5
Indian Athletic Club 151
Indianapolis Clowns 86
Indianapolis Freeman 50, 128, 167
Industrial Workers of the World 103; *see also Messenger*
integration 6, 11, 14, 17, 55–56, 80, 81, 87, 94–95, 119, 126, 132, 138–139, 178, 180, 185–186

Index

intellectualism 4, 7, 8, 9, 12, 14–16, 21, 22, 27, 38, 41, 43, 45, 47, 55, 57–59, 61, 63–65, 67, 78, 81–82, 93, 95, 96, 103, 104, 106–107, 113–117, 126–128, 132–133, 154, 173; *see also* Bohemianism; professionalism
International Club (London) 67
International Colored Unity League 177
internationalism 57, 67–70, 73
Interstate-Tattler 103, 104, 105, 126–131, 133–137, 141
Irish Renaissance 59
Irvington-on-the-Hudson 76

Jackman, Harold 14
Jackson, J.A. 165
Jackson, Tom 122
Jacksonville (Florida) 89–90, 122
Jacksonville *Daily American* 90–91
Jamaica 67, 144, 148
Jamaica (Long Island) 134
James, Bill 48
James, C.L.R. 69–70, 143, 145–147, 177, 189*ch7n*3; *Beyond a Boundary* 145–147
James, Winston 145, 148, 161
jazz 7, 15, 16, 21, 38, 101, 104, 105, 107, 119, 182, 185
Jazz Age 10; *see also* Roaring Twenties
Jeffries, James J. 23, 92, 95, 188*ch3n*2
Jenkins, Clarence "Fats" 135
Jersey City Athletic Club 151
Johnson, Charles S. 28, 35, 43–44, 103, 109, 128
Johnson, Fenton 128
Johnson, Helene 109
Johnson, Henderson A. "Tubby" 39
Johnson, Jack 7, 21, 23–24, 25, 62, 70, 71, 72, 81, 91–95 188*ch3n*2
Johnson, James Weldon 11, 12, 51–52, 57, 60, 64–65, 72, 80–97, 108, 113, 119, 120, 128, 129, 132, 137, 161, 162, 170, 184, 186; *Along This Way* 13–14, 72, 80, 88–89; *The Autobiography of an Ex-Colored Man* 14, 64–65, 83–85; *Black Manhattan* 13, 60, 80–83, 85–88, 89, 96, 137, 184; *The Book of American Negro Poetry* 13, 52; *Negro Americans, What Now?* 95–97; "O Black and Unknown Bards" 52
Johnson, Josh 44
Johnson, Rosamond 87, 120
Jones, Irving 87
Jones, Juli *see* Foster, William H.
journalism 8, 10, 24, 72, 82, 104–109, 111, 112, 116, 131, 142 149, 157, 162; *see also* African American press
Jubilee Singers 36–37
Justice Department 5–6; *see also* Congress (U.S.); U.S. government

Kansas 48
Kansas City (Missouri) 10, 55
Kansas City Call 107, 128, 167
Kansas City Monarchs 45
Kant, Emmanuel 53
Keats, John 52, 54
Keenan, James J. 126
Kelley, Brent 44
Klots, Allen 180
Kornweibel, Theodore 173
Ku Klux Klan 128

Lacy, Sam 87
Lady Nicotine *see* Dismond, Geraldyn
Lafayette Theatre 14, 165, 177
LaGuardia, Fiorello 87
Lamb, Chris 10, 138
Landis, Kenesaw Mountain 15
Langston, Tony 165
Latin America 75, 82, 188*ch3n*2
Latitia Athletic Club 151
Lawrence, Jacob 11
Lawson, Andy 6, 7
League of Nations 149
Leech, Harper 95
Leeward Islands 144; *see also* St. Kitts and Nevis
Leiter, Andrew 9–10
Lenin, Vladimir 68
Lester, Larry 168
Lewis, David Levering 9, 25, 27, 36, 40, 64, 94, 179; *When Harlem Was in Vogue* 9, 179
Lewis, Theophilus 114, 128, 173–174
The Liberator 69
Liberia 120
Liberty League 162
Lincoln, Abraham 177
Lincoln Giants 44, 86, 120, 122–125, 127, 129, 135, 137–139, 166–167, 170
Lincoln Motion Picture Company 165, 177
Lincoln Stars 120, 170
Lincoln Theatre 59
Lincoln University 101–102, 115
Lindsay, Vachel 63
Little Italy (New York) 76
Little Rock (Arkansas) 11
Livy 137
Lloyd, John Henry 44, 125, 135
Lloyd George, David 154
Locke, Alain 30, 41, 63, 107; *The New Negro* 41–42, 46
Loendi Big Five 140–141, 170
London 67
A Long Way from Home (McKay) 58, 66–68, 73–74, 75, 77, 78
Los Angeles 182, 183

205

Index

Louis, Joe 17, 21, 24, 88, 94, 109, 131–132
Louisiana 35, 182
Lundy, Dick 123

Mably, Jackie 59
Madagascar 5
Madden, Will 152
Madison Square Garden 93, 170
Malamud, Bernard 90
Malarcher, Dave 35, 49, 50–55; "Sunset Before Dawn" 51–52, 54–55
Manchester (England) 145
Mandel, Miriam B. 188*ch*3*n*2
Mann Act 23, 91
Marx, Karl 66, 68
Marxism 7, 27, 58–59, 66–69, 72, 73, 146, 161; *see also* capitalism; communism
Maryland 183, 187*ch*2*n*3
Mason, Charlotte Osgood 63, 64
Maxwell, William J. 69–70
McGraw, John 124
McKay, Claude 5, 58, 59, 63, 66–79, 82, 97, 113–114, 117, 142, 144, 181, 182, 188*ch*4*n*18; *Banjo* 67; *Home to Harlem* 59, 67, 77–79, 83, 181; "If We Must Die" 5; *A Long Way from Home* 58, 66–68, 73–74, 75, 77, 78; *The Negroes in America* 58, 68–73, 75, 79
McKenzie, Fayette 37, 38, 39
McKible, Adam 114
McLean, Larry 120
McMahon, Jess 166, 169, 171, 173
McMahon, Rod 170, 171, 173
Meharry College 36
Meisenhelder, Susan 64
Memphis Press 95
Mencken, H.L. 7–8, 110–112
Messenger 103, 110, 113, 114, 141, 144, 160, 173
Metropolitan Basketball Association 151
Mexico 188*ch*3*n*2
Midtown (New York City) 57
Mills, Florence 127, 129, 130
Milton, John 53
minstrelsy 80, 82–83, 85–86, 96
Mishkin, Tracy 59
Missouri 187*ch*2*n*3
Mobile (Alabama) 183
Monroe, Al 117
Monticello Rifles 171
Moore, Fred R. 119, 121
Moore, Richard B. 144, 145
Moran, Frank 23
Morton, Jelly Roll 182
Moscow 69
Moses, Alvin J. 126, 129, 133–137
Mount Zion Church 127
musical theatre *see* theatre (popular)
Myrdal, Gunnar *see* Carnegie-Myrdal

NAACP (National Association for the Advancement of Colored People) 9, 56, 81, 95, 108, 118, 127, 133, 139, 162
Naco Giants 3
Nail, John E. 162
Naison, Mark 148
Napoleon 157
National Baseball Hall of Fame 44
National League 106
The Natural (Malamud) 90
Nazism 27, 33
Negro American League 134, 135
Negro Americans, What Now? (Johnson) 95–97
"The Negro and the Theatre" (Dougherty) 174–176
Negro Daily Times 113, 128, 162, 163, 164
Negro League baseball 3–4, 9–10, 11–13, 21–24, 41–42, 44–58, 65, 79, 80–83, 86–89, 94, 96, 97, 118, 120–127, 129–130, 135–139, 141–142, 153–155, 164, 166–170; *see also* baseball
Negro National League 3, 21, 41, 47, 50, 79, 82, 122, 130, 153, 166, 169
Negro Times see *Negro Daily Times*
Negro World 4, 101–102, 104, 111, 113, 129, 131, 144, 161, 163, 177
The Negroes in America 58, 68–73, 75, 79
Nevis *see* St. Kitts and Nevis
New Deal 16
New England 34, 35
New Haven (Connecticut) 101
New Jersey 5, 44, 143
New Masses 132, 144
The New Negro (anthology) 41–42, 46, 60, 63; see also Locke, Alain; *Survey Graphic*
"New Negro" Renaissance 4, 7, 9, 12–13, 14, 15, 21, 34, 42, 53, 57–58, 64, 94, 104, 107, 109–110, 115, 121, 154, 160, 161, 179, 180, 186
New Orleans 183
New Orleans University 35, 49
New York Age 81, 82, 87, 89, 91–95, 103, 103–104, 110, 112–113, 114, 118–127, 137–138, 141, 149, 150, 163, 166, 167, 177
New York *Amsterdam News* 3, 4, 44, 68, 102, 103–105, 107, 109, 110, 113, 114, 118–119, 126, 128, 130, 137–138, 140–141, 143, 148–151, 154, 163, 164, 169, 171, 173, 174, 176–178
New York Black Sox 3
New York Black Yankees 86, 87
New York City Commission on Civil Rights 120
New York Cuban Stars 3
New York Daily News 105
New York Evening Journal 95, 134
New York Freeman 119, 148

Index

New York Giants 82, 120, 124, 125, 135
New York Herald Tribune 106, 156, 180, 181
New-York Historical Society 154
New York News 3, 6, 105, 128, 131, 134, 136, 140, 147–150, 165
New York Rangers 93
New York Rumor 119
New York State Athletic Commission 93
New York Times 10–11, 40, 181, 105, 120
New York University 48
New York World 110, 120
New York Yankees 86, 87, 135
Newspaper Guild of New York 176
Norfolk (Virginia) 29
Norfolk *Journal and Guide* 108
North Carolina Mutual Life Insurance Company 42
Northwestern University 95
Novak, Michael 76
Nugent, Richard Bruce 75
numbers *see* gambling

"O Black and Unknown Bards" (Johnson) 52
O'Brien, John, Jr. 61–62
Ogbar, Jeffrey O.G. 179
Ohio River 171
Ohio State University 50
O'Keeffe, Georgia 28
Oklahoma 15
Oklahoma City *Black Dispatch* 126
Olympic Field 86, 137, 170
Olympic Games 22, 23, 24–28, 55, 88; *see also* U.S. Olympic team
O'Neill, Eugene 14, 59
Only the Ball Was White (Peterson) 10
Opportunity 103, 107–108, 109, 110, 114, 115, 131, 144
Ottley, Roi 110
Ovington, Mary White 127
Owen, Chandler 162
Owens, Jesse 21, 22, 25, 26–27, 88

Pace, Harry H. 162
Pace and Handy Music Company 162
Pacific Rim 188ch3n2
Paige, Satchel 11, 17, 47
Palm Beach (Florida) 126
Pan-African Congress 70
Paris 23, 25, 70
Park, Robert 42
Patterson, Andrew "Pat" 48
Penn State (Pennsylvania State University) 44, 171
Pennsylvania 140, 168
Peterson, Robert L. 10, 50; *Only the Ball Was White* 10

Phi Beta Kappa 14
Philadelphia 82, 93, 123, 166, 168
Philadelphia Giants 137
Philadelphia Stars 169
Philadelphia Tribune 134, 167
Philippines 156
Pickens, William 162
Pittsburg Normal College 48
Pittsburgh 140, 170–171, 173
Pittsburgh Courier 25, 26, 55, 81, 104–105, 108–109, 110–113, 125, 134, 137, 162, 171, 173
Pittsburgh Crawfords 56, 135, 136
"Plain Language from Truthful James" (Harte) 172
Pochmara, Anna 9
Poles, Spotswood 125
Pope, Alexander 53
popular theatre *see* theatre (popular)
Posey, Cumberland 135, 136, 140–141, 170–173
Posey, Seward 173
Powell, C.B. 176
Powell-Savory Corporation 176
primitivism 9, 38, 62–64, 67, 181
"The Problem of Amusement" (Du Bois) 28–29, 30, 31, 33
professionalism 5, 8, 12, 22, 25–26, 37, 39, 44, 46, 49, 58, 61, 65–68, 71, 79, 80, 85–86, 138, 151–154, 171–173, 175
Puerto Rico 144
Pulitzer, Joseph 105, 157
Punta, Revolutionist (Dougherty) 142, 155–160

Quality Amusement Corporation 175

ragtime 14, 65, 84; *see also* theatre (popular)
Rampersad, Arnold 24, 30–31, 59, 60
Randolph, A. Philip 128
Rathskeller (135th Street) 122
Ravenell, James H. 152
Razaf, Andy (Andrea Razafkeriefo) 3–4, 5–7, 14, 141
Reed, Ishmael 11, 13
Reims (France) 70
Reisler, Jim 141
Renaissance Casino 61, 170
Renaissance Five 7, 61, 103, 140–141, 151, 154–155, 170
Reiss, Winold 14, 63
Reno (Nevada) 188ch3n2
Rhodes, E. Washington 108
Rice, Albert 75–77
Rice, Grantland 129
Rickard, Tex 92–93, 170
Riess, Steven A. 44

Index

Roaring Twenties 102, 104; *see also* Jazz Age
Robeson, Paul 14–15, 46, 62, 95, 131, 152; *Here I Stand* 15
Robinson, Bill "Bojangles" 86, 87
Robinson, Jackie 17, 21, 24, 55–56, 106, 186
Rockland Casino 7
Rogosin, Donn 44, 47, 48, 49
Roman Cities 89
Royal Ponciana Hotel (Palm Beach) 126, 127
Ruck, Rob 173
Runyon, Damon 106
Ruppert, Jacob 138
Russ, Robert A. 78
Russia 69; *see also* U.S.S.R.
Rutgers University 14, 95, 152
Ruth, Babe 9–10, 90, 94

St. Christopher Athletic Club (St. Christopher Machine) 141, 151, 152–154
St. Croix (Virgin Islands) 144
St. Cyprian Athletic Club 151
St. Kitts and Nevis 144, 151
St. Louis 183
St. Louis Cardinals 106
St. Louis Giants 120
St. Louis Star-Sayings 119
St. Paul (Minnesota) 55
St. Philip's Episcopal Church 140, 153
St. Thomas (Virgin Islands) 143
Salem Crescent Athletic Club 151
Sanders, Mark A. 184
Santiago-Valles, W.F. 155
Santop, Louis 125
Saperstein, Abe 61
Saturday Evening Quill 109
Savannah (Georgia) 88
Savory, P.M.H. 176
Savoy Ballroom 61
Schiffman, Jack 182
Schomburg, Arturo 144
Schuyler, George 64, 68, 81, 109, 110, 114
Scruggs, Charles 110, 114
Selma (Alabama) 11
Senegal 70
sensationalism 104–108, 117, 134, 157; *see also* journalism
separatism 5, 126, 131–132, 150, 161, 163, 178
Shadow and Act (Ellison) 15–16
Shakespeare, William 51, 85
Shaw, George Bernard 66, 68
Shipp, Jesse 120
Siki, Louis Phal 70, 71, 73
Silent Protest Parade (Harlem) 160
Simmel, Georg 7
Singh, Amritjit 62, 181–182
Slater Fund 36
Smart Set Athletic Club 151

Snelson, Floyd 126–127
soccer 147, 151
Society for American Baseball Research (SABR) 10
The Sound and the Fury (Faulkner) 10
Southern Intercollegiate Athletic Conference (SIAC) 37, 39
Southern Road 179, 184
Southern Workman 28
Southworth, E.D.E.N. 157
Soviet Union *see* U.S.S.R.
Spain 71, 73, 74–75, 156
Spanish-American War 142, 155–157
Spartan Athletic Club (Spartan Braves) 151, 152, 154
Sporting Life 88
Sporting News 88
"sporting" world 78–79, 181–184; *see also* gambling
Springfield (Massachusetts) 101
Stansell, Christine 84
Stieglitz, Alfred 28
Stovey, George 54
Straight University 35
Streator, George 39–40
Strivers Row 61
Strong, Nat 167–169
subculture 78, 80, 83, 84–86, 182, 184
Sue, Eugene 157
The Sun Also Rises (Hemingway) 77
"Sunset Before Dawn" (Malarcher) 51–52, 54–55
Survey Graphic 14
Sweatt, George 48
Sykes, Frank "Doc" 48

Talladega College 35
Tammany Hall 79
Tandy, Vertner W. 153
Tenderloin (New York City) 57, 85
Tennessee 37
tennis 42, 145, 163, 185
Tennyson, Alfred Lord 146
Tesreau, Jeff 122
Texas 72
Thanksgiving 101, 115; *see also* football
theatre (popular) 3, 9, 14, 80, 83, 87, 91, 96–97, 114, 120, 128–129, 150, 165, 166, 173–176; *see also* ragtime; vaudeville
The Theory of the Leisure Class (Veblen) 8
Thermopylae (Greece) 152
Third International *see* Comintern
Thomas, D. Ireland 165
Thompson, Louise 148
Thurman, Wallace 57, 60–63, 65–66, 75, 77, 78, 97, 107, 114, 179; *Infants of the Spring* 62–63, 77, 78, 107; "Negro Life in

Index

New York's Harlem" 60–61, 65–66, 75, 77, 107
Tijuana 183
Tillotson College 49
Toledo (American Association baseball club) 54
Toomer, Jean 64
Toronto Star 76
track and field 22, 26, 36, 58, 94, 121, 132, 152, 181, 183, 185; *see also* U.S. Olympic team
Trammell, Nat 47
Trinidad 145
Tucker, Henry 122
Tunney, Gene 93
Turner, Victor 33
Tuskegee University 15, 29, 30, 31–35, 36, 48, 49, 112, 118

United Negro Improvement Association (UNIA) 101, 150, 161–162; *see also* Garvey, Marcus
United Press 105
U.S. government 111; *see* Congress, Justice Department
U.S. Olympic team 136, 181
University of Chicago 42, 181
University of Virginia 36
Up from Slavery (Washington) 31–32, 33
U.S.S.R. (Union of Soviet Socialist Republics) 68, 69, 148; *see also* Russia

Van Vechten, Carl 28, 62, 63, 77, 78, 128
Vann, Robert L. 108, 110
vaudeville 59, 81, 87, 128, 150, 188*ch3n2*; *see also* theatre (popular)
Veblen, Thorstein 8; *The Theory of the Leisure Class* 8
Villa Lewaro 76
Vincent, Thoedore (Ted) 110, 113, 116, 126, 131, 132, 141, 142, 149, 150, 175
Virgil (poet) 23
Virgin Islands (U.S.) 5, 143, 144–145, 148, 157, 177
The Voice 144

Wagner, Richard 27–28
Walcott, Joe 57
Walker, A'Lelia 76
Walker, George 120
Walker, Jimmy 93
Walker, Madame C.J. 76
Walker, Moses Fleetwood 54
Waller, Thomas "Fats" 3
Walrond, Eric 144
Walton, Lester A. 89, 119–120, 150, 165
Warren, Edward H. 150

Washington, Booker T. 22, 30, 31– 34, 35, 43, 48, 49, 53, 55, 103, 104, 108, 112–113, 118–119, 125–126, 138–139, 148, 149, 162; *Up from Slavery* 31–32, 33; *see also* Du Bois-Washington debate
Washington, D.C. 5, 16, 75, 185, 187*ch2n3*, 101–102, 148
Washington *Sun* 148, 162
Washington Tribune 108
Waterman, Warren G. 36
Waters, Ethel 59
Weber, Max 8, 58, 65, 71
West, Cornel 27–28, 34, 43
West, Dorothy 109
Wheatley, Phillis 53, 55
When Harlem Was in Vogue (Lewis) 8, 179
White, Sol 133, 137–139
White, Walter 41, 55–56, 116, 132
White House 37
Who's Who of Colored Americans 161–162
Wilberforce University 137
Wiley College 48
Wilkins, Barron D. 121–123
Wilkins, Roy 17, 55–56, 107, 115
Willard, Jess 72, 91–93
Williams, Arnette Franklin 40
Williams, Bert 120, 150
Williams, Joe 127, 135
Williams, Raymond 83
Williams, Sterling A. 42
Williams College 42, 185
Williamsbridge Colored Men's Association 151
Wills, Harry 61, 72, 93, 129, 170
Wilson, August 11
Wilson, W. Rollo 55, 87, 109, 134, 162
Wilson, Woodrow 172
Wolters, Raymond 34, 37, 44
Woodward, Stanley 106
Work, John W. 36
Workers Party 145, 161
World Series 79, 120, 124, 134
World War I 34, 37, 70, 104, 125, 142, 143, 145, 148, 152, 154, 156, 162
Wright, Richard 9, 11, 17, 43, 51, 84, 131
Writer's Guild 181
Wyatt, Dave 50

Yale University 26, 101
Yankee Stadium 21, 138
Yeats, W.B. 59
YMCA (Young Men's Christian Association) 29, 123
Young, Frank. A 188*ch3n2*
Young, P.B., Jr. 107–108

Zimmerman, Heinie 124

www.ingramcontent.com/pod-product-compliance
Ingram Content Group UK Ltd.
Pitfield, Milton Keynes, MK11 3LW, UK
UKHW042000140426
5217IPUK00015B/894